Top Hollywood Acting Teachers

Inspiration and Advice for Actors

The Hometown to Hollywood Interviews Volume II

Bonnie J. Wallace

**Hollywood
Parents
Press**

For Simon, Claire, Chloe, and Lara
With love and appreciation, always
&
For all the dreamers
And the ones who teach them

CONTENTS

GRATITUDE

This book would not exist without the incredible generosity of the twelve master acting teachers who took the time out of their busy lives to speak with me on the *Hometown to Hollywood* podcast. Their success, and the success of their many students over the years, is a testament to their talent, vision, passion, creativity, and hard work.

A huge thank you to:

Zak Barnett
Diane Christiansen
Marnie Cooper
John D'Aquino
Patrick Day
Judy Kain
Anthony Meindl
Eric Morris
Lisa Picotte
Mae Ross
Scott Sedita
Marcie Smolin

Special thanks to Kristin Wolfram and Sarah Wallace, who volunteered to help edit this manuscript. Special thanks always to Bob Wallace, Kristin Wolfram, and June Wallace for their love and support.

Very special thanks to Simon, who makes my life beautiful, and to Lara, for sharing her generous heart with me. And to my daughters Claire Hosterman and Dove Cameron (Chloe)… with love always and always.

INTRODUCTION

Ten years ago, my youngest daughter Dove and I moved to Los Angeles from Bainbridge Island, in hopes of helping her break into the world of professional acting. We knew the odds were challenging, but we had faith that she had what it took to succeed, and we didn't want to live our lives wondering what might have been if we'd only given it a try.

After Dove reached a certain level of success, I knew I wanted to give back by helping other young actors. So I began a blog; wrote *The Hollywood Parents Guide* and *Young Hollywood Actors*; started the *Hometown to Hollywood* podcast; and began consulting, teaching workshops and speaking, and creating online video courses.

My mission is to educate and inspire. Education helps you make the best decisions for *you*. Inspiration is necessary so you persevere when the going gets tough—as it can for everyone.

This book shares that mission, and is the second in a series based on the *Hometown to Hollywood* interviews. I'm excited to bring the generous, wise, and inspiring words of these twelve top Hollywood acting teachers to you in these pages.

Each of these master teachers has been teaching for decades; each has mentored some of the biggest stars in film and TV, as well as many more whose names you may not know, but who have seen wonderful success. Each of them is well respected in the industry, and brings something unique to their acting schools.

Some are geared more toward adults, some more toward younger actors; most teach classes for both. Most are focused on acting for film and TV, and a few offer more commercial classes. Some use classical acting methods in their classes, and some have created their own approaches.

You will hear their philosophies, insights, and advice in their own voices in each chapter. You may feel that some are speaking directly to you, and that some resonate less with you. All of them have something to teach you, and can make you a better, and more successful actor.

I am proud to know all of them, and to call many of them friends.

If you enjoy this book, I encourage you to subscribe to the podcast, where you can hear the full original interviews, as well as many more educational, insightful conversations with top Hollywood talent.

Just go to *hometowntohollywood.supportingcast.fm*, and you can have access to every new episode, as well as the entire collection of well over 100 other exclusive interviews.

It's my hope that the wisdom, advice, and incredible inside information that these twelve master acting teachers so generously share here will help you learn what you need to become a more successful actor yourself, as well as inspire you to keep learning and growing creatively.

And if you decide you want to take classes from these amazing teachers and their schools yourself, I have some great news: as of this writing, most of them are now offering online classes. So you can be anywhere in the world—not just in Los Angeles—and learn from the best. You can find their contact information at the back of this book.

To your success and happiness,
Bonnie

BONUS CONTENT:

Download the free BONUS CHAPTER featuring an interview with actresses and acting coaches Audrey Whitby and Victoria Moroles at: www.hometowntohollywood.com/bonuschapter

ZAK BARNETT

Founder of Zak Barnett Studios

"This is not the art of pretending. This is the art of becoming."

Zak Barnett is the founder of Zak Barnett Studios in Midtown Los Angeles, which is billed as an acting studio for the whole self. ZBS provides classes, intensives, and private coaching for professional actors aged seven through adults.

Alumni include Madelaine Petsch, Danielle MacDonald, Storm Reid, Johnny Ortiz, Emily Robinson, Victoria Moroles, Gabrielle Elyse, Sloane Morgan Siegel, Lulu Lambrose, Jonathan Daviss, Jadah Marie, Greg Kasyan, Olivia Sanabia, Lauren Donzis, Gabrielle Elyse, and Eliza Pryor.

Bonnie Wallace: How did you get started teaching acting?

Zak Barnett: Well, I was an actor-writer-director from a young age. When my parents would ask me when I was a kid what I wanted to be, at nine I would say a poet. So it was never a policeman, or a firefighter. It was always a poet, and I feel like that's been the through line of what I've done, and studied, for all of my life. So ... in that way, I was sort of the lone artist where I was. Then I graduated early from high school.

I went to Tisch School of the Arts. I actually went for

1

playwriting, and it was amazing, because Tony Kushner taught in my program, Martin Scorsese ... I would see Spike Lee in the elevator, and I was this 17-year-old kid, surrounded by all of these incredible artists, and had this huge future in front of me. I actually had a traumatic event happen during that time, and I lost my proprioception, which is basically my mind's ability to know where my body is in space. So I was literally kind of grabbing at different parts of my body, thinking my back was on my front. I didn't know where my legs were, and I was sort of this being without a body.

Bonnie Wallace: That must have been terrifying.

Zak Barnett: I'm laughing at it now, as I think we do when we get through certain things in our lives, but it was absolutely terrifying, and no one could tell me what was going on. I remember I went to a psychiatrist, and without looking up from their prescription pad, they told me I was psychotic.

Basically, I had all of this potential. I was this kid with this destiny, and then all of a sudden, it was gone, and I was going to be in a mental hospital. That was sort of the forecast. I refused that diagnosis, and it set me on a journey to, like Humpty Dumpty, kind of put myself back together again. At that point in my life, the only tools I really had to understand anything were storytelling, writing, acting, and directing. So it really became the means in which I healed myself.

I just think I might have a different point of view than a lot of acting teachers, or a lot of actors, because for me, it was kind of foundational to healing myself, and bringing myself back to this world. So when they talk about, as an actor, you are your own instrument,

I really feel that literally I saw all the components of that, and figured out how they fit together.

At this point, it's very intuitive, and it's all reassembled. I look at the mechanism of the human instrument, and that's how I see an actor. So I see, "Oh, this is off. That's off. This is where we need to move that. This isn't open. We need to open this part." I think deeply ingrained in that is that this is a healing process. Now, it's not therapy. That's not the point of it. It is about expression, and it also is about perfection, but it is a healing process. So yes, that's the origin story. Then I got this opportunity when I was in my early 20s. So I dropped out of NYU. I moved to Japan.

It just felt like, I'm on a quest. I've got to figure out what life is about, and I was sort of set adrift into the world. So I moved to Japan, then I moved to San Francisco, and I had a theater company. I was the artistic director of a theater company, and we were doing experimental work, and it was fun, and wild, and we performed at this college, and the dean and the president of the college were there, and I think I was 21 at the time. They loved the work, and they asked me to create their bachelor's and master's program.

But I was 21, so I didn't have a bachelor's or a master's yet. So they put me through it, and they gave me a fake head of the program. I won't name the college so I don't get them in trouble. So for 10 years, I got to create this program for actors who wanted to create their own work. It sort of predated what is happening nowadays, which is so much actor-generated content. I got to do that 20 years ago.

It was cool. We had these big acting conservatories from London coming to study our curriculum, and it

3

was a wild time. What was wonderful about it was really… it was about people finding their voice, and their sense of purpose. So even more so than skill, or craft, it was really about voice. I really learned how to focus on getting that unique thing out of each person.

Then, when I moved to Hollywood, I worked at another acting studio, Margie Haber Studios, and I worked there for a decade. I started their youth program, but I also worked with their adults, and that was much more single cam, multi-cam, procedural drama, serial drama. It was just like, "This is Hollywood. This is how hard it is. This is how fast it goes. Figure it out." So I did that for a decade.

And then when I started my own studio, it was really bringing together those two elements. How do we meet the demands of the business, and how do we do it in such a way that it feels very integral to who we are, and also afford to have a compass to kind of keep us safe in the industry, keep us sane, and also keep us extremely singular?

So essentially, the way that I look at acting is, it is a self-study, it is a martial art, and this business is extremely demanding on every level. It's an incredible opportunity for, dare I say, spiritual development, an opportunity to become all of who you could be if you approach it the right way. If you approach it the wrong way, you can get lost. It can be utterly overwhelming. I know that was a mouth full.

Bonnie Wallace: But it doesn't have to be that way, and actually you're already sort of segueing into my next question. There are a lot of acting schools in L.A. You could throw something across the street, and you'd probably hit an actor or an acting school. So what makes your school different? What's different about ZBS?

Zak Barnett: One of the things I learned when I was figuring out the curriculum of that master's program that I taught was, in terms of finding an actor's individual voice, these three themes of spirituality, entertainment, and activism really hold life's biggest questions.

I don't have the answers to those questions, but I do know how to pose them. I know in the process of answering them, it distills someone's essence, purpose, presence, and their connection to themselves. So I always say to my students, "The more connected you are to yourself, the more connected you are to any character." It's like they walk right over, and they sit right next to you, but if you feel like you don't know what's going on with yourself, you feel disconnected, and you're always going to have to reach for that connection to the character. So much of what we teach is about really getting connected with who you are, and then we funnel that through the craft of acting.

There are seven different teachers at our studio. There are a number of different levels. Every level starts off with a meditation and a check-in, and people are doing outside work over the course of the week. They're doing morning pages. They're doing fear inventories. They're doing gratitude lists. They're learning how the instrument of their mind works, and they are really getting honest with who they are and what's important to them.

I know these are big questions, and sometimes the words can be scary, but when I say spirituality, I don't mean any particular religious affiliation. What I mean is a connection to one's self, and to the world around them, an access to their creativity. It's kind of like, as an actor, you're both a craftsman and a mystic. Right? You're actually assembling this, using your conscious mind, assembling a character. But there has to be a point of release, and if you think that you are alone in the universe, you will never let go enough to become another character.

Because this is not the art of pretending. This is the art of becoming. We are having something come through us. That's why we love this so much. That's why you keep coming back. What's this magical thing where I can be both myself and someone else at the same time? All of a sudden, my identity isn't rigid. I'm not separate from the world. There's some intuitive thing passing through me that I don't know. In order to find that, you have to trust more than your will.

Bonnie Wallace: That intuitively makes all kinds of sense to me. I was thinking this morning … why are people so interested in actors? There are a billion things to do with your life in terms of a profession, but why are actors so focused on? I think it's because actors make us feel things.

They're like our avatars. We see the actors, and the characters that they bring to life have these experiences and feel these feelings, and we feel those with them, which is why we feel such a strong connection with the actors.

Zak Barnett: I'm going to need you to teach my class.

Bonnie Wallace: But it only works if the actors are connected to what they're doing. And if it works all the way through, there's nothing like it.

Zak Barnett:	There's a reason why there are 5,000 TV shows, and why we have an entire culture that rotates around sitting in front of this screen or that screen. It's because people are looking to find themselves through other people and to experience themselves through other people. There are actually neuroscience studies done with audience members watching actors where the audience member fires the same neurons in their brain as the actor does in theirs.
Bonnie Wallace:	They're doing the mirror neuron thing, right?
Zak Barnett:	Yeah. This goes back to the whole poet/ seeing the unseen thing, in that there's this incredible level of communication that's happening that our culture really doesn't understand, or talk about, or value actors for that reason. It's hard. It's like actors are either royalty or they're nothing. But why?
Bonnie Wallace:	They may be more like priests. They're like high priests, because to me, it's a very sacred calling done properly.
Zak Barnett:	Yes. They're healers. So I think also, that's part of the mission of this school, to orient people towards that purpose, so they don't get lost in the fray. I know first-hand, from being an actor myself, that this town is overwhelming at any age.
Bonnie Wallace:	Let's talk about love versus fear for a minute.
Zak Barnett:	I love this question ... I love the idea that the ego is kind of a wall that separates our unconscious and conscious minds, and when we're young, when we're kids, we

believe that there's a monster under the bed, and we're convinced of it, because that wall is not fully formed, that sense of protection over the unconscious. But as we get older and we get injured, that wall gets erected, and then fear really is the guard at that wall. So it's not that fear, in and of itself, is bad. I think it's a signifier of growth, or that we're about to grow. Right? That's what fear is letting us know.

We're at the edge of ourselves. This is as far as we can go.

Bonnie Wallace: Or have gone.

Zak Barnett: Or have gone, yes exactly. This is as far as we have gone. And I love the orientation to being on this planet, that my job is to evolve. It's not to be comfortable. I think we are taught in our culture, we are reinforced in every which way, that we're going to find joy in comfort, and the truth is, when we get comfort, we just make a smaller and smaller cocoon, until we're afraid of everything and everyone.

Bonnie Wallace: And it's a straitjacket.

Zak Barnett: Yes. So it's this idea of yes, we are going to get to the edge of ourselves, and we are going to walk through, and I really see the audition process as that, too. It's like you walk into a room with all of this creative capacity, and then you see a bunch of producers, and a casting director, or a network exec, and fear walks into the room.

Bonnie Wallace: Yes, in a suit.

Zak Barnett: Yes, fear walks into the room in a suit, with this fragile creative thing, and you can retreat, or you can walk into it, and if you walk into it, you grow. And in that growth, there is this cathartic spiritual experience, a beautiful experience, that people get to witness, and that you get to experience. You're going to walk out, and you are most likely going to feel, "I totally screwed that up. I need to move home." Because the wall is going to come back up, and it's going to say, "Don't do that again. You need me." And the truth is, I need you, but I need you less and less.

Right? And what I really need to do is to constantly walk towards my fear so that I can grow in this lifetime, and not shrink.

Bonnie Wallace: I love that. I had a wonderful guest on my podcast a few weeks ago, Diana Elizabeth Jordan, and we were talking about comfort zones, and she said she doesn't think of it so much as going beyond your comfort zone. She says, "I just think of it as expanding my comfort zone."

Zak Barnett: Yes, and just a little bit each day. You know, along the line of your question, I heard this great quote the other day, which is that the mind creates the abyss, and the heart crosses it.

Bonnie Wallace: Oh, I'm keeping that one. That's wonderful.

Zak Barnett: Yes, so that's the business that we're in. We're in the business of creating and transcending, and you must move through fear. You don't get to the places of greatness if you don't, so what a wonderful opportunity. For me,

9

I never knew that this would become my purpose on this planet, but it has, and to walk people through that, to walk people into this process is a gift so much greater than I knew I would receive, so I feel very honored to do what I do.

Bonnie Wallace: I think it's easy these days for people to lose sight of the fact that actors are artists, because film and TV—and even Broadway—are big business. It's millions and millions of dollars, and high stakes, and huge companies. We can get dazzled by that side of it; but what makes an individual actor successful in that world, is if and when they are deeply and thoroughly in touch with what you're talking about. That's what's necessary for them to be believable, for us to identify with them, and go on that journey with them, whatever that may be in the storyline.

Zak Barnett: Yes. It's so easy to look at the shiny thing and wonder why you're not there.

Bonnie Wallace: The red carpet, the magazines...

Zak Barnett: And let me tell you, from having seen a lot of those people in those positions now, and the paces that they went through in order to get where they went, the process is messy, and beautiful, and hard, and no one gets there without persistence, and walking through fear every day. They're still walking through fear every day.

Bonnie Wallace: It doesn't change. It's just a higher level maybe, or different.

Zak Barnett: Higher level, and higher level of ego obstacle that you've got to get through.

Bonnie Wallace: I want to talk about your emphasis on community, because this is a different aspect to what you do, but it's unusual in this industry.

Zak Barnett: So our three tenets are spirituality, entertainment, and activism. I talked a little bit about the spirituality part. The activism part, I really make it as simple, in the study of acting, as *what do I really care about.* Not *what am I taught to care about.* Not *what does culture tell me I should care about, or anyone else tell me I care about,* but my test is always *if there's a bulldozer about to knock over an old tree, I'm not about to step in front of it.*

                      I can say I can care about the environment, but I'm not going to do that. But if someone's getting assaulted on the street, I will probably jump in because there would be something in me that catalyzes me, despite my better judgment, to get involved, and that's saying what my value system actually is. So once I really start defining that, I get connected to a deep sense of purpose, and in terms of story, that's need. Those are the guts of a character. Right?

                      So we're talking about the transcendent element of creativity in the spirituality, and a lot of what we're talking about in activism is the human element, of, "What do I really care about, and how do I use that energy within the course of my acting?"

                      When I think about community, and activism, I think about, "How do I take that impulse, and who can I serve with it? Who shares similar values? How can I be of benefit with what I do and love, to people that

11

have similar value systems?" That process of identifying, that is part of you creating your own community.

I guess in Buddhism, they call this a sangha. It's like a spiritual community of people that are going through a similar process of finding something, and they're on their own path, but they're doing it together. It doesn't necessarily have to be Buddhist. Again, there's no particular religious affiliation, but it's this idea that we all have really high values, and we are all in a very difficult business, and we are doing this together. And this is a lonely town. You know?

Bonnie Wallace: It really can be, until you find your people. You move here. You leave all of your people behind, generally, and there's a sense of competition. It can take time to find your people, and your community, and to build that.

Zak Barnett: Yes, and then we reinforce it in all these different ways. We have movie night. You know what I mean? And even some of my students that have been there for a long time, some of whom you know, like Victoria Morales, Shelby Wulfert... they're both student mentors. There are a number of them, but they come into the younger kids' classes, and they assist me, and the kids can reach out at any time if they're struggling. So it's not just a concept. Again, it's the *how* of it.

If you stay attached to the meaning of what you're doing, if you stay attached to the beauty, if you stay in line with generosity, and keep your business open at the same time, the thing grows because it's true. It's the same way that I see when a student has integrity, why they become successful. I'm hoping to follow their lead with our business. There have been some great people benefiting over the years.

Ethan Herisse was a scholarship student who now is in the new Central Park Five series, *When They See Us*, with Ava DuVernay. Another one of my students, Storm Reid, is in it. They're killing it. Johnny Ortiz who was on *American Crime*, he was a scholarship student. So there are all these just incredibly worthy kids. You know what? If you're going to come, and you're going to have that level of humility, and discipline, and gratitude, and you're going to kill it, and I got space in class… we're going to figure it out.

Bonnie Wallace: I love that. So this scholarship program, how can people learn about that?

Zak Barnett: Well, this year, they've already been allotted, so I guess just stay tuned.

Bonnie Wallace: So get on the mailing list, and then you'll know about it.

Zak Barnett: Yeah, yeah. Send us an email, for sure.

Bonnie Wallace: Every actor on the planet wants to know, "How can I get noticed? How can I get cast?" Increasingly, the answer is along the lines of, "OK, create your own work. Don't sit around waiting to be chosen." I believe you're developing something for that?

Zak Barnett: Yes. Well again, this goes back to my roots actually, because this is kind of where I started with that initial master's program, and bachelor's program that I created, but it's evolved, and it's always evolving. It is so exciting

13

to me. I'll talk about the faculty shortly, but our faculty meetings are just amazing. There's so much passion, creativity, knowledge. I've been teaching for over 20 years, and I think I'm kind of in the middle of the teachers. We've been really developing this curriculum more in depth over the last month, this particular intensive.

The *Create Your Own Work* intensive, it's kind of based on the principle that ... you know how they say every writer has one story, and everything they create is somehow a variation of that? Well, I would say that that's true of every person, and of every actor. Much like how I led off by talking about my story, and this foundational experience that I had that really set my life into motion. A lot of it is starting off with a process of them identifying what that is, and maybe they're in the middle of it. Maybe they haven't gotten to the other side of it. Maybe they're just beginning.

Part of what started my story is, I remember being this kid in suburban New Jersey ... I remember the street I was on, and looking out at the sky, and nature, and feeling separate from it, and that I just didn't belong, and I didn't know whom I belonged with, and how I was going to get there.

So maybe that's the inciting incident of my journey, and then it went through New York, and then I had this experience, and then I put the pieces back together again, and then I was able to be helpful to all of these people. So maybe people are in a place where they're just sort of identifying the beginning of their story, or people have been through something, but it's definitely this idea of *your curse is your gift is your brand.*

What is the thing that you have gone through, that you are an authority on? Where have you been deeply uncomfortable, and so as a result really have some insight to share from your heart?

The first part of that week is really getting people to begin to understand that aspect of themselves, and begin to understand sharing it with people. It's going to start off with a series of exercises. We're going to start writing monologues from the point of view of that. People are also going to learn how to give feedback in a really constructive way to one another. They're going to learn how to collaborate.

We're really going to refine that story, and then we're going to take that story, and we're going to say, okay, let's take the essence of that story and drop it into a buddy comedy. Let's take the essence of that story and drop it into a sci-fi. We start with message, and then we go to voice. What are all the different ways that the heart of this can be manifested into different styles, genres, et cetera?

Then the final thing will be, now let's talk about the medium. Is this a pilot? Is this a short film? Is this a feature film? Is this a performance art piece? Is this a novel? And starting to get people to think in those different structural ways about how this different story can manifest.

The idea is that we're giving people a process. We're getting people connected to the heart of their story. We're getting them to play with their voice, how that story is expressed, and then we're giving them tangible outlets, in terms of form, and saying, "Okay, what's your next step after that? Where are you going to go from here?" So it's super exciting.

The week prior, there's another intensive. These two intensives, there's a section for teens, and there's a section for adults. We have other intensives for kids that are amazing, and I can talk about them in a second. But the week prior is called *Art of the Breakout*, and it's really, well, what makes a breakout? I've seen a lot of breakouts, and there is this level of self-acceptance, and of working with the elements that someone else might want to hide.

Everyone has this idea of how the role is, and maybe the parts that they should exclude from themselves. The people who include those things are the people who get the parts. You know what I mean?

The *Art of the Breakout* is really about, "What don't you want us to see, and how can you start to reclaim the power of that?" so that really becomes your star quality, your magnetism.

That leads into *Creating Your Own Work*. There's a week of *Art of the Breakout*, which is completely actor-focused, and then it's okay, so now you've connected with some heart there. Let's now translate that into some stories you can tell from the heart.

Bonnie Wallace: It sounds like these intensives stand on their own feet. They don't have to be linked up with other ones, but they also kind of build on one another in some ways.

Zak Barnett: Exactly. And then just to kind of round it out, in June, we have what we call our *Young Professional Actor Camps*, which are definitely more fun. You know what I mean? Not that those aren't fun, but those middle ones are kind of the soul-searching deep stuff. This, there's one focus on film, and one focused on TV. There are student mentors, who are wonderful, so a lot of young actors that the students would have recognized from shows growing up are going to be their camp counselors. One of them was in the *This is America* video, as a dancer.

So we're even going to have a *This is America* dance party, and we're going to go see a screening of a sitcom. But then they're also going to be working with all of the teachers, which is wonderful. It's great for people from out of town, because they get to find a coach they really connect with, and then have an ongoing Skype relationship with. And these are also back-to-back, so theoretically, someone could come for two weeks, do one focus on TV, and one focus on film. There's a great panel with agents and managers. So that's super fun.

Then in August, we have an episodic intensive, and there's a kid section, a teen section, and an adult section. It's more career focused, in terms of we're going to focus on auditioning for guest stars and recurring guest stars in the upcoming episodic season, and what that means in terms of a breadth of genre, and how is it different to going for a single cam on this network versus that network, and what about a multi-cam, what about a procedural drama, what about a serial drama, what about all these different gray areas? It's really going to be prepping people for the grind of episodic season.

Bonnie Wallace:

I'm happy that you started to break that down, because I think it's surprising to a lot of people when they come here, with whatever background they're bringing, in terms of acting training, that they really do need different approaches to these different genres.

17

Zak Barnett: Yes, I think about it like you wouldn't say that singing jazz is the same thing as singing classical, is the same thing as singing rock…

The way we teach it is both structural, in terms of understanding what the writing is doing and being able to really see on the page, and then is also intuitive, and physical, and experiential. We talk about something called the core experiences, and this is a through line through a lot of the classes. There's this expression, "Actors are the only people that try to feel. Everyone else tries not to."

Bonnie Wallace: Oh, that's great.

Zak Barnett: Right? The reason why actors try to feel is because it connects them to the character. It makes them feel that they have an experience so they're not in their self-consciousness. It also connects the audience to the actor.

But going after emotion is counterintuitive to the human instrument. Right? So it will look like you're pushing. It will look like you are a "bad actor," like you're soaking it up. Right? So how do we approach emotional life as an actor? I developed this thing, and again this is part of what I was talking about, of understanding how we're assembled. I've broken up 12 different core experiences.

One of the core experiences, for instance, is fear. Fear is not an emotion. It's an energy. I can feel it in my body when it's happening. It is the fuel for an emotion when it meets a circumstance. I walk into an audition, and Steven Spielberg is on the other side of the camera, and he gives me a smile. All of a sudden, that fear turns into joy, vulnerability. It starts to radiate an emotion. If he gives me the stink eye, and he's like, "Why are you here?" then I feel sad. I feel angry. I feel lost. I feel all of these things. We can, through our awareness practices, begin to really become aware of what we're experiencing energetically in our body, and interestingly enough, these correspond to genre.

People don't watch a procedural drama, a CSI, or an NCIS or whatever, because they want to experience joy. And the actor is not going to paint with that color palette. They will paint with empathy, loss, fear. These are the colors ... Now, of course someone can die in a sitcom, but people aren't coming to process loss when they watch a sitcom. We still need that sense of play that it's being filtered through, so as an actor, you need to be in touch with yourself enough to know the paints that you're coloring with, if that makes sense.

What we teach when we teach genre, or we teach auditioning, is that these are the genres. These are the color palettes that exist within the body, and this is how the structure of the writing works. Then this is how the particular room works. How do you deal with scaling a wall? Like scaling a mountain, and you're in an audition room. There's also the practical aspects of it.

Bonnie Wallace: Who is your ideal student?

Zak Barnett: Someone who is humble, hungry, interested in other people, not afraid of looking at the parts of themselves they don't like. Everyone's afraid of it, but willing to. I mean, when I look at the common denominator of the people that have been successful, they are the people that are focused when other people are working. They actually do the outside work, not because they're told

19

to, but because they're excited by it. And they're there whether they're booked on a series or not. If they can make it to class, they come to class.

Some of the students become family over time. I have a number of students that would probably refer to me as their second dad. I don't always think that I'm old enough to be a dad, but I'm so old. When did it happen? I'm in my 40s. Of course I'm way old enough to be a dad.

But some of them I've had as students since they were 13, and now they're 22. And those relationships are just so beautiful, and I feel so blessed to have had them. They are one of the great gifts of my life. So I guess I'm interested in students that are in it for the long haul too, because it's great to watch someone go through all of that, and watch their career come to life, and watch their lives come to life. I guess I would say those are the ideal.

Bonnie Wallace: You just expanded your studio space significantly. Tell me about what you've got to offer now, in terms of the space.

Zak Barnett: We were on the second floor of a two-storey building, and we took over the bottom floor, so we have the whole building now, which is amazing. We have six studios, and a couple of big event spaces, which is wonderful, because they really get to be community spaces.

When students are in between auditions, they can come hang out, and work on their sides. We also have a little mini bookstore in there, of cool books that will help an artist grow, so people can come and just read the book, or they can buy the book, or whatever. We have a screening room for students, so when they book big projects, and they want to show their family and friends, or agents or whatever; we have an event space if we do a showcase, or when we have industry events.

There's just a tremendous amount of versatility within the space. We're also getting to work with some of the different unions and whatnot, and bring some of those folks in, which is cool. Our students really get exposure to the industry in a way that feels very organic, and it's beautiful. Certain folks have referred to it as the "Equinox of acting studios."

Actors are used to being kind of dismissed, so we really wanted to create a place that honored their creativity, inspired their creativity, so that they can find greatness.

Bonnie Wallace: Your success rate's kind of crazy. What is the average success rate of actors?

Zak Barnett: I guess SAG actors, 4% booked last year.

Bonnie Wallace: Booked at all. We're not talking about "worked steadily," we're talking, "had a booking." 4% of SAG.

Zak Barnett: Yeah. I think ours last year was somewhere around two thirds.

Bonnie Wallace: So around 67%. That's astonishing.

Zak Barnett: I can't take all the credit for this because one, we do have great relationships with agents and managers. People come here because this is what they want to do. They come devoted. But then I think, whether

I'm working with a younger actor or an older actor, it doesn't matter.

The job of all of the teachers in this studio, and this is one of the things that really unifies us, is we meet the person creatively where they are and we have a dialogue from that place. Our job is to see what is happening with them and help them shape it, help them understand, nudge them past where they're comfortable, and continually expanding and all of that stuff. I think the orientation is towards humility.

It's humility, it's consistency, it's curiosity, and it's support of one another. All of them, I love the way they talk about it. It doesn't feel competitive; they feel inspired by one another to kind of one-up each other.

I've been really fortunate to work with some great people and be a part of their journey in some way or another. The list is kind of long. But the other cool thing is the teachers that I bring in. I'm very much of the mind that a lot of studios are structured where there's one master teacher, and a lot of "mini-me's" and I thought, if this is my purpose, I need to be challenged by the best people that I can find.

My own teacher teaches at the studio, and she's currently Jane Fonda's coach on her show. She was Rami Malek's coach in *Mr. Robot*. One came from the Royal Shakespeare Company. Another worked with Philip Seymour Hoffman extensively. You're not going to go wrong at my studio. Sandi McCree was on *The Wire*. She also just won an NAACP award for her work on *The Bobby Brown Story, The New Edition Story*, but she's been teaching for 35 years.

Martha's been teaching for 35 years. Michael's been teaching for 25 years. The amount of humility that is in those teacher meetings, and the amount of excitement, I'm deeply proud of that. It is not something where I'm telling everybody what to do.

Bonnie Wallace: I really love that you brought that up, because I have seen a lot of that, where you have the one master teacher, who opened the studio, and then you've got a bunch of highly transient, much younger teachers who don't have any kind of the equivalence of experience or ability.

Let's be honest. Just because you can do something—if you can—that doesn't mean you can teach it. Teaching is truly its own gift and skillset. So that's a big deal.

Zak Barnett: Yes. It also just makes it fun for everyone. It makes the studio a place where I can say, "Okay, you're tired of me? Great. Go study with Michael." You know what I mean? Go try it out.

Bonnie Wallace: I'm thinking about the age range of the people that you work with. A lot of acting schools in L.A., they tend to say, "We cater to kids," or, "We cater to adults." I find it really interesting that you say that you work with professional actors age seven and up, and you and I both know there are a lot of truly professional young actors out there. Those kids ... they're more professional in some cases than the adults.

How do you make that determination? For example, is the kid a professional because they've got an agent, or they've got representation, or they're working? If somebody was new, and they just landed here, could they work with you? Could they take classes?

23

Zak Barnett: Well, they can come in; we kind of place people based on resumé. Most of the time we ask people to go through the whole thing, but if someone has been a series regular on a show, we'll just put them in the Master Class.

We'll find the right place for them. Currently, we've been word of mouth this whole time, and we haven't done any advertising, so we don't get many people that are kind of fresh off the boat here. I think maybe 85 or 90% of our people come through agents and managers. So we're just starting to now kind of advertise in a broader market.

Bonnie Wallace: But that's going to definitely affect the readiness of the kids that you're working with. I was looking at your website, and you've got a pretty nicely broken-down age group division, in terms of the way you group the kids together. So you don't have a 9-year-old doing the scene with an 18-year-old. From a parent's point of view, I appreciate that.

Zak Barnett: For so many reasons. The truth of the material and the truth of the actor's process and the truth of what I'm seeing in any given actor is the same. But, how I relate to them, not only depends on their age, but it depends on who they are, what I perceive their strengths and limitations to be, and we have a creative conversation from there. So there's more commonality in a group of 9 to 12-year-olds in terms of how to speak to them and where they are. They might not have all the experience to draw from, but they have sort of a faster natural inclination to the truth. It's kind of closer. They can kind of stumble into doing it well if you just kind of distract them and bring them over this way.

It's interesting, the distinction for me, really, between coaching and teaching is essentially giving them the tools to evolve in their own process and create a sense of ownership over their own process.

Coaching is, *I'm a director, and I am going to get you where you need to go.* So those are two very different things.

Bonnie Wallace: And you do both?

Zak Barnett: Yeah, we do both here. We also do Skype and Face-Time coaching and Zoom classes.

Bonnie Wallace: It's funny, a lot of people still don't understand that Skype or Zoom is just as good, really, as being face-to-face. You and I are talking face-to-face right now, but there could be a screen in between us, and it wouldn't be different. You get just as much out of it.

Of course, it's nice to be in the room together… but video is absolutely valid.

Zak Barnett: You see the truth in the actor's eyes, and you hear it in their voice, and you see it in their face, all of that stuff. I don't need you in front of me to do that, I can see what's happening, I can see where you don't understand what you're saying and you're trying to prove it to me.

It's so funny, actors lie the same way that all people do. If they're not connected, they'll push to try to prove that they're connected, they'll stonewall you, they'll look away. They'll do all these telltale signs, and you say, "Okay, that's not real. We have to make it real, we have to make it specific."

Something really cool that I love to talk about in class and work with is that the unconscious doesn't know the difference between highly developed fantasy and memory. So if you start using your imagination, which is really sort of a bridge between your conscious and unconscious, if you start using that specifically enough and tell stories from the point of view of the character, you will get connected to their world. Because they'll start to have emotional responses to the things you're saying, and then it lodges there.

If I were to talk about what I did last week and I was on camera and I'm telling the truth, you would see how I felt, what I thought about everything that I experienced. If actors don't know that the language is representing experiences that they've had, and they don't make those specific, they're going to push. They're going to try to prove it, which is overacting.

Bonnie Wallace: Which is where it doesn't feel real, and which is where they lose everybody.

Tell me a little more about your programs and classes. We talked about some of these intensives and summer camps that you've got coming up, which are super cool. But what about your more ongoing programs and classes?

Zak Barnett: Well, we have classes for kids, teens, and adults. The first course is called our CORE course. Most people do come from agents and managers to us, and the level is generally pretty high, so it's not a beginning acting class by any means. We're teaching those 12 core experiences that are fundamental, so even with the kids, we create workshops around fear. We create workshops around joy. We create workshops around empathy.

They're really getting to understand this as an instrument, and then getting to apply it to the audition process across four major genres, so single-cam, multi-cam, procedural drama, and serial drama. It's self-investigation, and craft, and industry, and career.

The second level course is kind of a conservatory course. It's voice, physicality, imagination, and connection. These are the means with which an actor creates. Now that you've got the connection to yourself, and you understand the material, how do you link the two creatively? These are the tools that do that, if that makes sense.

The level after that is an intermediate on camera class, and now we get a little bit more into individual process, but also different circumstances that they're in. We cover self-tapes. We cover auditions. We cover testing, and we cover on set. That's, again, three weeks in each of those, but it's also about process, and it goes to the whole unconscious and incompetent, to unconscious and competent journey.

What are my different tools at different stages of creation? Here are 15 in this category. Here are 15 in this category. Here are 15 in this category. Because in any given day, I am different and my script is different, so this is a moving target. I need all of these tools to find a way to attach this to this. It becomes a self-created process by being exposed to all these tools, and then funneling them through self-tape, audition, blah, blah, blah. Right?

Bonnie Wallace: Until they become intuitive.

Zak Barnett: The next level is an advanced scene study class, and that is "let's get unconscious." It starts off with a 45-minute-long meditation. It gets you deep into your intuition and your unconscious, so your choices ... it's like a digestion for all that information that you've just learned, so now that your choices become much more intuitive. They don't become conscious.

The last one is the Master Class, and that is a combination of audition work and scene study work, but now it's really a question around personal development. What's the edge of yourself? Where do you meet fear?

We choose a different theme every session. We also read a book together that we discuss in the beginning. I ask that everyone do the meditation, the morning pages, the peer mentor... There's a big check-in about that. For instance, the theme this session is change, and resistance to change. I ask everyone weekly, at the beginning of the session, "Name some place in your life that you feel you're resistant to change." I want them to track that over the course of the week with all of these practices, and then ask that same question of the material. It's amazing how it lights up the material, and the reason why it lights up the material is because the deepest part of them is interacting with the script. Right?

There's this expression, "A problem once articulated is half-solved." When you ask a question of yourself, the universe conspires to give you an answer. Either you answer it mentally: the world comes to you and says, "This is your answer," or you have a physical experience of change.

We're doing this kind of work while we're working on scenes, and bringing those questions to the characters in the scenes. Of course the scene, every time you do it, is going to reveal itself as new. And that's what makes it alive. There's nothing worse than an actor that has decided what to do in every moment of the scene, because that's not acting.

Bonnie Wallace: It's like recitation. It's dead.

Zak Barnett: Yeah, and fear will make you want to do that, because it's something you can control. I'm going to do this here, and do that here, and do that here. The truth is, each time you try to do that, you are that much less likely to be able to do it. There are diminishing returns every time you enter that process. But if you go into that audition room… here's a suggestion. You go into that audition room, and as the character, you ask a question through the text, you will discover it again. It's not that your existing choices will go away. They will have created a groundedness within you. It will just light up all the discoveries you've made through a new lens.

Bonnie Wallace: I like that. That's good advice. Any other advice for auditions?

Zak Barnett: I think a lot of it's just having awareness of what's happening, that your fear voice is going to come in. It's a sign of greatness coming. You just have to be strong enough to walk into it. Don't shut down. Step into it. Don't rehearse something that you're going to perform. Create an experiment for yourself, where you actually have a creative experience. I know this is said over and over, and it's almost impossible for an actor to hear when they're afraid, but the people on the other side of the camera want you to succeed. It means they get to go home, and they get to go home happy.

Bonnie Wallace: It's that basic. It is. They're on your team. You can't say this enough. It's so critically true.

Zak Barnett: But when fear gets in there ... they talk about the limbic brain. It's that fight, flight, freeze thing that comes in, and you only see danger. There is stuff happening in your brain while you're going through the audition process, and to start becoming aware of that, and start working with that instead of blocking it, instead of thinking that you can just muscle your way through it, start working with yourself intelligently, and remember the mind creates the abyss, and the heart crosses it.

Bonnie Wallace: That's beautiful. That is great advice for life. What about rejection? That's a conversation for everybody in the industry. Parents worry about how to help their kids survive the pain of rejection, and adult professional actors are always grappling with it. How do you frame that? How do you hold this whole idea of rejection?

Zak Barnett: I don't know if there is an easy answer to it, but what I do know is what doesn't kill you makes you stronger. It is expansion. Look, I get my heart broken, I can decide not to open my heart again, or I can open my heart, and when I open my heart, I open it even wider. We talk about the sacredness of being an actor. To find who you really are is not easy. It's not given to everyone.

Bonnie Wallace: It's not light work.

Zak Barnett:	It's not light work. It's going to hurt. It is that constant breaking of your own barriers that is going to make you a tremendous force, not only as an actor, but as a person. You just need a really good community to be inside of it so you don't feel isolated within that experience. You need good mentorship; you need people that you trust to help you navigate it. But ultimately, I don't know what is a better teacher than rejection. There's this quote, it's so dramatic. It's at the beginning of the play, *Angels in America*. It's not from the play itself, it's from something else, but it says, "In murderous times, the heart breaks and breaks and lives by breaking."
Bonnie Wallace:	That's wonderful.
Zak Barnett:	We can expand with it. Again, I think actors have a sacred purpose in this world. We are healers, and we have to know our own pain to know our characters'.
Bonnie Wallace:	And then to be able to connect enough with that, that you're able to connect with the audience, which is what the audience is hoping for, it's what they're looking for. That's why people tune in and show up, they want that experience of connection, an authentic connection.
Zak Barnett:	Yes, I think it gives the audience the experience of, "I'm actually not alone." It helps gets rid of the illusion that we are separate. Again, it goes to the unseen.
Bonnie Wallace:	Any advice for young people who want to be actors? You talked about yourself growing up in New Jersey, and feeling that you didn't belong there, and I know that the world is filled with passionate, creative young

people who feel like they want this thing. What's the bridge from here to there? How do I do it? How do I get there? What would you tell someone who actually can't just pick up and come out here right now, but what could they do to maybe start putting stones on the path that they can walk on?

Zak Barnett: Well, find your tribe. I remember when I was 16. Again, there wasn't much in terms of arts programming ... and I was selected for this thing called Governor's School for the Arts in New Jersey, and basically for a month, they chose 10 dancers, 10 actors, a symphony, a bunch of visual artists, and they put them up at this college, and they gave them daily training.

I just remember being there and thinking, "Wow, I have found my people." I didn't know they were out there. And the power of that is ... I don't know what's more significant than finding your people in the world. Find your people locally. Maybe it's just an hour away.

This is very precocious of me, I know, but I remember I had this mantra in my head. When I was a kid, my mom would always call me a poet savant, because I never knew what words meant, but they somehow ended up meaning the right thing. I remember I had this mantra in my head, and I didn't know what it meant, which was, *truth has its own momentum.* You will make it here. You will make it here. You know? If that's what you are supposed to do, you will make it here. So just keep connected to that truth. Keep knowing what you know. Try to find other people that know the same thing, and we'll see you soon.

Bonnie Wallace: That's beautiful. Anything else you'd like to share?

Zak Barnett: I'd just like to welcome your listeners to reach out to the studio. This summer, we do have a number of intensives. We have I think 15 weekly classes right now, so there are lots of ways to interact for kids, teens, and adults. We also have a great pilot season intensive, if you're looking a few months out.

Then, like I said, just want to say this is a really beautiful path, so go into it with an open heart, and I hope to meet you one day.

DIANE CHRISTIANSEN

Founder, Christiansen Acting Academy

"If you have gone one direction with your career and you're
not getting the results, let's reinvent, let's recreate."

Diane Christiansen is an award-winning acting teacher and founder of Diane
Christiansen Coaching in Los Angeles as well as the brand new Christiansen
Acting Academy in Agoura Hills. She offers weekly classes to actors from age
three to adult, broken down by age and focus, and including scene study, audition, technique, improv and character development, as well as offering commercial classes, casting director workshops, demo reels and private coaching.

Alumni include Hailee Steinfeld, Miranda May, David Henrie, Spencer Daniels,
Danielle Panabaker, Jason Dolley, Amy Bruckner, Joey Luthman, Malcom
David Kelley, and Joy Lauren.

Bonnie Wallace: Can you describe your approach to acting? There are
a lot of different ways to teach acting, and I'm always
curious about the differences between teachers and
techniques. How do you do it?

Diane Christiansen: For me, I was inspired by the work that I did at the Actors Studio. So I'm a "Method Girl". My sensibilities
are definitely deep rooted in the Method, and I trained

with some of the greatest teachers in the country: Academy Award nominee Sally Kirkland, and Joseph Bernard in New York. It transformed my work, becoming a Method actor; it really changed what I was doing. What I was doing was always natural as an actor, but those techniques took me down a path of truth that threatened me and challenged me on every level to be more of who I was. In that self-discovery, I found my gold as an actor. It only enhanced whatever I had done up until that point, and changed everything.

I'm not against throwing in a little Meisner, throwing a little of any of the five American Masters in my classes, but my adult class is a twelve-week Method conservatory, and I love teaching those techniques. I love seeing what happens to actors with them. It's not for everyone, but 90% of the actors love it, really love it. I teach it to kids and teenagers.

They're getting a lot of Method Techniques too. They all respond well, they all are very proud to be Method actors.

Bonnie Wallace: I think there's nothing more exciting for an actor than having a sense of discovery, and there's nothing more exciting than for the audience to feel as though they're watching somebody in the moment of self-discovery.

Diane Christiansen: When it's organic and truthful. I say to the actors, "If you have altered the electricity in the room, you're doing your job."

Bonnie Wallace: You've got extensive experience coaching young actors who audition for a really wide range of projects, from serious films to the Disney Channel. Are there any differences on how you would approach an audition for a Disney show versus one for say, a TV drama or a film?

Diane Christiansen: So much so, I made a video about that. Adjusting your style to different scripts. I made a video for Master Talent Teachers, which is our free virtual university for performers, mastertalentteachers. com. You can also watch over 300 archived training videos on YouTube from Master Talent Teachers ... in fact, Miranda May is in that video, when she was maybe 15. She's in that video, giving an example of how you adjust.

It's really easy to work with theater actors, because they come in with all of this energy, and they play out a full emotion, with their full instrument, and it's very easy to dial them back to film and television style, or even to underplay. But it's very difficult to take a film actor and bring out what you need for a multi-cam show, for a sitcom. Very difficult. Plus, theater actors understand stagecraft, so that's easy.

First of all, a great actor's a great actor's a great actor. If you've got that to work with, you can go anywhere. But I think that an actor who wants to be a film actor, but has no idea about stage craft, will be lost, because the blocking, and all the things that happen on set are pretty much the same things that happen on stage, and you need to understand how to function within that structure.

So we teach the structure, and we encourage actors to come to class and treat it like the set. If you understand that structure, you can have as much fun in that structure as you want, and we encourage that.

Bonnie Wallace: Just about everybody I talk to in this industry comes from that point of view. Whether they're directors, or casting directors, or agents, they all say if you have good theater training, that's such a leg up for you.

Diane Christiansen: I think theater is to an actor what ballet is to dancers. What the classics are to music. It's the best foundation to have.

Bonnie Wallace: So how would you change your approach for an audition for say, a Disney show versus a TV drama, or a film? Would you approach those differently? Obviously you would, but how?

Diane Christiansen: Well, having been an on-set coach for Disney and Nick, it's all about energy, pace, and cramming a lot of dialogue in 22 minutes for a half-an-hour multi-cam show. It's all about energy, and it's very theatrical.

It's very much like theater. It's very much about allowing yourself to be very animated and over the top, whereas the dramas and the single cam shows are much more internal, and it's enough to play your thoughts as opposed to playing out a full emotion.

I've seen actors just raise an eyebrow, and it was so effective. Of course, their internal landscape was filled with something; it wasn't empty, so they've learned to fill it up with the kinds of things we do in our Method classes. You can play your thoughts on film and camera, and the camera will read it.

But you can't do that in theater, you've got to reach the back row.

Bonnie Wallace: Let's talk about pilot season.

Diane Christiansen: It's traditional pilot season right now.

Bonnie Wallace: Traditional pilot season, I love that you frame it that way. There's a lot of anxiety about it for a lot of actors. Thousands come out to L.A. every year between January and say March, April, but more and more shows are being cast year-round, and on top of that, movies are cast year-round anyway.

Diane Christiansen: And commercials.

Bonnie Wallace: And commercials, right? What are your current thoughts about pilot season?

Diane Christiansen: Well, it's changed in the last seven or eight years. Mostly because there's more on television, and there is Netflix, and there are reality shows, there's just so much casting. But pilots traditionally did cast, back in the day, between January and April, and now, a lot of those green-lighted projects are shooting their episodes already in January. We're already casting characters for second and third episodes, so I'm seeing a lot of that. But this year I was shocked. We were coaching for network pilots in July, in August, in September, in October, November and December. A lot in November, and a lot in August.

A lot of new shows. And some of them are already green-lighted. They were shows that were not just pilots, they were already picked up and casting, they were casting early. I really believe it's because the networks especially want the best actors on board and attached as early as possible. I don't even know what early is anymore.

Bonnie Wallace: There's no line.

Diane Christiansen: I think there's a little hiatus in May.

Bonnie Wallace: Where everybody collapses after so-called pilot season.

Diane Christiansen: Everybody collapses and then we have all that end-of-school stuff and there's a little lull in May, and then they start casting episodes of the new pilots that are picked up in June, and they're full tilt by August with episodics. Honestly, for the people that are thinking of coming to L.A. for the first few times, or for pilot season with their children especially, you can come in summer, and if you have a good agent, and you're getting good auditions, and you're right for the part, there are pilots casting in the summer.

Bonnie Wallace: And there are movies casting in the summer.

Diane Christiansen: And lots of commercials.

Bonnie Wallace: And there are networks for which pilot season is neither here nor there. Disney, Nickelodeon, and Fox don't pay any attention whatsoever to pilot season.

Diane Christiansen: It's always happening. I do think though, that when you see a lot of it in the fall now, they're getting those actors attached.

Bonnie Wallace: I always thought that fall was a nice time for actors to come out because that's when you get the opportunities for the episodics; and you can cut your teeth on

39

some juicy guest star roles, which is a very good way to build your resume.

Diane Christiansen: Most of the actors that I've trained in the last five years that come out consistently are coming in the fall, and they're coming in the winter.

Bonnie Wallace: Tell me more about your new space.

Diane Christiansen: We're just opening a second studio, Christiansen Acting Academy in Agoura Hills. So this is a huge time for us. And I thought going into it, "Well, I want to do this for Tess for the future." But I'm in it and I'm all in. Now I'm excited and ignited and ready again.

Bonnie Wallace: So just for clarification, Tess is your daughter.

Diane Christiansen: She's my daughter and she's been teaching for nine years now. And she had a career as an actor her whole childhood. In fact, she just stopped last year after starring in two movies and she told me, "I love being in the studio teaching. I don't enjoy going to auditions and being on set anymore. It's just not fun for me anymore."

Bonnie Wallace: Well, and if it's not fun, you need to stop. You need to change gears and reinvent.

Diane Christiansen: It's a shame because she's really good. But again, being true to yourself and reinventing yourself. She is so excited about the studio. By next year we'll have camps too.

Bonnie Wallace: So you're going to end up with two locations? You're not letting go of your old location in North Hollywood?

Diane Christiansen: Not at all. We'll still be there. And we do our Agent Showcases there and we want to keep that location primarily for our Agent Showcases.

Bonnie Wallace: Well, let's talk about those Agent Showcases right now because what you offer with the showcases is such a big deal. It's so hard to find. You're the only person I know of in L.A. that's reputable that offers essentially standalone professional showcases. And they're affordable.

Diane Christiansen: Well, that's the whole point. The whole point is to reach as many actors of all ages as we can. We did present showcases for years that were end-of-session-presentations, like a recital, if you will, and agents have always come. Not as many as come to this, but we're in our 14th year of separating our showcases from our classes and making them a standalone workshop.

So people audition to get in, actors age six to adult, and they have to pass the audition. We feature singers as well. But the wonderful thing is the A-list reps keep coming back and back. We have that strong core, even though we have different agents and managers attending because they know they're going to see people ready to work. And because it's a four-night workshop, we spend the first night branding and giving a parent's seminar, which is just so important.

Just trying to get everybody's resumé in standard industry format is a huge thing. And that is the first thing that agencies see when they come and open their packets, and if they know that that's being done, that's very encouraging. And then we add another layer. We encourage branding both on their visual content and in

41

their scene work, which is my favorite thing about the showcase, which I think contributes to it being special, is once everybody auditions and we find the best people to present, I get to choose all the scenes. And it's fun.

That's really what I love to do. And I think I do that best. Tess will keep an eye on everything I'm doing and she's very intuitive and she'll say, "That's not going to show the best of what that person could do. Let's change the scene." And she might do that with one or two because they're her students primarily, and she knows them a little bit better. So we coordinate on that and we wind up with a very well-branded seminar.

Bonnie Wallace: Tell me more about branding with the scene choices.

Diane Christiansen: It's really casting. What I'm really doing is casting. And being a director, I love that. So we have a file of showcase scenes that are very character-driven, that are very specific types. And then we keep adding to that as we do showcases because obviously we have new types come in and new brands come in.

Branding is probably the hardest thing for an actor to do for themselves. In fact, they stress over it the first night. "Well, what's my brand?" And I tell them, "You're making it harder than it needs to be because you want to show your range," which is normal. We all want to do that as actors. I wanted to do that.

I didn't want to be limited by one little niche when I was an actor. But the truth is, that's your best way to get started. The best way to get a foot in the door is to be something very specific that nobody has to think about, it's just presented there for you. And agents love that because they're starting to say, "I don't have anybody like that in my roster. Never thought about a person like that." We had a showcase on Monday and some of the actors were asking me how I honestly thought in my professional opinion they would do. And I said, "There is no answer."

Sometimes the person that we think is outstanding and that people are going to fight over just doesn't happen. And sometimes the people that we think, "I don't think they're going to..."

Bonnie Wallace: So four nights in and out, done. Not weeks or months?

Diane Christiansen: No, no, no. And people don't have to be our students. Usually half of them are.

But then we audition as many as we can, and they come from everywhere. We had people in from New York and Miami, for this one, Atlanta. So it's drawing nationwide.

It used to be a three-night workshop, and then we added the branding seminar and the parents' seminar and made sure that it was mandatory that a parent attends for anyone under 18. And we have four worksheets for them. We do a branding exercise with the actors. They love it, and it really gets them thinking and on track with creating a branded resume, just getting their stamp on everything. The looks, the colors, the fonts. It's all important. And it's fun.

Bonnie Wallace: It's a business. It's a creative business, but it's still a business and this stuff applies to all businesses.

Diane Christiansen: And when that business side to anybody's career is missing as an actor, there's just too much competition now. You have to be the package, you just do.

43

We also do casting director workshops. And when the casting directors come in to Actors' Platform, we talk about self-tapes a lot. And 50% love taped auditions, 50% do not. Mostly they want to be in the room with the actor and know who they're hiring. And of course they have to wait for the callback for that. They do like seeing more people, but they also know that anybody can make a self-tape look good.

And it might not even be a good actor.

Bonnie Wallace: They might have taken 30 takes.

Diane Christiansen: So that's the good thing for actors—they can make themselves look really great on camera. If they're not coaching and collaborating, it's not going to be as good. But in an hour we can pretty much get anybody looking good with coaching and taping. We've had bookings on our self-tapes. Straight bookings, which is amazing to me.

Bonnie Wallace: That's wonderful. Almost 30 years teaching acting in L.A. You've worked with some incredibly successful young actors. You've been named best L.A. Acting Coach for Backstage Choice twice. What do you think explains your success?

Diane Christiansen: I really believe hard work. I built this business from nothing when I lived in the mountains in a small community and found I had a lot of industry people living in the mountains, a lot of writers, musicians, and actors. But then we had a community theater up there and I really think, first of all, doing what you love is the key to success. As Marianne Williamson says, "Wherever your bliss is, there is your treasure." And I agree with that 100%. And that's what I taught my kids, as I know you did. You just figure out what you love and do that because life's too short to do anything else.

Obviously we have a lot of people that have been with us a long time and I think that loyalty is really another mark of success, more so than any amount of money or popularity. Loyalty and the long-term commitment that actors have with us really make me the happiest. I mean, they're finishing one workshop and asking, "What can I do next?" They're finishing the session in there, "What can I do next? Can I train in both locations? So seeing them just ready for the next thing, always wanting something new, which actors do.

They want to do as much as they can. So I think part of the success is maintaining long-term relationships for years. Our newest instructor, Duncan Barrett Brown's been with us seven years.

Bonnie Wallace: And you're doing your own rebrand. It's been Diane Christiansen Coaching, but now you're moving into The Christiansen Acting Academy. What does that mean for an actor? Is it any different from one location to the other? What are your offerings?

Diane Christiansen: Well, we had a meeting trying to finalize how we're going to do that last week. To start all this, I should talk about the fact that we're reinventing.

Bonnie Wallace: Reinvention is a juicy subject.

Diane Christiansen: It's a necessary addendum to an acting career. Absolutely. And it's one of the things we talk about when we're branding. If you have gone one direction with your career and you're not getting the results, let's reinvent, let's recreate. Ask Madonna, ask Lady Gaga. I mean, they're constantly putting something new out there in regards to their brand. And I think that they're great examples of just using your creativity to the max. It's another way to use your creativity and it's necessary. And you and I hear actors all the time say, "My agent doesn't love my photos and I love this and they like this, but I'm not getting calls." And I say, "Okay, it's time to rebrand."

It's time to rethink what your niche is, what your type is, how you're putting yourself out there, who you're being in social media, who you're being in the world, and what are you presenting on your website? What are you presenting on all of your social media sites? And honestly, you and I know that you need content. The goal is to be an actor; it's to be a performer, a celebrity, and a recognized personality. So we encourage reinvention.

Bonnie Wallace: I think it's a necessary conversation for all of us just as humans, because life is not static, and we need to kind of roll with it. And we do need to reinvent ourselves as time goes by.

But I'm thinking about young actors in particular. For example, you may have incredible success as a child actor and then hit a kind of a wall when you hit your teens, and your face and your body are changing. You don't look like you looked when you were a cute little child actor, now you're a teen actor and it's different. And then from the teen actor transitioning into the young adult actor, that's another big bump for a lot of kids.

You're not less talented, in fact you're probably more talented because you've got even more experience. But then who are you? You do need to sort of come to terms with the fact that you're not who you were; you're someone else now. People see you differently.

Diane Christiansen: Absolutely. And that's another topic that comes up quite a bit because we have so many child and teen actors that do emerge into their adult career. And I've seen some of them do that very smoothly and I've seen a lot of different kinds of stories in their reinventing.

David Henrie for example. David was with us a long time, including for his first pilot, *The Pitts* when he was 13. He's the same age as Tess, so they were in class together quite a bit. And the Panabaker girls, they were all in the same class. Joy Lauren. It was just a hugely talented class. And he went from *Wizards of Waverly Place* to a voiceover to a Miyazaki movie at 18.

He's had great luck. He and Hailee Steinford are two of the Cinderella stories. But he definitely moved into his young adult career with voiceover, which I thought was brilliant. I thought that was really fortunate. And then there are others like Miranda May who lost a hundred pounds between 16 and 19.

She was always brilliant. She was doing standup at 10.

Bonnie Wallace: Let's talk more about your new school. I have seen with a lot of acting teachers who start their own schools, that it can become almost a personality cult, where the temptation is to feel like if you're not working with the founder, it doesn't count.

Diane Christiansen: It's come up. I would never have a teacher in our studio who hadn't fully experienced our curriculum or
brought something to the party that was so needed.
We have had a few teachers over the years that weren't
our students. Well, actually only one; every other teacher we've had has come from our studio and they're
fully immersed in the curriculum and it's very Method
based, I will admit. So it's very specific, especially with
our adults and teenagers. Because I'm an Actors Studio
actor so of course I'm going to bring what I love.

People can come to the Agoura Hills location and
try as many classes as they want. And we're going to
have studio membership, which we had never done in 28
years. People just paid for their sessions. But now we're
going to have a six-month membership and a one-year
membership and people can buy either one, and take an
enormous number of classes under that umbrella.

So we're creating something new there too and
we're going to have homeschool classes during the day,
for kids and teenagers.

And I think people have offered that, but I don't
know if they've offered it in Agoura Hills. So we're
excited about that, too. And Tess did homeschool for
part of her teen years and she's familiar with what
that's like, and she did some homeschool acting classes
too, that I taught.

Bonnie Wallace: You were saying that you use *The Method* because of
your background.

Can you talk a little bit more about that?

Diane Christiansen: Again, it's doing what you love to do. I know we have
all of our awards for kids and teens over the years, but

we've always taught adults. We would always incorporate a little Method into our curriculum, my favorite things. And then all of a sudden one day I thought, I want to reinvent my adult class, and I changed it to Actors Core House of Method. I created a Method curriculum for 12 weeks. There are about 25 Method techniques that are very specific to the Actors Studio, which was my alma mater. And I created an all-Method class, which may be my favorite class now.

I don't know. I love the teenagers quite a bit. I really love that they're on the brink of their dreams. It's a very exciting place to be with them. But Method... we do 12 weeks and then we do another 12 weeks and you pretty much get all the Method techniques, and then we repeat. And people have stayed for years. But you're going find that a lot of the Method techniques cross over into all of the other sensibilities being taught out there, because the five American Masters all came from Stanislavski.

So they all have the same training. They just branched off, Uta Hagen and Elia Kazan and Meisner and Stella Adler and Strasberg. Those are the five American Masters. So they are similar, even though they claim to be very different.

They're all under the same umbrella. But the thing that I think the Method helps people learn the most about is themselves, because we're going to dig down into some gritty stuff. As Lee Strasberg used to say, "Your pain is your gold." I wish I'd said it, but I didn't. He also said, "You know you're in the presence of true talent when the electricity in the room is altered." And he said that when he saw Eleonora Duse first perform back in the 20s. He said that she alters the electricity in the room. We had that in Monday night's showcase with one of our actors. When she got up, she transformed the energy in the room and that's when you know you're in the presence of something really great.

I was just reading an interview on Casting Frontier and there were four or five actors that talked about why they don't do the Method. And one of them was Charlize Theron, who I felt understood the Method better than anybody else that was quoted. And she said, "I liked it, but I can't do all that digging. That deep down, it's exhausting for me. And for me, I just can't do it when I'm on set because it's too much of my own stuff." And yes, the Method is about using your own life in the work. Of course, we have it as a technique.

Of course, we have the *Magic If,* and we work off the top of our head and in the moment. We have a lot of those techniques, but we also are willing to go in and pull out and use some of the most difficult parts of our life in the work. And for me it changed my work completely.

Completely changed me as an actor and it simplified my work because there's something about organic and truth that's very simple. It's not complicated. But it's not for everybody.

Bonnie Wallace: Nothing is for everybody. And that's one of the many things that I've come to love about Los Angeles: there's a true range of people to work with and learn from. And you can find your fit, your tribe, your people.

Diane Christiansen: Exactly. And the people in that class stay a long time because they've connected with the Method.

Bonnie Wallace: Something you said a minute ago struck me. When you said, "We've got a 12-week program and then there's a second 12-week program and then we do it again." I just flashed on how a lot of people think, "All right I've taken that class, I'm done now... where's the new class?"

Diane Christiansen: The new thing. There's a ton of that.

Bonnie Wallace: But it's not really like that. There's a classic model for child development that's a spiral. And the idea is that you keep revisiting the same stuff over and over and over again, just at a different level. So you're going to want to take the curriculum again and again and again because you're going to be a different person in it each time. Bringing a different level of understanding to it.

Diane Christiansen: And life experience. One of the things that I've noticed about actors—actors are movie buffs, right? They love to talk about movies, they love to go to movies, love to sit in the dark theater and absorb it all and to feel something and all the things we go to the movies for. But I always tell them, "Get out of the movies and get into your life. Go out there and get a little messy because you're going to need it. You're going to need to be whole and complete to be a great actor and you need to be out there living your life and not just sitting in the movies."

Bonnie Wallace: Yes, you need some real-life experience to bring so you can make a role come alive.

Diane Christiansen: It's true. And without that, that can be a missing. As you approach being the package, it can be a missing.

I see people just being too cautious or scared. And so when I say that our class really teaches people about themselves, I think that's what they learned the most about, honestly. And obviously they get the tools to use. I've had actors come in and go, "Well, I'll never be that person that cries on cue. I'll never cry in front of anybody." They cry right on the beat that they need to cry on now. And they've been there three years. And I remind them that they said that when they came in.

And I look at the class, especially the people that have been there three years and more, and I think, these are Method actors. These are real Method actors. They're using the tools, they're using the techniques, they're living through their own past and they're allowing it, they have faith in it, they trust it. And it's really exciting because we go on task every session. On task is where you go out and you live through the life of a character for a week. You go live your life as that character for a week.

Bonnie Wallace: That sounds like fun.

Diane Christiansen: It's very fun. I do it in the teen classes too. Every six months they go on task. So they're out there being somebody else for a week and seeing how that affects them. So that's my favorite Method technique, is being on task. And if you look at our great actors, I mean Michelle Williams is one that goes on task for everything. And you look at all the things that people do to prepare for a role, that's what we're doing. We can talk about the business, we do. We talk about audition technique and we separate those classes. But you get into a Method study class and you're going to be working like a working actor and it changes their lives because when they commit to that, then other things happen.

Bonnie Wallace: I'm just thinking about what that does for someone on a human level. I mean, I don't think you can be a real actor and not develop an extraordinary sense of empathy for human beings.

Diane Christiansen: Absolutely. And for the human condition in general.

Method things we don't do with the kids too much. Our tweens start to get a little bit of it, certain techniques. So it's incorporated throughout our curriculum pretty strongly and that makes me happy.

Bonnie Wallace: Well, it absolutely works gorgeously for some people, and it doesn't make sense for everybody. And that's the whole thing for me… if you try something and it's not a fit, okay fine. It's not a fit for you. It doesn't mean it's bad and wrong or you're bad and wrong.

It's just, "Okay, that's just not a fit." So you look until you find your fit, and when you do, then you run with it.

What classes are you offering currently? It sounds like you're about to broaden your offerings now that you're getting a second location.

Diane Christiansen: We're reinventing everything except Monday nights. Monday nights are pretty much going to stay the same. We have screen teens at 5:00 pm and we have my Actors Core House of Method class at 7:00 pm. I will be having one of our students who's been in class for seven years teach the Actors Core class in NoHo. Duncan Barrett Brown, who is starring in a new Netflix series—he's an amazing working actor, he's a triple threat—will teach the Actors Core class. He's fully ingrained into the curriculum.

I will be teaching Actors Core in Agoura Hills, I think on Wednesday nights. And Saturdays we'll be changing, we'll be doing audition technique in NoHo for kids and then one for adults. And then we have our tween class, that doesn't change from 4:00 pm to 6:00 pm. That is a very, very strong class and always has been. And Tess and I share that class. I do two weeks, and then she does two weeks. I think that's another reason why it's so successful because they've got the eye of two teachers on them with the same curriculum.

Bonnie Wallace: That's great. I'm a very loyal person, and I have a lot of friends who are acting teachers, and still I feel that it's important and beneficial to get coaching and teaching from more than one person. You're inevitably going to learn different things from different people because we all have something different to offer, right?

Diane Christiansen: Absolutely. Sometimes after three years, if somebody's still with me, and they're not growing, I will say, "I think it's time for you to get another coach. I still would love to coach you, but I also want you to find some other techniques to help you grow."

The most successful people that I've trained are training with a couple of people, two or three people. Hailee (Steinfeld) trained with three coaches for a year before her mom would let her get an agent.

And Lucas Barker, one of our other very successful child actors ... I can't say the name of it yet, but he's working on a huge feature film with the Coen brothers.

He's got a huge role and it's a film with Denzel Washington and Frances McDormand and I just can't say more beyond that. But he has always had two or three coaches. Most of our successful people are training with more than one person.

Bonnie Wallace: I don't think that's disloyal, I think it's smart.

Diane Christiansen: Miranda (May) always had somebody for stand up and she had us for everything else. So she always had two coaches.

Bonnie Wallace: Let's talk about auditioning for a minute. Because in between the training and the coaching and the success, there's auditioning. And you don't get the success without being good at auditioning.

Diane Christiansen: I think that's one thing that a lot of actors overlook. They might not look at the fact that audition technique is very specific. What you do in the room at each of the four stages of an audition is very different.

But it's very important to know what happens at the audition, the callback or the producer session, the executive session and network testing for series regulars. And when you get into the network testing for series regulars, it gets very gritty and people don't realize how much is coming at them at that point, including contracts, which are placed before you before you go into the network testing.

And yes, it's done with the agents and yes, it's done with the parents, but it's still in their head going, "I could be making $40,000 a month, I could be making $200,000 a month." I mean all of a sudden, it's a money mindset and that can really hurt you as an actor. Because it's the wrong focus.

Bonnie Wallace: And you have to sign all that stuff before you go in for the final round.

Diane Christiansen: That's having quite an effect on you. No matter what your socioeconomic standing is in the world, it's going to have an effect on you. So we have techniques that help you refocus on what's important and what to be thinking about. And I think when we get to that point with our actors in that fourth class, in our four-night workshop, we have it for adults and we have it for kids and teens. It's kind of like the NBA or the NFL hire coaches to come in and mentally prepare the players to go into that game. It's the same thing.

Bonnie Wallace: Mindset is everything.

Diane Christiansen: It's everything. "What are you thinking about when you walk throug that door?" We give them very specific things to visualize and think about and present the moment they cross the threshold. It's incredibly important and we make it so affordable. I would love to see actors know that those four classes are going to change your life—even parents, because there's a lot of paperwork that we distribute, and we give examples of contracts and we give examples of the kinds of things that are going to be coming at you when you get there. And we really specifically help them understand what to expect at an executive session when you've got 20 suits there.

Bonnie Wallace: Which can be absolutely intimidating.

Diane Christiansen: It's very different than an audition with the casting director and a reader.

A lot of people never get past a producer session. I would say 90% of actors never get past, they don't get into the executive sessions, the network testing, but they could if they knew a little bit more about those four stages. I really believe that.

Bonnie Wallace: Everything I do is driven by a desire to educate and inspire. And the whole education piece breaks down to: the more you understand about how this works, the better choices you can make.

Diane Christiansen: Knowledge is power.

Bonnie Wallace: It is. I feel so passionate about this, it's so clear to me. And it's really kind of arrogant to assume that you don't need to understand this stuff. And you can succeed without understanding. Everything is possible, of course. You could, but wouldn't you like better odds than that?

Diane Christiansen: I mean, you may have a dazzling, charismatic personality that's just going to win over anybody no matter what. Some people have that. Obviously Jennifer Lawrence has that, but it can also be developed.

So it's important to learn how to pop and how to stand out and what to do and what not to do. I think what not to do is just as important.

Bonnie Wallace: Agreed. Any special advice for audition self-tapes? Because that's becoming more and more important. Even if you're here in L.A., the first round of auditions is often self-tapes. With a self-tape, there's no excuse for turning in a bad one really because everybody knows you had a number of takes to make it. But still there are things that you can do to make them better or worse.

Diane Christiansen: First of all, try not to tape against a white wall. That's probably the least appealing. A beige wall is much better. A blue wall. Film yourself against a colored wall or curtain. Wear your best colors, wear something complementary to the background, no black, white or gray. You should find the best reader you can, because that's the one place the reader can be good, that will help the self-tape, whereas in the room, the reader will generally read pretty quickly, and without any emotion. But on tape, it's very good to have a good reader, and make sure the reader stands away from the camera, because the camera has a microphone in it, so we don't want to hear more of the reader than we do the actor. So those are a couple of technical things.

Bonnie Wallace: The loud reader and the quiet actor is one that I think a lot of people stumble on.

Diane Christiansen: Casting directors now try to confuse you in the way that you title each clip and they say that the reason they do that is because if people can't follow instructions, they don't want to work with them. So self-tapes are becoming a whole universe of their own. And when I heard that, I asked a casting director about that and they said, "Well, there are so many people in self-tapes now that if we see that they don't title each clip correctly, then we're not going to watch it."

Bonnie Wallace: It has a little test built into it.

Diane Christiansen: They say it's a test, that's the quote from Casting Frontier, "We're testing you to make sure you can follow instructions."

I get it, I do. With the number of actors, I get it. They have to weed through those who can take the time to follow instructions. And we teach this in our seminar now. We gave you a checklist, and if you can't look at that checklist and read one email a week during those four weeks, then you're not going to be able to cut it with an agent or a manager.

This is it. You have to step up now. And we had 75% of our people really wanting to step up last week, and that other 25% sort of caved.

They realized they had to do more than be cute and talented and they're not going to rise to the occasion. So back to self-tapes though, I think that's the most important thing to know that I've learned in the last month.

Bonnie Wallace: Follow instructions.

Diane Christiansen: Follow the instructions to the letter. And the nice thing about collaborating with a coach: the coach does it for you.

I mean we're the ones that title those clips when we get them all together in one link. We do that for you. And I remind them: you have to learn how to do this if you're going to do this without us.

So that's also the value of collaborating with someone who's got their finger on the pulse of the industry as opposed to just doing it yourself.

Bonnie Wallace: What if you don't live in a major market, you don't live near L.A. or New York and you have complete clarity that this is your path, this is what you want to do with your life. But you can't come out here. What could you do right now? What would you tell that young person? What could they do where they are?

Diane Christiansen: Well, they can do local work to start to build their resume and their experience. They can train somewhere. I mean, I go back and teach in Chicago, so I know that kids come from Ohio and Iowa and Wisconsin and Minnesota to take those classes. So find something near your home, wherever it is, and start training as consistently as possible. If you don't have the resources or the money to do that, ask if you can help out at a studio because we have a work/study program, we've always had it.

And I find some of our best office workers and studio help from the work/study program. So people can do that. The Master Talent Teachers have a free training site. It's for all performers. The teachers are Joe Tremaine for dance and Holly Powell for casting. I'm the kids and teens teacher, Carolyn Barry taught commercials. Steven Memel is the voice coach. He's Adam Levine's vocal coach. Kimberly Jentzen is the adult acting teacher. Susan Lyons, a huge producer, teaches the business of acting. It's a powerhouse.

Mastertalentteachers.com still exists. We're also on Facebook, and people anywhere in the world can train by watching those training videos. It's all free.

You can get training. Even if it's not the best training, it's about working out your instrument. It's like going to the gym. And I tell actors, even if you're not training with us, train somewhere because you need to be working out that instrument and putting those units in the bank, so to speak.

Bonnie Wallace: The 10,000 hours.

Diane Christiansen: That's what Sally Kirkland used to say to us, as Strasberg would say, you're just putting units in the bank and those will all come back to you. And I believe that.

And when things aren't moving along in your career, whether you're a kid or an adult, anywhere you are, as quickly as you'd like, keep working out as an actor, keep learning, keep training, keep going to training like you go to the gym and making sure your instrument is strong and ready.

Bonnie Wallace: Then when the opportunity comes up, you can be anywhere technically in the world, but certainly in this country. If there's a big role that they're trying to book for a big project, and they need someone really specific for that, they will shake the bushes, they will look everywhere to get the right person.

Diane Christiansen: Especially Disney.

Bonnie Wallace: Especially Disney, very much so. And those roles really are available for people who aren't necessarily in the major markets. And will you be ready? Have you been doing the work?

Diane Christiansen: A lot of people have been found that way. By major players. Even the boy who played the Cameron Crowe character in *Almost Famous*, that kid they found, I think in Phoenix or Colorado from a self-tape years ago. I saw that self-tape once and it was brilliant, and he was amazing in that movie.

Bonnie Wallace: Talent is everywhere.

Diane Christiansen: That's true. And I look at how many kids over the years we've had move out here with their families. And I will say this about moving to L.A., if you have the resources and the means, by all means do it. If you don't, don't. Train remotely, train with Master Talent Teachers, and listen to Bonnie's podcast. Train wherever you can. We Skype, I'm Skyping with people in Australia. We Skype every day.

Bonnie Wallace: I Skype. Actually, I've moved to Zoom now. It seems more stable. But I do most of my consultations online. We're still face-to-face.

Any final thoughts?

Diane Christiansen: Be very open to reinvention if you're a young adult, very open. Because sometimes it's as simple as changing curly hair to straight hair, changing the color of your hair. And I've seen some of my young adults go through all the hair colors, all of the facial hair options until they found something that clicked.

Bonnie Wallace: And when something clicks, all of a sudden it all just opens up.

Diane Christiansen: And that that's the perfect reason to check in with your agent. That's the perfect thing to talk about, is to call in and say, "What do you think of my photos?" If you're not getting calls. Is it working?

Bonnie Wallace: "Should I consider getting new headshots?"

Diane Christiansen: Absolutely. Or should we go back through that last photo shoot and see if we can find something to help rebrand me or reinvent me a little bit? I think that has to be a constant with any creative person.

So reinvent yourself, rebrand yourself, recreate what you're doing. In between you and the world, the only thing we've got is communication. So make it count.

Bonnie Wallace: Sometimes you'll get a resume where there's a whole bunch of stuff on it that just doesn't make sense. It feels like, why are you including this? Because what's on a resume is basically shorthand for telling people who you are and what kind of roles you want.

And if there's stuff on your resume, because you've done it, but it's not indicating where you want to go, what you want more of... maybe that should just be taken off. Just because you've done something doesn't mean it needs to be on your resume.

Diane Christiansen: Or maybe you're going to put something back that you left off last year. That you edited so your resume would fit on one page. You might want to go back and draw from that again as you represent yourself. And I don't think there's really a limit on that.

I think it's really important and it's fun, and I think that I just proved that to myself going into this new venture. I was thinking it's for my daughter and her future, but really, I'm the one over there with the contractors. I'm the one choosing the colors, I'm the one delegating and suddenly it's this beautiful bouquet of all of our input that's unfolding and I'm very excited. I'm excited about rebranding and reinventing.

Bonnie Wallace: Is there anything else you'd like to share, Diane?

Diane Christiansen: Just how grateful I am to be in a business that I love in the land of milk and honey, with such beautiful people on this path.

MARNIE COOPER

Founder, Marnie Cooper School of Acting

"You need to get comfortable being uncomfortable."

Master acting coach and talent manager Marnie Cooper has been teaching, acting, and coaching clients for over 25 years, and she works with kids, teens and adults. She teaches beginner through master classes as well as private coaching in her studio in Studio City, California. Marnie also does on-set coaching and works with actors all over the world via Skype and FaceTime.

She's also the author of *Teaching Kids to Act for Film and Television.*

Alumni include Miley & Noah Cyrus, Danielle Panabaker, Skai Jackson, Jennette McCurdy, Olivia Holt, Chandler Kinney, Vivien Blair, Skyler Samuels, Brenda Song, Paul Dano, Arlen Escarpeta, David Mazouz, Ariana Greenblatt, and Isaak Presley.

Bonnie Wallace: Marnie, how did you get started as an acting coach?

Marnie Cooper: Well, I was a frustrated actress, and ironically, I was complaining about somebody who really didn't do their homework very well. It made me bananas, and I went on a tirade. And somebody overheard my conversation, and knew somebody who was looking for an acting teacher and recommended me. I met with the person and I said, "I'm underqualified." He said, "You're overqualified." And I said, 'I'll take the position."

It started there, and it just happened that the kids that I had coached for this workshop, all of the ones that I had worked with were of great interest to casting directors, managers, and agents at their showcase.

Bonnie Wallace: So you had instant success.

Marnie Cooper: Yeah, I did. I really did. It came to me for sure. I did not go after it. I thought I'd rather die than teach acting, and here I am, loving it.

Bonnie Wallace: Life is full of surprises that way. Can you describe your approach to acting? There are a lot of different ways to teach acting, obviously, and I'm always curious about the differences between teachers and techniques. What do you do?

Marnie Cooper: I work with kids and teens primarily, and the bottom line is to get them natural. So whatever that means. It can be using what's called *substitution*, so that we're substituting someone or something that we don't know for someone or something that we do know to make it more real for them. We also use their imagination, of course. We can use *As- Ifs*, meaning ... kids are so creative that they can just create something in their mind and work off of it. It's very easy, but sometimes we need something solid, too, to work off of, if that makes sense.

Bonnie Wallace: Totally. It's absolutely true that one size does not fit all with acting training. Even among individual artists, it's not like one thing is always going to work all the time.

Marnie Cooper: Exactly. Sometimes I'll work with people with what's called *actions,* which are assigning verbs to different lines. Sometimes I won't. Some people get too much in their head, and so that just makes them stiff. Whereas, a lot of people, you need to do it because you don't want it to just be one color. What happens is people in real life use many, many different colors to get what they want, and then when they go to their acting, they get on one color and they stay there, and it gets boring. It's a technique that's just used to make sure that they're not hitting the same color every single time.

Bonnie Wallace: Kind of like one music note.

Marnie Cooper: Yes, and that's a big note that casting directors will say, "I need more colors," which means "I need more levels," which if you think of it in music is, "I need more notes."

Bonnie Wallace: More richness, more tones all at once, chords instead of single notes.

Marnie Cooper: Exactly. I think it's interesting that if you ever see one of those paint wheels for people who paint, there can be so many greens. That, to me, is a way to think about it, just because that's where you're going with it. There are so many different hues, if you will.

Bonnie Wallace: It's not just primary color green. There's really an infinite range of possibilities there.

Marnie Cooper: Yes. You want to be able to break down your script, but you also want to leave everything alone. It's a funny process. I always say it's one of the only professions where you don't want your hard work to show. You want to work really hard, and then you have to let it all go.

It really is different with every person, but inevitably they all have to let the work go. You just don't want to go in winging it. That's what a lot of people do, is they think that "Oh, I'm going to be really natural. I'm just going to wing it," but that's not a way to go either.

Bonnie Wallace: I think there's a ton of confusion around that. Everybody knows pretty much that casting directors and directors want you to be natural. Of course, we want to see a natural performance. We want to see a performance that feels so real that it makes us feel something, but that doesn't mean random and unprepared and untrained.

Marnie Cooper: Right. It bugs me to no end that a lot of the times casting directors will write on the breakdown, "Do not get coached." To me, it's the antithesis of what I do. I've even spoken to some of those casting directors, and they go, "Oh, Marnie, we don't mean you." It's frustrating because I want to coach you so that you are completely natural. If I coach you well, they should think you're not coached.

Bonnie Wallace: Parents can tear their hair out thinking ... "Should I get my kid coached? This is a really, really big audition. It's a really big callback. But I was told not to get them coached."

Marnie Cooper: Come to me, and tell them you didn't get them coached, and it should all work out. That's what I do all the time, because it's a game and you have to play by their rules. I'm not saying you should lie, but I'm also saying don't tell them, "Marnie said hi." You want to be careful about that, because what they're really saying is "We want you organic," and whatever you do to get organic is what they want you to do.

Bonnie Wallace: That's really it, I think, in a nutshell. They want you organic, but whatever it takes to get you there. For different people, that's going to be different things.

Marnie Cooper: Absolutely. I highly recommend people work out. I recommend that they meditate. I recommend that they go to school and do all their normal things, that you don't treat an audition like freeze-frame, let's not breathe. Because then by the time you get to the audition, you're a mess, and it should just be a part of your day, not your whole day. Don't put everything centered around the audition. Do everything that you have to do, but don't set yourself up for failure.

By making it so important, it just puts your head in the wrong place. You're just going in to give them a piece of your art. You're not going in to get anything from them. It should just be like when you come to a coaching. It's the same kind of feeling, "Ooh, I'm going in to strut my stuff. How fun," a workout, and that's it.

Bonnie Wallace: I read somewhere the other day, and I'm not going to remember who said this, it was a very famous actor, but it was something along the lines of, "Any day that somebody gives you a free room to go be an actor in is a good day." You didn't pay the rent for that space.

Marnie Cooper:	That's right. You get a full 10 minutes, or whatever it is, where all eyes are on you. That's amazing. That's great. Even if you're wrong for the role, I highly recommend you go in because a casting director immediately will say, "They're wrong, but man, they're good. I'm going to bring them in for something else." That also is a pet peeve of mine, when someone goes, "I'm wrong for this role. I can't believe my agent is sending me out." You should be grateful.
Bonnie Wallace:	That one took us a little while to get. I remember vividly a few auditions that Dove went in for early on before she was really booking anything, and we'd just look at each other and say, "Why does anybody think you should be going out for this?" You look at the description and the breakdown, you look at your kid, and you think, "I don't see it. Are we wasting our time here memorizing these sides that are really long and then driving across town?" But the answer is no, you are never wasting your time, because it's an opportunity to get in front of a casting director.
Marnie Cooper:	Yeah. There are a lot of workshops where you pay a lot of money to meet the casting director. You're meeting them for free. And they really want to meet you. They might not be bringing you in for this particular project. They may be just interested in seeing your work.
Bonnie Wallace:	If you can knock their socks off, even if you're obviously totally wrong for the role, you never know. They could rewrite the role. They could fall in love with you and have another project. They could be just tracking you for a while until they find the right project for you.

Marnie Cooper: I, in fact, went in for an on-set job, and they already had a coach, and I was thrilled to go in. I knew there was nothing at stake, so I could be 100% me. End of the meeting, they said, "You know what, we're going to tell the other coach we'll give her a job another time. You're so right for this. You've got the job." That was a really great experience for me to share with my students, which is: bring the stakes way down. Just go in to meet them. Just go in to do your work without anything attached, and you're a lot freer.

Bonnie Wallace: Yes, the old "book the room, not the job." There's so much truth to that.

Marnie Cooper: Just go in to make an impression. That's all you're doing.

Bonnie Wallace: I love that. And what an opportunity that is all by itself. How many actors would give so much, to just have that opportunity? That is something to celebrate all by itself.

     Now, you teach acting classes as well as the private coaching. What are the differences between your teaching and your coaching?

Marnie Cooper: There's actually a great difference. When I'm coaching, my goal or my objective, if you will, is to get you the callback and, inevitably, the job is what I want to get you. Want to help you get. I certainly can't get it for you. My head is in that place, and I'm going to do whatever it takes to get you there, which might be the dreaded line reading. Yes, which I rarely will do.

     I really, really want the kid to get there. But even this morning, the kid was too young to really understand

71

what they were saying, and they even kept saying the line wrong. So I went, "Listen, it's really like this," and then there was a little epiphany and he got it. But it was convoluted to him, so I demonstrated, if you will, what they're trying to do, and then he got it and did it his own way.

With coaching, my goal is to get you the call-back. I'm not there to help you grow necessarily. I want you to grow, but that's not my goal, which is very different. In a class, I'm just there. I pray you make all the mistakes in the world, so I can guide you and help you. Take risks. Don't connect with your scene partner, so I could help you to connect. Do it all on one level, so you learn that you need a lot more levels. Only use eye contact, so I can teach you that there are other places that we look as an artist. We're not just glued to the other person's eyes. When we go inside ourselves, we actually look at a very different place.

I also will show clips in class, which I love. There's one clip that I show all the kids where Bryan Cranston, who I think is absolutely one of the most brilliant actors, is doing a monologue talking about his father in Breaking Bad. Just the pacing, he is so in the moment. There is no rush going on. Kids, so often they pick up a monologue and they zip right through it.

And boy, you could watch this man say anything, and everything he says, there's such a deep reason and there's such clarity. The specificity in his work is awesome, and that's what I teach as well.

Bonnie Wallace: I love that you show clips. I've actually been telling any-one who will listen to me, for years, that this is one of the best ways that young actors can become better actors, no matter where they live. You can live in a tiny town in the middle of nowhere with maybe no real access to good acting instruction—but you can watch top-notch performances all day long, and you can learn so much by studying that.

Marnie Cooper: Absolutely. That's why, for example, I'll talk about specificity, and how if you're describing something, you see a picture in your own mind before you speak. Even if I were to say to you, "Describe your kitchen," you would take a moment, think of your kitchen, and then you'd actually be picturing it in your mind as you're telling me. I will have them do that, and then I'll have them watch the clips. We're talking about specificity, and we're talking about pictures in your mind. We're always using pictures. I say to them all the time, "If you don't see it, they won't see it."

Bonnie Wallace: That is one of my favorite things about a really fine actor: it feels like you can see their thoughts rippling across their faces.

Marnie Cooper: Yeah. That's the inner monologue that we talk about all the time. That's also what young people really struggle with, the little ones, because they're not yet very good at what you're doing now, which is nodding, "Yes, yes, Marnie, I'm listening to you." They're not really good at that in life, so it's hard for them to be really good at it in their work. That's something that we have to work on, to listen and to really take it in.

I tell them that it's like an apple. If you take a bite of an apple, you can't just swallow it whole. You have to chew it. You've got to chew it. That's really them taking in the information and chewing on it. Processing it.

Bonnie Wallace: What do you think are some of the biggest differences, from an acting standpoint, between theater versus film versus television? Then what are some similarities?

Marnie Cooper: Well, I taught in New York for 10 years, and I had a lot of kids ... I think at one point I had 11 kids on Broadway. But they were doing *Les Mis*, so there you go. I can't even remember the plays they were doing, but a lot of kids were in them.

Obviously, projection is one thing. Where is the other person? Who do you want to reach? In film and TV, it's just the other person. They're right there for you. Just the other person. Whereas, on stage, it's got to be the very last row you need to make sure. I'm a stickler on that, because they paid money and they need to hear you. I hate when you can't hear the people. My grandmother used to go "What'd they say? What'd they say?" She shouldn't have had to do that.

Bonnie Wallace: Not for those ticket prices.

Marnie Cooper: That's right. Obviously, using your diaphragm is different in film and TV versus the theater, but the technique should be very much the same. Your listening may be a little more dramatic, maybe a little bigger, but the processing, as we talked about, is still the same. You still have to take in the information. It's the same thing ... you could say that about a drama versus a musical on Broadway. You still have to listen actively, but what it looks like might be a little bit different, if that makes sense.

In TV and film, here's something I find that's very interesting. In drama, you've got to love your pauses. Really take those pauses, because they can always edit out a pause. They can't create a pause. If you go a little too long, better that way. They can just go in the editing room and shorten that. But if there's no pause, if there's nothing going on, they just do the other point of view.

In fact, I had an experience like that, where I was working on *Touched by an Angel*, and I said to the girl, "You can do better than that. There are more colors. Take that again." I asked the director, "Can she do that?" He said, "No, we don't have enough time," which is also a big difference between film and TV. I was just so frustrated, because what did they do? They just put the point of view on the adult because the kid didn't have enough going on. That just made me nuts because I knew she could do it.

That's a big difference in film and TV. Film, they go, "Oh yeah, let's try again." TV, "No, we got..."

Bonnie Wallace: You're racing.

Marnie Cooper: The meter is running.

Marnie Cooper: A soap opera is one take these days. One take and they're done. When you ask for another chance, "Can I have another shot?" Boy, they're looking, "Ugh." They do it very often these days. It's like a machine. One take.

Bonnie Wallace: I've heard it was getting faster and shorter.

Marnie Cooper: Really fast. Now, it also depends. I worked with some great directors who took many, many, many, many takes. When I worked with Ron Howard, he loved to take different takes. You're working with the genius of Ron Howard and then Jim Carrey, and both of them were saying, "Let's try it another way; "ooh, let's try it another way," "Let's try it another way." You're very lucky because you get to have all those takes. But at the end of the day, they're going to pick Jim Carrey's best take, so you better be on all the time.

Bonnie Wallace: So much wisdom here. You've got extensive experience coaching young actors who are on every different kind of genre, from serious dramas to Disney Channel. Any differences in how you approach these performances? This is a variation on the question I just asked.

Marnie Cooper: Very differently. Disney is a different animal, but Disney is getting less Disney.

It's so funny, because I once had a conversation with a Disney casting director, and they said, "Oh, we don't want it Disney," and I wanted to say, "But you're Disney. What are you talking about?" That's important, too, that Disney is turning down the volume, and that's good.

But it's still a different energy. If you don't have the energy, then you're not going to get called back. You need to walk in the room, and everybody has to look up and go, "Who just walked in this room?" I work with Skai Jackson. She has that energy. She comes in, and I sit up. She just demands attention.

Bonnie Wallace: Energy is important. Film and TV are subtler than stage. But that doesn't mean lackadaisical.

Let's talk about auditioning. We've been talking about it a little bit at the beginning, but it's really its own skillset.

Marnie Cooper: It is. You can be a great actor and a bad auditioner and never work a day in your life.

Bonnie Wallace: How tragic, right? I imagine you see this.

Marnie Cooper: All the time. There's one actress that I work with who just gets so nervous, and I've sent her to different people, a meditation person. I've just recommended different things for her to try out.

Hypnosis is a great one. I know somebody else who goes to a great hypnotist. You've got to do whatever it takes to make sure that when you walk in the room, you're just meeting another human being. They don't walk on water. They want you to do well.

Bonnie Wallace: They want you to be the one they're waiting for. They are so on your side.

Marnie Cooper: Especially because if they don't find it, they get fired. You just go on with your day, especially as kids and teens. There was no great, horrific thing that is going to happen if you blow your audition. But if they don't find the person, they're out.

Bonnie Wallace: Yes, that is a really, really good point. Casting is motivated.

Marnie Cooper: They are. They want you. I cannot tell you how many times I've heard casting directors say that, "I want you to be good." My deal is I always recommend that kids bring notebooks to their auditions, journals, and journal from the character's point of view. It does two things. One, it gets your head in the right place, but it also gets you away from talking to the other people, because that's where you get wackadoo.

Also, there's a "no phones allowed policy" in my world, because once you get into video games or whatever it is, again, your brain goes to another place, and it's not easy to switch out of that gear. Keep your head in the right place. Journal. Stay with your character's point of view.

If your dad left you, try to remember the last thing he said before he left. If it says in it, like a script I was working on last week, that the brother smoked cigarettes, what brand did he smoke? What did they smell like? Why did it bother you so much? Obviously, smoking bothers people, but did he always have a cigarette in his hand? Was he a heavy smoker? Were you afraid that he wasn't going to put it out and the house was going to go on fire? Let your imagination really go. That's what an artist is.

Bonnie Wallace: This is great advice. Any other audition advice?

Marnie Cooper: I would say even with the little kids, if they're even too young to journal, color. Have them color. What does your house look like? What's your room look like? How is your room decorated? That's one thing I always ask the kids, "How is your room decorated?"

It tells me so much about them. Then I say, "Now, how is your character's room decorated?" They get to have that epiphany of "Oh." Your room is a sacred

place. Generally, it's a place that you're allowed to decorate and says a whole lot about you. That's what I want.
Open up the imagination. Really, how would your character decorate their room?

Start with you. What do your parents do for a living? How does that influence you? Okay, now what do
your character's parents do for a living? So that you
have an awareness. It's not just "I'm in school answering questions," but you want to have a lot of aha
moments.

Bonnie Wallace: So by starting with yourself as reference, you're laying
the track for those feelings and those associations that
have a genuinely real feeling.

Any special advice for audition self-tapes? There
are so many self-tape auditions now … you've got to
get good at them, no matter where you are.

Marnie Cooper: Absolutely. I mean, there's the basic stuff. Put just one
color behind you, only one person. It's just the ac-
tor. I like a blue curtain because it really makes their
eyes pop. Make sure the lighting is good, no shadows,
just because that's distracting. Have somebody read
off-camera.

You don't want your mom to do it if it's a boy-
friend-girlfriend scene. It's just not going to fly. I think
a lot of people do that. Seek out some other actors.
What a great experience to have another actor read for
you so that you really get the essence of what's going
on in the scene, or an acting coach.

Oh, pet peeve. Be off-book, please. Every time you
look down, it's a moment that you're not present. If
you're at an audition, it's a little bit different. Certainly,

you want to be off-book, but it's still different when you're in the audition versus when the camera's just on you. Every time you look down, it's a nightmare. It really looks horrible. If you need to sneak a peek, I get it, but let's not be doing that up-and-down thing, because you might as well not send it in. It'll be a disservice if you send in a tape like that.

Bonnie Wallace: I was talking to a young actor the other day, and they said, "What am I supposed to do? There just isn't enough time to memorize." But you know what, everybody else has the same amount of time you do, and lots of other actors are going to have found a way to memorize those sides and do it well.

Marnie Cooper: Listen, I was always horrible at memorizing, so every audition was a little bit of a trauma for me, but you've got to do it. I explain it this way: memorizing is like the pencil in a test. You have to bring your number two pencil to take the test, but it has nothing to do with the test. It's just that you have to memorize so that you can play.

But just memorizing isn't great acting. People say this to me all the time: if I had a dollar for every parent that said, "My kid can memorize."

Bonnie Wallace: Good. That's step one.

Marnie Cooper: I get that that's a skill. But that does not make for a great actor. That makes for an easier time getting off-book.

Bonnie Wallace: It helps. What are your thoughts about working via Skype?

Marnie Cooper: Honestly, I'm still an '80s girl. I like the person in front of me. I like them to breathe in front of me. I think if you have the opportunity to go to a great coach versus sit in your living room and go on Skype, get in your car and go to the coach. However, I do a lot of Skype. I Skype with someone in Singapore these days. They're getting up and I'm going to sleep, but it works.

Skype is great because it allows my team to bring people to the highest level that we can while still being in another country. However, if you just don't want to drive over the hill and you don't want to be in traffic, so we're doing a Skype for that reason, that makes me nuts, because there's nothing... It's really about human connection. You don't quite get that human connection.

The other thing about Skype that is interesting... I once Skyped this girl and I thought she was quite good, and then she saw me in person and she's very wooden, because I couldn't tell. I only saw so much of her body. She was very stiff, and I thought, "Wow, that's the same person I Skyped with?" But it was a different experience.

Also, I'll have people who will ask me to come to their house. As much as I would love to go to their dreamy house, and in some cases they really are, it's better you come to me because I don't want you comfortable. That's the whole point. I want it to be more like it would be at an audition. You might be brilliant in your living room, but that's not the point. The casting director is not coming over to your house.

It's always important, get them out of their comfortable environment. They can still, if you will, bring that environment in their mind with them, but it's best to do it in a studio or wherever the coach is in person. Second best is Skype or FaceTime.

Bonnie Wallace: What you just said is so important because you need to get comfortable performing, whether it's for an audition or if you book the job, in an unfamiliar, maybe less than cozy environment. Sometimes these environments are downright-

Marnie Cooper: Intimidating.

Bonnie Wallace: I think about some of the places that Dove has had to work, for example 14 hours in the snow in subzero temperatures. Under such adversity, sometimes you can't believe what these actors have to pull off. They need to not be thrown by that.

Marnie Cooper: Right. I always say you need to get comfortable being uncomfortable.

That's what you are, and that's what you're paid to be. Nobody wants to see somebody happy-go-lucky— maybe for Disney and stuff—but really you are showing parts of yourself that nobody really wants to show.

And that's your job, so I need to see that discomfort.

Bonnie Wallace: Those emotions need to read through, despite whatever else is going on, despite whatever your environment might actually be.

Marnie Cooper: Yes, and I always say, "Use it. Use it!" When things happen that are negative, ooh, good, use it, because life is not a bowl of cherries. Nobody understands that. No kid just understood that reference, not a one.

Bonnie Wallace: How has your experience as an acting coach informed the way that you manage clients, and vice versa?

Marnie Cooper: Well, as I said to you, I only manage five clients. They are people that are with me for a long time. I'm not taking on new clients. This is something that I got into many years ago, and the clients that I have, I've been working with for so long and I believe in wholeheartedly, that I would never want to let them go, but I'm also not building that business anymore.

How it's helped me is before I managed, when the actor would come in and go, "I can't believe I'm not getting the audition for this," I would think, "Yeah, you should be getting an audition for this."

Then I started managing and I thought, "Oh my God, I can't get this person in the room. It doesn't matter what I do." That really helped me to spread that message, which is "Your agent or manager might be trying so flipping hard to get you in, and maybe it's something that you can do, as opposed to something your team needs to do," if your pictures aren't good enough, if you don't look like your picture.

It's a drag, but you've got to spend a lot of money on a great shot. You can't do whatever is on sale, that you want to save money. This is not a business to make money, and if you're in it to make money, you're in the wrong business. You have to invest. It's not to say that you have to go to the photographer that charges $1,000. I'm not saying that at all, but you have to go to a photographer that is competitive and that is really, really good, and that might cost you a pretty penny. That's too bad. That's part of the gig. It could be that.

It could be your resume. Very often, it's the resume. You just don't have enough on there, so you need to get out there and get the experience, not your team. That really has taught me a heck of a lot about where the responsibility lies.

Bonnie Wallace: The usual answer back to that, if you're a young actor who's very frustrated that they don't have much on their resume and they're not getting those auditions, is "Well, how am I supposed to get stuff on my resume when..."

Marnie Cooper: Well, yes, but there's so much you can do. You could do a student film.

Why? Because that's going to help you get yourself in front of the camera, so that when you go on your audition, the camera is not even there. All the little things. You can join a gym. You can go to the dermatologist. There's so many things.

You need to look at yourself, sadly ... that's why I say most people shouldn't do this business. You really need to look at yourself, as this is what you're selling. So if you're all broken out, I'm not going to want to buy the kid who's all broken out when there's somebody next to them that's got a beautiful complexion. Go to the dermatologist.

Bonnie Wallace: Or the nutritionist...

Marnie Cooper: I hate, hate, hate this, but you also have to be cognizant of your weight.

The reason why I hate it, is because I was in the business and I was anorexic for a while, and I get it.

It is a business that promotes bad eating. You've got to get yourself a nutritionist so that you're eating well and you're healthy. I am so big on actors being healthy because so many of them are not.

Bonnie Wallace: It's a serious struggle, and a lot of actors are finally coming out and talking about that. I think that's really healthy because our whole culture is struggling with it right now, and it's good for people to know that they're not alone. Healthy is everything.

It's a strange thing. This business is literally objectification. And that is a very uncomfortable feeling, to be objectified. It doesn't feel good.

Marnie Cooper: Absolutely, no. I say to kids all the time, "Hey, you know what? I've got gray hair going on here. If I were still acting, I couldn't have that. I've put on some weight. Well, that couldn't be. But I'm not acting. You chose it. I didn't." Now I get to kick back and do whatever I want because I'm not the product anymore, to a certain degree. I still have to shower and brush my hair and all those wonderful things.

Bonnie Wallace: What would your advice be for a young actor who lives very far away from L.A. or New York, and they don't have the possibility of moving here right now? What are some of the best ways for them to move toward their dream where they are right now?

Marnie Cooper: Well, I think that's a good point, because you can come to L.A., and have absolutely no credits, and you're no closer getting into the room, so be that big fish. Go ahead and find an agent close to you, if that means five miles away, 10 miles away, wherever. There is an agent, because this industry is all around the world. Find that agent, get some experience, and get some films under your belt, whether it's student films, or independent films, so that you are getting that experience. The more you're in front of the camera, the less you'll be intimidated when you do come here.

You can also Skype and FaceTime, as much as I said, "No, don't do it." Yes, here you should, because you want to get the most accurate, the most up-to-the-minute coaching. You don't want to get coaching from the '60s. So often you're in ... no offense, but if you're in Oklahoma ... I tease my client, who's working all the time, who's from Oklahoma.

You're not going to find the greatest coach probably in Oklahoma, or one that really knows what the industry wants at this time.

Bonnie Wallace: That's a really good point. There are people who've been in the industry, to some degree or another, everywhere, but how long ago were they really working? If it was decades ago-

Marnie Cooper: There's a problem with that. It's the same thing. I don't teach commercials. I'll do it in my evaluation because I can certainly get a sense of how you'll do commercially, but I have another teacher who does commercials because she's the expert and I'm not. People say, "I want to come to you." No, you don't. I want you going to the best, and I'm not the best for that. Chrissie knows her stuff, and she books a million commercials. She gets kids who aren't booking to be booking quickly.

Another thing which is really, really hard—and when my daughter was in it for 10 minutes, I broke this rule—don't over-talk about the audition afterwards. Don't ask, "What did she say? What did the casting director say, and what did they mean?" It's muddying the waters. Just let the kid have the experience and go on with their life. The less you say, the less important it will be, and that's what you want. Again, go back to "It's just a part of what I do. It's just a part of my day." Of course, the parent is dying to know, but don't over-analyze. It's like anything. You overanalyze it to death, and you kill it, so less is more in everything you do.

JOHN D'AQUINO

Founder, Young Actors Workshop

"Erase the 'no's' that are in front of you, until finally, someone says 'yes.' You can't give up. You must believe."

Veteran actor and master teacher John D'Aquino (*Cory in the House, Shake it Up, CSI, Hannah Montana, Seinfeld*) has starred in six TV series, and recurred and guest starred on dozens of hit TV shows in his 30-year career. His love for performing is surpassed only by his love for teaching, a love inspired by his mentor, teacher, and friend, Charles Nelson Riley, who instilled in his students a passion for helping actors create dynamic performances by reaching deep into the human spirit. He teaches weekly classes, as well as private audition coaching and videotaping sessions in his studio in Burbank, California, and workshops for actors of all ages across the U.S.

Alumni include Kira Kosarin, Jack Griffo, Noah Centineo, RJ Cyler, Owen Atlas, Madison Iseman, Josie Totah, Siena Agudong, Garren Stitt, Katelyn Nacon, Audrey Whitby, and Izabela Vidovic.

Bonnie Wallace:	Do you think that your breadth and depth of experience as an actor gives you an edge as an acting coach?
John D'Aquino:	It's a good question. I think yes, obviously, because you understand what it takes to get those jobs. Some

of those jobs, as you well know, can be a process of five and six auditions before you have that job, when you're testing. In some cases, it happens so relatively easily, it's really interesting. It's almost as if it's meant to be. I think as a teacher, possibly it's the thousands of failures that inform how I teach, and maybe make me better suited for this than the average person.

I'm always thinking, "How can I save this young actor the agony that I went through, or the learning curve that I went through?" I was lacking mentorship. I had some really wonderful people in my life, but it would have been terrific. Some of them passed away early on after I met them. Fantastic people, but I think I could have benefited by the mentorship along the journey.

Bonnie Wallace: Mentorship is huge. I know it's been incredibly central to my growth as an artist, and as a person in general. Would you say that mentorship is something that you offer as an acting teacher as well?

John D'Aquino: Yes, I think it's part and parcel. In a way, it's what every gymnastics and little league coach is doing with their kids. If you're really meant to be a coach, and if you really are invested in how a child's life, or a teen's life further develops, it's an honor to play that role in their lives.

Bonnie Wallace: I love that. Can you describe your particular approach to acting? There are a lot of different ways that people can teach, and I'm always curious about the differences between various teachers and techniques. How do you approach that?

John D'Aquino: Well, I think it's changed, number one. There are different approaches that I'll take for various genres. Obviously the Disney/Nick sitcom is a particular, brightly colored genre. Then, if you move on to major network sitcoms, it's going to be a much more subtle delivery. Yet, it's still broad. If you move over to cable, then you're going to be using sharper brushes, different colors. Then, once you move into one-hour drama, well, is it *Law & Order*, and just give us the facts? Or, is it going to be a highly stylized *CSI: Miami*, where you have to tilt your head to the side and then perform? It just depends on what the show is. You have to be well-versed in all of those genres. I've had the good fortune of doing most of those genres, so I think I understand it.

I think my own personal approach has changed, in the sense that when I was a young actor, I would want to predetermine what was going to happen into the room. I realized that's not a very good idea, because your audition room is going to add a particular energy itself.

Improvisation really plays a big role in that, but also sensing the room, feeling the room; let that inform your choices.

I guess what I'm trying to say is now I want to prepare very, very well. I want to know who my character is, and I want to know how they will be in most circumstances. I don't want to know the next moment. It's that delicate balance where the actor knows the script, but I don't want my character to know the next moment. I want it to unfold organically and I want to be as surprised as anyone; because typically the reason why I go to the movie theaters, or I want to watch a particular show is because I want to watch my favorite characters discover.

Then I want them to discover again, and now look, they're discovering again. I want to go on that journey. When it's really crafted well, I'm on the journey. I'm not watching the mechanics of how this was put together. I think as an instructor, I know that there's a math to situation comedy, and that's what I teach often on the road and in Los Angeles.

That's why agents and managers will send me their clients specifically for that. There is a math, and it's not rocket science. You don't have to be a genius, you just simply have to understand it and what they're asking for. When it gets to the real complex, subtle type of styles, then you don't want to know. You don't want to predetermine, because then it's fabricated and it doesn't feel organic. It's interesting. How I will work with each actor may depend upon what they're bringing in the Periodically, somebody walks in the room and I realize, "Oh, wait a minute. I can't coach them the way I coach most of the kids, because this kid's bringing in something organic, different, idiosyncratic to their own personality, and I have to first honor that and see what else they can give to this piece." Then, it offers the casting director a different choice, something that maybe paints outside the lines and is very unusual to what the other kids or teens may be delivering.

I say "kids and teens." I love teaching adults, and I do a lot of that on the road. Our business in Los Angeles seems to be primarily more kids and teens. It is a good fit for me personally, and a good fit for us as a staff because quite frankly ... once you get to a certain age, often times, our young adults will walk in and ... their bags are fully packed.

You want to tell them, "You need to kind of empty your luggage before you walk in here, because if we're going to do something that's new and fresh, you're so predetermined ... and then you have your blockages." With kids, there tend to be fewer blockages.

Bonnie Wallace: I like that. Kids naturally have that sort of beginner's mind, if you will. I imagine that anybody that's gone through a BFA program or whatever has a certain number of things on their resume. They figure they pretty much know what they need to know, which makes them less open to what you might to contribute.

John D'Aquino: To that point, when I was at Florida State University, Burt Reynolds was coming in to talk to us. I remember a masters student scoffed, and I heard him say, "What does Burt Reynolds have to teach me?"

I thought, "Wow, let's see. Burt Reynolds is top box office on the planet, and you? Who? What's your name again? So I'm guessing a few things?"

Bonnie Wallace: Maybe just a few things! You teach acting workshops, both in your studio in Burbank, and also in different cities all across the country. What do you do in your workshops?

John D'Aquino: Well, they vary. We do three specific workshops each year, two in pilot season. We call them "pilot season prep." In reality, they're an audition technique workshop. Basically, we examine everything from the point where the actor crosses the threshold and enters the room, body language, interview skills, hitting the mark, taking a breath, delivering your slate in a way that sends a message to casting and the producers that you're ready. Then, backing it up with your performance, and your preparation, and getting ready to deliver something that's going to be remembered. You want to leave an indelible mark in the room. You want to live beyond the time you exit that room.

Anyway, we examine that; and then we'll do one in the fall called "episodic prep." Sometimes we'll do scene work for casting people, we'll bring them in. Sometimes we'll have representatives come in. We'll have an agent, a manager, or multiples of such, and bring them in to educate the kids on what they're looking for, how they find the marketplace.

In Los Angeles, we do a summer film camp, which I think is probably the best thing we do all year. It almost kills my staff to do it, because it requires a lot of preparation. We have students flying in from various cities to be a part of it. Sometimes they fly in from out of the country. We have some people coming in from Australia this year that we're excited about. That is a 12-day film movie making camp, so literally it's not only the classes. It's not only the seminars, the information; then it's the scenes. It's the rehearsals. It's the group table reads, the private coaching on your scenes. It's character development.

Then, we hire a professional crew, all people who work on various shows around Los Angeles. We want to give our students that experience. These are real crew people. It's not like they're coddling our campers, if you will. You have to adapt to the professional environment, and that's part of it. We don't really make it any easier. We try, in our preparation, to get them ready for the moment, because on set, we don't want to create this false expectation that you're going to be coddled. You have to live up to the expectation that's placed upon you.

I know you're experienced with Disney. I have a lot of experience with Disney where we'll have an excellent writer who writes a particular joke and because the young actor didn't invest the time into that joke, the joke dies and the network cuts the joke.

Bonnie Wallace: Yep.

John D'Aquino: It wasn't the fault of the writer. It was the fault of the actor. Even though we try to treat kids like kids on set, behind the scenes, I heard what that guy said about that kid.

I can't say it in this podcast, but that was one angry writer; and rightfully so, because the kid was lazy in that moment and didn't invest into the joke.

Bonnie Wallace: Unfortunately, people do talk. Then, that stuff gets around; if the kid can't really deliver...

John D'Aquino: We're not going to be writing those jokes for that kid in the future, and we're going to focus on the ones who honor. Then, as you know, these kids have to show up at 7:30 in the morning, go to school, and then they have to have their lines ready at 9:00 a.m. ... that's a lot of pressure.

Usually, these kids we work with are so professional, they're the ones who have their lines prepared where the adults are floundering to get their lines.

Bonnie Wallace:	It's true. So in the summer camp, you basically give your campers the experience of being in a full professional production.

| John D'Aquino: | One of our kids who's done really well, Kira Kosarin, is the lead of *The Thundermans*. We're blessed to have three of our homegrown kids on that one particular Nickelodeon show. Jack Griffo and Audrey Whitby, who is also the star of *Bad Fairy*, which John Beck produced. The John Beck from *Liv and Maddie*. |

At any rate, Kira credits these summer film camps with ... I think she had one line on some other show ... For *Shake It Up*, or *Austin & Ally*, but that was it. That was her only other television experience. But, because of this experience, she credits the camps. That being said, Kira Kosarin's one of the smartest people I've ever met ... your own daughter is sort of one of those super children ... no one's going to get in your way of doing well.

| Bonnie Wallace: | Yes, and yet Dove's first experience on a real set was when she was cast in a guest star role. It would have been great to have a summer film camp behind her. She had five years of theater, which was fantastic training in my eyes, and a lot of people think that theater's a great training for film and TV. |

| John D'Aquino: | But not necessarily specific to what was being requested. |

| Bonnie Wallace: | No. It was much more challenging than it needed to be, because if she'd just had some sort of experience before doing it, she would have had less anxiety. She |

95

would have literally understood the context that she was stepping into. It is something that I think that everybody should get an opportunity to do in some way or another before they're thrown into the water at the deep end.

John D'Aquino: Before we go off on that road, we do workshops as well. They vary.

There are probably 15 or 20 standard courses that we'll take out on the road. Typically, to your point, we are working with kids who have a lot of musical theater background. Therefore, the job becomes getting their performances abbreviated for the camera. I'm a stage actor way back when, and it's interesting.

The camera sees the world very differently. An actor is typically myopic, seeing the world through their own point of view. They have to begin to understand how the camera sees the world, and then you adjust toward that lens. We spend a lot of time, especially with the teens, getting them behind the camera to understand how everything is affected by a single move of an actor. Not only are they learning by doing, but they're also learning by filming. They're learning by editing. They're learning the global composition of what it takes to put film together, or television together.

Bonnie Wallace: That is huge; so you get the kids behind the camera, too?

John D'Aquino: Yeah, as a matter of fact, we'll begin that cycle for our on-camera class, taught by my very gifted associate, Japheth Gordon. I'll be joining that course next Saturday.

That's something that will be ongoing. Gloria Garayua, who's a wonderful actress, leads our scene study course, which is really developed exactly like a course that you would go to in your 20s and 30s in town. That's for our mid-teens, older teens, and early 20s students. Then, at the end of that cycle, we'll have an industry person come in. I will accompany them. We will give our notes on the scene, just so that they understand how the professionals are viewing their work, and give them some greater clarity.

Bonnie Wallace: One of the greatest issues for any young actor is finding representation.

Just getting a meeting with a potential agent or manager is so challenging. One of the best ways for that to happen is for them to be in some sort of showcase, where agents and managers come to see who might be out there, new talent. That's something that happens in your workshops, or some of your workshops.

John D'Aquino: Yeah, we can't guarantee it. It's really based upon the kid's performance. We take extra care, because unlike another workshop, possibly, where the reps are going to ... They don't know the kids, they don't know the teens, and we typically know them. I've met them on the road, or my staff has met them on the road in advance of them getting to Los Angeles. We have a lot of industry people that are very friendly to our school: agents, managers, casting people. We want to be able to show to those buyers the strength of this particular young performer.

We are not a profit participant in their career, but we work in association with our industry friends to basically be a conduit to them getting represented. We cannot fool a representative, because they're very smart. They see it. They know it in a moment. What we can do is maybe inform the work. Often times, my associates and I are writing the scenes, especially if the kid has a very particular talent.

In the showcase that you sat through, one of our boys happens to be a hip-hop dancer. He's also a singer, and an actor. We wrote a scene that allowed him to showcase what he does, and he does so wonderfully. In other cases, it might be a girl who sings, et cetera. We want them to know how special the kid is, and then if they have room on their rosters, they'll call in for interviews. Often, they'll get placed. That's always a point of pride for us. I wish we could guarantee it, but it really is reliant upon the level of the child and where they are on their journey.

I get a special satisfaction when maybe a child enters, and they're green. Then a year later, they come back and do another workshop; and the same people who were there a year before are going crazy for the kid, because they see the development in a year. That always makes us very happy. Those kids are represented, and then they're doing pretty well.

Bonnie Wallace: I love that you take the time and have the ability to create material for the kids sometimes. That's extraordinary.

John D'Aquino: It's often done at 11, 12:00 at night. Or, I'll get up at 5:00 in the morning just to do that before my daughter gets up for school. My associate, Japheth, has two children. He'll do the same thing. One thing I love about my staff is I'm really blessed in that they care about this as much as I do. They're all working actors. They're all really talented. We basically cover for each other when we're working. We create this safe place where they have work to come back to, and they're very invested in their students. They're very invested in getting them to the next level.

Bonnie Wallace:

Earlier, you were talking about what the camera sees. It's not what the actor sees. A lot of people feel strongly that theater is great training for this sort of thing, except, guess what? The camera catches all kinds of stuff that you don't catch when you're in the audience watching somebody on stage. What would you say are some of the bigger differences between theater versus film and television, and what are some similarities in terms of acting and technique?

John D'Aquino:

I find that theater is very similar to situation comedy, especially if you're playing before an audience, because you have to present in a way that the audience can see it. For sitcoms, you have four cameras. In a way, that fourth wall is your audience. It's very wide. I was working with Jason Earles. Japheth and I were asked to come over to that Disney Show, *Kickin' It*, in the first week. They had a young cast. They asked us to come in and sort of get them ready.

Jason, who's really smart, sat in with us. He didn't need to. He was on *Hannah Montana* for many years. He's older. He's very skilled. Jason has a way of presenting for sitcom that everything is toward the fourth wall. It's almost like a tennis backhand or forehand. He then hits the final syllable over to the person next to him, which is this energy that goes flying in that

99

direction. Basically, every camera can pick up what Jason's doing in that format.

It definitely changes as the genres change, and as you go to a delicate one-hour drama and film ... I'm thinking of what my wonderful, amazing teacher, Charles Nelson Reilly, would teach us in class. Charles was a product of the Uta Hagen School in New York.

Charles would say, "It's what's not being spoken that speaks the loudest." It took me years to really understand the overall value of that. As you get to film in a close-up, you're not presenting anything. It's what you're not saying. It's the secret you're holding onto. When I teach on the road, it puts me in a position where I have to make an actor better in three hours. How can I do that? I challenge myself.

My favorite American male actor is Robert DeNiro. The reason why I love Robert DeNiro is because there's something alive in his performance, 100% of the time. Often, it's when he's not speaking. As you can imagine Robert DeNiro doing, he's usually asking...

Whether he's saying it out loud or not, he's asking, "Are you lying to me? Are you lying to me?" He's looking right through them. It's like he reaches into their throat, goes down their chest, yanks out their heart, rips it out and is looking at it to make sure the person's not lying.

I think that we, as humans, are constantly asking active interrogation questions. That's what I like to call this. I don't like talking in terms of things that are difficult to grasp. I want to give them tangible tools to leave with. Active interrogation informs every single line, because a young actor and sometimes adults who come to us, they're merely going to the next line. You don't see the light on in their eyes whatsoever. If I'm a human being, and if I have a pain my stomach...

I think, "What is that pain? Why do I have a pain in my stomach? Oh, wait a minute. Am I hungry? When did I eat last? What did I have for lunch today? When am I having dinner tonight? What am I having for dinner tonight? What did I have last night?" It's a series of interrogations that go on constantly.

Two ladies meet outside church. The first thing they're going to do, that the computer chip in their brain is going to scan all the way up and down to find out, is if that's really a Prada purse. Is that really a Rolex watch? Is that Bentley leased or rented? Is this old money or new money? Guys will do the same thing. There are so many things that we don't ask, because we're being too polite, but as an actor, I love that stuff.

I love when I'm picking up on people talking to me who are not saying something, and I like saying it out loud.

Bonnie Wallace: I like to see that flickering behind an actor's eyes. To feel as though I can see into their thoughts, even though they're not saying a word. That is one of my favorite, favorite things.

John D'Aquino: The director and an editor will love you for that, because when we cut to you, you have so much going on. You're actually pushing the plot forward.

Bonnie Wallace: Silently. But effectively, and powerfully. That's not the same as mugging for the camera, which takes us to my next question. You have a lot of experience both acting and coaching on Disney.

Disney has a very ... we can say "broad," we can say "colorful, brightly colored style." I think you said something like that earlier. I liked your color analogy. It's got a heightened style to it, and different genres have different styles. A lot of kids who want to be actors, want to be actors on *The Disney Channel.* It's got its own style, but it's not the same as mugging. It's got its own rules, right? How would you approach a performance for a Disney show?

John D'Aquino: Each character's different. They're all drafted according to what the writers need. The writers are going to need a particular collection, a composition of characters to come together. For example, I played the President of the United States on a Disney show. Well, he wasn't the sharpest tack in the shed, this particular president. He had delusions of grandeur. He enjoyed the sound of his own voice. As I start to put the character breakdown together, I started to realize ... he's a do-gooder. He wants to do good. In essence, he was kind of like the village idiot in the form of the President of the United States. Everybody had to come to his rescue. In a way, there's this dial. It goes from one to ten. It just depends on how brightly you need to paint this performance.

It's interesting, in *Liv and Maddie* ... I know because my daughter has it on constantly. You can get some really cartoonish guest star characters on that show. It's to the point it's gone beyond comedy. It's on cartoon. Then, the writers are allowing for those moments when Liv is having a crisis of faith or something, and then all of a sudden, it's going to have that dramatic moment. What's the style? Even within that one particular program, where are we? Certain programs on Disney or Nick ... the one thing I will say, and I have to laugh...

Casting directors will say "No, no, no. This Disney or Nick show is different. This is real. It's going to be really grounded," and we go through this thing. They go through three months of casting, and when it gets on air, I'm sorry, I can't distinguish between that program and the next one, in terms of brightness. I think what ends up happening is people start to want to play it safe and fall into the same formula as they go along. I think the biggest thing is it's still the truth. It's all the truth, but to what degree is it dialed? Is it at one and a subtle tone? Or, is it at ten?

One of my favorite punctuations ... I love to do classes just on punctuations, because often a young actor does not carry the sound of their line to the punctuation. They start to drift off, and they lose effectiveness.

You don't want a producer in the back of the room going, "What did he say? What did she say?"

As soon as they go into that mode, you're not getting that job. Just like a female gymnast at the Olympic launches off of her apparatus, she has to stick the landing.

If she falls forward or backward, there are points off. I feel the same way about punctuations. We do a fun game where the kid has to say "period" after the line.

"I'm having a really nice coffee with Bonnie, period." If I turn that into a question, "I'm having a really nice coffee with Bonnie, question mark?" I have them say 'question mark,' because I want them to carry the feeling through the punctuation. Or, "I'm having a really nice coffee with Bonnie, exclamation point!" I'll have them be enthusiastic through the punctuation. Then, there's my favorite punctuation, which is the "interabang," which is half interrogative, half bang. It's an old printing term, because when the printers ... The old printing machines would make the exclamation point, it would send this huge bang through the company, through the room. They created a term called "interabang." The interabang is incredulous. When I first started acting, they would never use that.

In parenthesis, prior to the line, they would say, "Incredulous, you cannot wrap your mind around it."

On a Disney show, it may sound like "Wait a minute, you turned dad into a toad?!" You're going to have that heightened dial-up to number ten reaction.

It just depends where you're at, and what character you're in. We often need that grounded character. On a major network, I really enjoy playing the point of view of the audience. I got to do this on *Third Rock From the Sun*. When everybody around me is a satellite insane being, and I have to be the grounded person so that the audience sees all this through that person's eyes.

Bonnie Wallace: You were talking about how even just lack of punctuation or not being in touch with the lines can lose a producer in a room, and that takes us to the whole conversation about auditioning. Auditioning is really its own skill set. It's a critical one if an actor's going to actually succeed in the business. What advice do you have for your young actors who are approaching an audition?

John D'Aquino: Well first of all, I think that the universe of an audition is vastly different than the universe of having the job and being on set; in the sense that you're going to have your TV family. You're in your TV kitchen. All of the individuals, the characters are there for you. It's so easy. All you got to do is pick up the piece of bread, take a bite, and say the line. It's so easy. For the audition, you have to manifest the entire universe.

Bonnie Wallace: In your mind.

John D'Aquino: Yeah. We do a lot of work with, first of all, projecting the eye lines to camera. There's a delicate science for that, because primarily, you want 80, 85% of the lines going to the casting director or the reader. You want to make as much eye contact as possible with that person. You want to feel like they're very much a part of it. If you have another character or two in the scene, you may have to honor them with the periodic glance.

You don't bring props into an audition. That's the general rule. There have been a few people like myself who can break that rule, but you better be a pro to try and do it; because you'll get in trouble. Then, it's a very delicate thing. Assuming that you cannot bring a prop into the room, you can still create an activity that the character is coming in with.

Every great acting class talks about the moment before. I often talk in terms of a dynamic entry. How am I going to make this audition indelible, where they have to see me again? I want to bring something into the room, and I want to bring an energy. Where have I been, and where am I going, and what is my expectation upon entering this room?

Then wait a minute, now you're telling me this new information, which creates this conflict and how many people am I talking to? That's why working the camera is so critical.

In fact, I teach a technique called 'the magic rectangle.' When I started teaching teens and kids, I started to realize I couldn't find a book on film technique. I wanted to make this tangible. It's a basic math. As a matter of fact, my adult actors around the country appreciate it even more. I think it's because it simplifies the math for them. Essentially, the math sends you in a direction of teaching you how to be intimate to the lens, especially with those subtle dramas.

Getting back to the audition, you have to bring the universe of the environment. Environment is huge. A great actor, in my mind, can change the temperature in a room by ten degrees if they truly believe it. If they're more completely committed to their environment than what is happening around them. If they're hungry. A great scene, every great scene has a ticking clock. What is the urgency that you're lending to that? The audition is a one-dimensional experience for the viewer. You have to bring those other dimensions to it. The actors that can do that typically have an advantage and will get to callback. Does that answer your question?

Bonnie Wallace: Yes, that's really nice. I've just seen enough kids auditioning where it feels like the world doesn't begin until the beginning of the sides.

John D'Aquino: Television writers are notorious for writing ... The scene begins in the middle of the scene. We're going to skip all the politeness, "Oh Bonnie, so nice to see you again. How are you? How are the kids? What's going on in your..." They're going to skip all of that and get to, "Where's my money?"

Bonnie Wallace: You need to have constructed some understanding of where that came from, too.

John D'Aquino: I think the better you understand what the writer's intention is, then the better you're going to be able to deliver that performance.

Bonnie Wallace: Which is where doing a little research on the writer can be useful.

John D'Aquino: Right, and also understanding writing. For our teen students, there's a certain point where I don't want to be responsible for sending out a legion of actors waiting for the phone to ring. If they're really bright, we're going to start to get them writing, maybe get them behind the camera, get them thinking in terms of being a producer.

My ultimate goal is to start to get some network executives and studio executives out there, because we get such bright people that are attracted to this profession. I don't want them to be victims waiting for the phone to ring.

Bonnie Wallace: I love that you brought that up because so many people in this town and in this industry began because they were in love with acting, but they found that they ultimately were happier and more fulfilled doing something just adjacent to that, like casting, or directing, or writing, or producing. I think that young actors should always have that in the back of their mind.

John D'Aquino: If they don't write, and writing is not for everybody, then they should be finding young writers and cultivating work. They should be constantly studying, asking, what is the next medium? Can I go make a six-minute movie, and get that out? How can I afford that, create that network, put those people together? Or write, just try writing. Learn from the Masters. A great artist, especially during Renaissance time and impressionist period would be handed a blank canvas.

Then, they'd say, "Okay, now copy the Mona Lisa," or "Copy a great classic." In the journey of understanding how the Master put that together, they became a great artist themselves.

Bonnie Wallace: Teaching may be the best way to truly learn something deeply.

John D'Aquino: Exactly, exactly. Exactly.

Bonnie Wallace: Speaking of new mediums, and that sort of thing, I want to know what your take on video teaching is. A lot of people feel weird about coaching over Zoom or Skype, but some people just love it. Where do you stand on working remotely?

John D'Aquino: Well, I Skype often. Obviously I prefer to have them in person, if it's possible. The only time that I find it a real hindrance is when we have to work on a lot of physical comedy, because then it requires me standing up, allowing them to see something that I'm offering them, and then me watching how they'll interpret it, and what they want to do to change it.

Those are the only times that I find that a problem, because actually, I'm in close-up, and they're in close-up. It's a very intimate sort of experience where I can get into their minds and see are they informing their characters with active questions to keep alive in the scene? I don't have a problem with it, and I think it's a great tool. It allows an actor in Texas, or Atlanta, or in the Midwest, to tap into a great teacher in New York, Los Angeles; whether it's a vocal coach, or anything. I think it's fantastic.

Bonnie Wallace: Yes. Personally, I love the democracy of it; that you don't have to be location dependent to work with somebody wonderful. I also love that it is very similar to acting for the camera, because guess what? That's basically what you're doing. Being on Zoom or Skype, you're seeing, more or less, what the camera sees.

John D'Aquino: Good point.

I've been asked to give classes or teach classes for introverts. I really want to study that more, because I think that there's such a great need. One time, I was teaching at a university in the South. I got surrounded by the faculty the night before at a cocktail party. They were kind of circling in on me.

Eventually, the question came up, "Hey John, what are you teaching our students tomorrow?" I also recognized that I was being interviewed at that moment.

I thought I'd play back a little with them, so I said, "Well, I don't have any idea." They all looked at me, kind of wide eyed. I said, "Because I haven't met the students yet, so I don't know what they need."

Bonnie Wallace: Yes.

John D'Aquino:	Interestingly enough, I have a friend who's a shaman, lives in Boulder, Colorado. He was asked to speak in front of 300 doctors. He told me the same story, and he was asked by all these people in advance, "So what will you be discussing today?"
	He said, "I have no idea. I haven't met them yet." Then, you just have to understand, what's the need?
Bonnie Wallace:	Yes, and then show up for that.
John D'Aquino:	Exactly.
Bonnie Wallace:	Now, what about the kids themselves? I get asked daily what a kid can do to break into the business. What would your advice be for some maybe 12-year-old kid who lives far away from L.A. or New York. They live somewhere away from the major centers. What do you think some of the best ways for those kids to move forward toward that dream might be, right where they are?
John D'Aquino:	Well, I'm just thinking of the way that I had to learn because there was no money to educate me. I had to study the greats. Peyton Manning just won the Super Bowl. I can remember when he was in college, ESPN would go and show how he studied tape. Nobody studied tape like this guy. Then, I'm mindful of Mike Tyson. His manager recognized that he had this beast of an athlete in front of him, but he forced him to become an expert on boxing. He had him watch the greats from going back to Jackie Lewis.
	I've had the pleasure of meeting Steven Spielberg, and people like him, these experts, and Scorsese,

JJ Abrams. They study film. In Dallas, I'll be teaching a class to try and educate people how to study film, how to study television. How to understand the genres.

Zendaya, who's on Disney, I was talking to her father early on when she was just on *Shake it Up*, and I was on the show. He told me how she studied the work of Raven Simone. Well, I've had the pleasure of working with Raven. Raven is a modern Lucille Ball. It's just amazing that she can do audibly, physically, how she captivates that audience constantly. In the same way as the great artists were studying the Masters, Zendaya was studying Raven; I was studying the great Masters of my time. That's where I learned the comedy from, and comedic delivery.

Then, I was lucky enough to get people like Burt Reynolds, who created a space for young actors in Florida, and Charles Nelson Reilly came down to be the master teacher. Then, we had people like Dolly Parton, Liza Minnelli, Sly Stallone, and then Julie Harris from Broadway, Vincent Gardenia, five-time Tony award winners, coming in. We as kids were interacting with them, working on stage with them, sweeping the stage afterwards in classes with them ... Vincent Gardenia, this wonderful actor, taught me how to cook pasta. We were at Burt's beach house in Florida. He said to me,

He says, "So, you want to be an actor?" I said, "Yes."

He says, "Good, then you have to learn how to cook pasta."

Bonnie Wallace: That's hilarious.

John D'Aquino: I said, "Okay." It's like a scene out of *The Godfather*.

Bonnie Wallace:

Well, I love that, because it's true. Most kids don't have parents who can pick up and move them to L.A. or New York. Many kids don't have parents who can even afford acting classes. There's usually some kind of class available where you are, but not necessarily. You really can learn a lot in your room watching YouTube, watching great films, watching incredible performances through television.

Any final thoughts for young actors hoping to make a career in film or TV?

John D'Aquino:

If you're a young actor, and there's no money in your family, and you're someplace in America and you feel you can do this, do it. That's why Nike makes so much money, *Just Do It*. That was my circumstance, just put one foot in front of the other. I had this dream of getting inside that television box. It was a box back then. They were having so much fun. It just felt so alive in there. I just kept on my course. Then, you have to become the best actor in your category, period; so that you erase the "no's" that are in front of you, until finally, someone says "yes." You can't give up. You must believe.

There was a great football coach one time who said, "It's okay if you out talent me, but shame on me if you outwork me." I'm certainly not the best actor in Hollywood, but I have outworked a number of them to get my jobs. I've been gifted with some great teachers, and I have a wonderful family, and so the support has been there. You just have to be willing to outwork everybody, and you'll be fine.

PATRICK DAY

"Analyze, personalize, memorize; relax, listen, then react."

Patrick Day is a veteran acting coach and director of Young Actors Space, an acclaimed acting school in Los Angeles. Young Actors Space offers classes aimed at students from age five on up. They also offer workshops, on-camera audition technique, dialect classes and individual coaching.

Alumni include Emma Stone, Zoey Deutch, Sabrina Carpenter, Aly & AJ Michalka, Shailene Woodley, Karan Brar, Tia and Tamara, Xolo Mariduena, Jack Griffo, Julianna Harkavy, Jason Dolley, Lilliya and Lola Reid, Nichole Bloom, and Brittany Curran.

Bonnie Wallace:	Patrick, tell me a little bit about the history of Young Actors Space.
Patrick Day:	Young Actors Space was started in 1979 by Diane Hill Hardin and Nora Eckstein, who was her partner in crime at the time. It was really the first school to work professionally for children on-camera. Back in '79 and the '80s there would be shows on three networks: ABC, NBC, CBS. There was usually a family, and there were usually kids within that family, and most of them were coming here because this was the place where you were doing real work for on-camera stuff.

Bonnie Wallace:	That's quite a history! Young Actors Space has launched a huge number of successful young actors. What do you think accounts for the extraordinary high success rate of your students?
Patrick Day:	I think it's magic.
Bonnie Wallace:	Magic. You heard it here first.
Patrick Day:	Yes, exactly. No. Honestly, well first of all, thank you. We seem very lucky to get these faces in here pretty much every day and I think what we try to do here is find the best version of the actor that shows up. So, we're not one of those schools that's here to tear you down in order to build you up. I've never subscribed to that theory. I think it's a bunch of hootenanny, to be honest with you.
	I think what we want to do is to find what you're bringing to the table and then use that to make the best version of you that's possible, because after all, this is an art form. So, you need to be comfortable when you're going in these rooms, and I think that's what we're focusing on here.
Bonnie Wallace:	That would explain a lot of success. You can't be successful if you're not grounded and comfortable in yourself.
	Can you describe what your approach to acting is? I'm always curious about the differences between schools.
Patrick Day:	Diane came up with this, it's on our wall out front: "relax, listen, react," which is our motto here. After teaching

for a while, I added a couple things to that. You want to analyze; you want to personalize and then you want to memorize.

So you get a set of sides, and you want to analyze them, look at them, discover them. Then you want to personalize them, figure out how that affects you or if you were that character, how would you behave under those circumstances. Then obviously get the lines down and memorize it so you can go in and then when it's time to audition or perform, relax, listen and react. That technique has seemed to work for us.

Now what we do in classes is, our classes are half improv and half scene study. The goal is to make the improvs look like the written word and make the written word seem as if it's an improvisation. So usually in classes we will do both. We'll do improvs for the first half and then we'll get into scene work after that.

Bonnie Wallace: I like the combination of those two things, and having each of them try to be as much like the other as possible. I don't think I've heard of that approach before.

Patrick Day: It feels super important because as an actor, as a young artist, whatever age, you're going to come in, you're going to want to make certain choices and you're going to go into a casting and hopefully they're strong and specific choices based on that personalization. But on a dime, that casting director is going to give you a note and you have to change. So you can't be locked into anything that's not playable and plus, as you're aware, if you get a series, you might have a different director every week. One director might speak Meisner. One director might say, "I don't need any of that." One might

115

go Spolin. One might go, "Just shut up and say the lines."

And you have to be in the position as an actor, that you are in life, totally pliable, because life is an improv. We want it to be specific, we want it to be planned out. We should have our plan, but at the end of the day, life's an improv.

Bonnie Wallace: I want that on a bumper sticker. Life is an improv. I love that. The thing you just mentioned about directors is something that I think is probably not widely known. We didn't know it. If you're doing TV, you have a revolving door of directors. If you're fortunate enough to get on a series, you're not going to have the same director every week and that keeps you on your toes. It can be an ongoing Master Class if you're lucky.

Patrick Day: Well, you learn every day on set and at every audition. That's the goal, is to keep your eyes open and your ears open and be aware, because it is constantly evolving and changing.

Bonnie Wallace: Yes. How do you structure your classes other than what you just mentioned, which is that you've got a 50/50 emphasis on improv and scene study?

Patrick Day: When I got here out of college and I first started teaching, there was this hesitation about what I was going to be able to give back, and so I would do schedules and outlines and this is what we're doing, and this week we're hitting this and this week we're going to do this and treating it more like a college class. Now I had just come out of college so, that would be where my head space was, and I realized after a couple of years that was starting to get in my way, because what if somebody from last week is still working on what we were working on last week? And now you're leaving that behind and you're moving forward.

So, the reality is when I come into class, fortunately after doing this for so long, it's an energy. I'll feel what these guys are bringing in and on one day I may come in with a plan of doing something and the moment we warm up, there's a different feeling in that room, and we're going to throw it out and we're going to go with this.

So, oftentimes I'll dictate where we're starting, but that's never where we end up because as I said, it's all an improv. So you've got to be open to the energy in that room. Now there are certain nights that we have here that I'll have to give them a week in advance because I might have them prep to bring something in, but even within that improv-wise, it's going to change because something may come up where it's an opportunity to teach and that's really what you're looking for. It's a lot like parenting. You're constantly looking for an opportunity to teach. And oftentimes it's the learning moment at the same time.

Bonnie Wallace: Because our children are our greatest teachers. It's interesting because in reality, for kids who fall in love with theater and discover acting that way—you get weeks to memorize your lines and get up on your feet and get the blocking and stuff. But in reality, in film and TV, you might get 24 hours, if you're lucky, to memorize those sides. Frequently, it's even less time than that to have your shot at it. So, it's nice to give actors a little bit of time, but they don't have that much time in reality.

Patrick Day:

Right. One of the most difficult things about once you've gotten the job and you're learning your lines and you're going to set, is the days where you show up and they go, "Hey..." I remember working on a soap opera years ago and you'd learn 70 pages of dialogue, because it's all narrative, and you show up and they'd say, "Oh great, Patrick, we're ready for you except your scene partner called in sick today. So we're doing Friday's schedule today and we'll do today's schedule on Friday." So now you're learning another 50 pages of dialogue.

Now you're the visitor on that set and the writers come to you in the morning and say, "We've changed the script just a little bit." And those little changes for me personally, those are always the hardest. Once I've memorized it in a certain way, then if it's two or three words that are out of place, it becomes harder for my brain to lock out of it. So again, it goes back to be ready to improvise on the fly. I always say deliver that first take as written because you want to make sure the writers get what they want and then if a director says you're free to improvise, then you can play, but you've got to do the work first before you can come in and be able to do that.

Bonnie Wallace:

Exactly. It's super common on TV especially for the lines to change as you're filming. The writers are going to huddle and say, "Actually-"

Patrick Day:

"This isn't working, let's try this."

Bonnie Wallace: Yes. So, the more flexible an actor can be, regardless of how old they are, is so important. You could be an eight-year-old actor and have new lines thrown at you as you're filming. They're not going to exempt you from that just because you're 8, or 18, or whatever.

Patrick Day: It's part of the game.

Bonnie Wallace: Now, you also offer these summer intensives besides your regular classes. Talk to me about those. They look really fun. I'm here in your studio and I can see all these pictures up on the wall, and the kids' faces are just shining.

Patrick Day: Yeah. I look forward to summer like I'm 10 years old. So Nora Eckstein, who I had mentioned earlier, is one of the founders of the school. She's now living up in Seattle, and we bring her back for the summer intensives because she's our writer. So that none of the children is a spear-carrier.

She comes in, we meet these kids and on day one we have a loose idea of what we're going to do. This is for the theater conservatory and we start improvising with them. By day two, Nora has a pretty good idea of where the script's going. By day three, we start to have a script. By day four, we cast the script and by day 10, we're performing an original one act, which with your theater background, you know what's involved in that.

So, we really create a piece of art in 10 days and it's insane and exhausting and beautiful all at the same time.

Bonnie Wallace: It sounds glorious. It sounds like the best part of the year for some of these kids.

Patrick Day: It's really a wonder, and this was the 16th year that Nora and I did this program, and we have kids that are now adults and are having children of their own and bringing them back for the Summer Conservatory.

They've made lifelong friends, and one of the great things about social media is you see these friendships that were created here that go on in life, and it's really wonderful.

Our other intensive, which we started a couple of years ago, is an on-camera intensive, and again, we'll fly Nora in, and she meets the kids day one. Now this is a one-week intensive. It's a little bit shorter and she'll write a one to three-minute scene based on their personality and what serves them best for their reel.

And then on day five we'll shoot these scenes that we've rehearsed throughout the week and they walk out of here with a real hands-on, practical idea of what it's like to be on set, and the limitations that are involved in that. We almost killed ourselves this year because we try to limit it to 15 because we want everybody to get plenty of work, but with our intensive sometimes we'll go between 15 and 20 actors, depending on the year and what we can get in.

We built nine different sets over two days, and we have three rooms here. So we've got one set to go in here, and we'll shoot it out and then we'll come in here and shoot it out, then go in the other room, shoot the other set, strike the sets, build three more sets and get the kids in here. They have a small window of time to show up and hit their marks. The practicality ... there was one set where we built a roof. The scene took place on a roof. So we had roofing towers in here, and they have to learn that they can't lean back on a set or put their hands here. Because it's still-

Bonnie Wallace: Like life on a real set.

Patrick Day: Exactly. So it's insane and exhausting, but I wouldn't change a moment of it. It's really a wonderful time.

Bonnie Wallace: That sounds like fun. Can you tease apart some of the differences between acting on stage versus acting for film versus TV?

Patrick Day: Sure. Obviously you can't lie to the camera, and it's really close to your face. So the idea is, and obviously depending on the genre it may change as well, but if we're doing a play, they're looking more for athletes than actors.

                    They want you to be an actor, but they want you to be an athlete as well, because the process you're building this show for, in our case 10 days, but in most cases longer, and the physicality that's involved ... the stamina, the taking care yourself, the showing up every day, the getting the lines down, the rehearsing and then the having to change in a moment because now we're going in different direction, they really want athletes as well as actors. I'm not saying that doesn't happen on film as well and TV. Sometimes it does.

Bonnie Wallace: That's been Dove's experience, that exact description. To be a lead in a show or a movie requires a profound amount of stamina and frankly, physical fitness and health to just get through it.

Patrick Day: Yeah. And I think it was Martin Landau who said, and this is a great analogy, "When I do a play, it's like eating a nine-course meal every night. When I do a film, it's just like having appetizers every day." Which is really a great description of how it feels, because you're shooting out of order on set when you're doing a film and, "Oh. I remember we did the scene before this two weeks ago." And you've got to review your notes.

But as the character when you're doing a play, you're going through this process from the beginning to the end, from the moment you're sitting in the makeup chair and you're hearing the audience coming in, to the moment you're taking your final bow and there are accolades hopefully of applause, and then you walk backstage and you pass out because you're exhausted and you get ready to do it again tomorrow because it's ethereal, and it's going to disappear, and the only people that are going to experience that magic are the ones that are in that room that night.

Oftentimes with film and television, quite honestly, you're stuck with it for the rest of your life, and then when you go back to it, you think, "I wish I could change this moment or do that or do this differently." So we're trying to figure out how to make it all perfect when in reality, all those flaws are the perfection.

The whole art form is about behavior.

Bonnie Wallace: It's humanity. I love that. Let's talk about auditioning.

I think of auditioning as really its own skillset. It's a critical one obviously. If you're a fine actor, but if you're a lousy auditioner, no one will ever know.

And weirdly, the reverse is true too, because if you're a really fine auditioner but then once you're hired, you can't hold up your end of the deal, it's disastrous. So, especially now that so many auditions are done on tape, talk to me about some great approaches for actors to step into an audition and do their best, and get their best shot at actually getting the role?

Patrick Day: I'm going to go back to this, Diane said it: "relax, listen, and react." And that's one of the hardest things when you're going in to the audition because as we discussed, you have that green room psychology going all around. Am I good enough? Do I deserve to be here?

Nora always says, "There's always somebody *more*. There's always somebody more tall, more short, more fat, more skinny or more blue, white or brown haired and you can't worry about that." And that's one of the hardest things when you're sitting in that room and you're trying to be your best possible version of you and the character when you're worried about all this other noise that's going on around.

I know we haven't spoken about the on-camera yet, but as far as going in the room, if you do the work beforehand, the *analyze, personalize, memorize,* then you're a lot freer to *relax, listen and react.*

Now, sometimes you're just going to have a day. You're going to be dealing with traffic and you're hopefully not late, but maybe you got lost on the way or something and you want none of that to be in that room, and it's a very difficult thing to manage that. But the reality is if you can manage that and you find techniques that work for you, you're always going to have a better audition.

Most actors tend to rush. So, oftentimes if you can take your time, you're setting yourself ahead of your competition. I still put myself in those rooms intentionally because I want to know what that feels like, and some of those rooms are great. I had an audition last week where I had a drive-on parking pass onto the lot, which is rare here.

It's rare because they usually tell you, "Actors, park in the back and find your way." So now you're walking in feeling great, but that's rare because there are other times where you're dealing with street parking and possible ticketing, and they need you in an hour. And either you're living on the West side and you're going to the Valley, or inevitably you're living in the Valley and going to the West side, and that can get in your way.

But for me, I feel that it's always better if you can get in the room. Look at it as an opportunity. The casting director is not an enemy. They have chosen to meet you, and if this stuff is fun, then you're doing the right thing. If you're worried about the other crazy stuff that doesn't belong in that room, then that's going to get in your way, but if you're going in, go in thankful for this opportunity.

If I have the opportunity to perform for the people that are making this decision, and if I've done my work by the time I go in that room, I feel like I should be putting that on my resume because I had the opportunity to audition for Hamlet, for the people that are doing Hamlet.

And if I look at it just as that, and then the moment I walk out of that room, forget about it, I feel like I'm doing my best work.

Bonnie Wallace: I think it's always preferable to get directly in front of the casting director and be face-to-face, but unfortunately these days that is less and less the case for various reasons, including budget constraints and everything else. So, even if you've done whatever it took to move to Los Angeles or maybe New York to be available in the big market, you might still be doing a lot of self-tapes.

Any self-tape advice?

Patrick Day:

I've had more clients in the past three years booked directly off tape, never meeting the director until they show up to set. I had a client who worked on this HBO show a little bit ago, and he had sent in a tape in May and casting kept calling back going, "We're doing this show and we still want to see this person." And he finally was booked and flew to New York in December to shoot from a tape that he'd done in May.

Bonnie Wallace:

More often than not, you find out sooner.

Patrick Day:

Because television moves quickly, and we've had that too. I had a woman come in here, she happened to be an adult and put herself on tape. The director was in Canada at the time working on another film. She was from London and this project was being shot in Australia. She came in here, we shot her. A week later she went to Australia having never met anybody, she booked off that tape and then she calls me six months later. I asked, "How was that experience?" She said, "Incredible. So much in fact that the director is now doing another movie in Atlanta and wants me to play the trophy wife of William Shatner." So she booked two movies basically off of one tape.

So there are advantages as well. You might be getting a callback when you're sound asleep or you're celebrating your birthday and some producer is watching that tape and calling you in, you just never know.

So there are advantages and disadvantages. As far as advice for on-camera, they will deal with not the best quality camera, and cameras are relatively inexpensive now. It's not like the old days of VHS where you had to cut tape to tape and all that, but you should have clean sound and good lighting.

Bonnie Wallace: That alone is such a step in the right direction because so many people don't even take care of that at all. That'll help casting at least want to look at your audition.

Patrick Day: And hear you. As a matter of fact, for those of you out there that are looking to set up your own rig, I would strongly suggest investing in a decent microphone before I would suggest investing in a really high-end camera.

Bonnie Wallace: Good advice. Any particular mic you like while we're at it or are we getting too technical?

Patrick Day: We use a Rode mic here because they're relatively inexpensive and they adapt pretty well to anything. But I'm sure there are others.

Bonnie Wallace: You mentioned a moment ago that you were working with an adult actor and I want to take a moment to just point out that just because your school is called Young Actors Space doesn't mean that you only work with people under the age of 18. Can you talk about that for a second?

Patrick Day: We have three adult classes here. We have our on-camera class, and then we have two of our regular half improv, half scene study classes, which now have turned into—I hate the word showcase—we call them demonstration classes, but these adults are now putting on realized shows sometimes at the end twice a year with the work they do in class.

It's because, I think a lot of our kids have grown up and still like what we do here, and we might have people in class that are on a series, and we might have people in class that have never done this art form before but have always wanted to. We don't divide by, just because you're working, you're advanced, because everybody can learn from everybody.

I learn every day I teach. If I'm not learning, I should retire because that is, honestly, the reality of what's going on here. You're going to show up to set and you're going to get a series and oftentimes on that series you're going to be cast opposite somebody that has never done anything in their life. They might have a great Instagram following and so you can learn from them, and they can learn from you.

So, we don't differentiate by degree based on resume. We all come here to learn from each other, and we do. Somebody walking in off the street might have great behavioral stuff that I might borrow after having read and done this stuff for 30 years.

Bonnie Wallace: It's true that on a set you will be in a cast with people of every different experience and ability level, so it's great that you don't differentiate that way in your classes because that's reflective of real life. What you do in fact with the kids, is make pretty fine slices with ages, and I really like that. As a parent, that's cool. I don't want my 7-year-old doing a scene with a 16-year-old. I just don't.

127

Patrick Day: Right. Or hearing what they're talking about not only when they're doing a scene, but when they're rehearsing the scene, because we don't want the little ones annoying the older ones and we want the older ones being respectful of their language and subject matter around the little ones.

Now, they're going to work with younger ones and older ones on set. So occasionally we'll have our makeup class, which is all ages where they all get to work together and those are fun, but really we're broken down by age because that is the subject matter they're going to be working with at that time.

One of the things about Young Actors Space that is super important since day one is that this is a very supportive environment. We want to make sure that everybody's comfortable and that doesn't mean that we're just here to tell you you're doing a great job, but if you're not feeling supported and you're not treating the work with respect and each other with respect, then how can you get up on stage and be vulnerable? How can you get in front of a camera and be vulnerable? You have to have that respect with each other and that support to go to these dark places sometimes, and to feel okay with it.

Bonnie Wallace: You have to feel safe in order to create an authentic performance. And it's true that on a set, like theater and real life, you are in mixed ages. But for the purpose of classes I like that the kids are in different developmental spaces.

What a 7-year-old is able to grasp in terms of how to approach character is not the same as what a 14-year-old is able to grasp.

Patrick Day:	Correct. I mean, the reality is, our goal is to teach to the top.
	So, let's say we're in a tween class, a 10 to 12-year-old class, and that 12-year-old is becoming a 13 or 14-year-old and evolving at a quicker rate than their scene partner. At that point, after we know them for a while, we'll say, "Maybe check out this class and see if this is the right fit." Now, occasionally they'll come to that class and go, "Whoa. There's too much going on. This is too teen for me." And that's not, "Oh. Now you're going backwards." That's just, "Stay where you're at until you're ready to evolve forward." And that's okay too.
Bonnie Wallace:	But you can't possibly make that call until you get to know the actor a little bit. You wouldn't do that just as they step in cold.
Patrick Day:	No. We have people call and say, "We're on a series. We should be in an older class." And we say, "You know, not necessarily. Let's see where your instrument is, so we can best benefit your instrument."
Bonnie Wallace:	I know that some people feel weird about coaching over Zoom or Skype, but it's the 21st century. Some people love coaching remotely, and getting coached remotely. What are your feelings? Do you do a lot of coaching here?
Patrick Day:	We do. Thankfully yes, and we have clients all over the world really at this point. There are upsides and downsides obviously with Skype or Duo or Face-Time, or whatever is the latest version of that. We're

so lucky they exist, because when I was doing this stuff growing up in Nashville, there was none of that. I had no idea what was going on and to be able to actually see somebody and communicate with them, it is beneficial. Oftentimes if they're doing something on camera, I'll have them set up the camera and read with them as if I'm a casting director, and that way they have an eye line for me, and they can talk. So we do that as well.

The downside is, sometimes Skype hesitates or stutters or pixelates and if you're doing a take, that can ruin a take. Also, the downside oftentimes with doing it on Skype as opposed to in the room, is, especially with comedy, you want to keep it clipping along and if there is that hesitation and you're missing the joke or you're not on top of it, it can affect the way your coaching is going. However, at the end of the day, I'm so grateful it exists because it's far beyond what we were dealing with even 10, 15 years ago.

Bonnie Wallace: It allows actors from all over the world to be able to work with you and get your coaching, and it allows you to help them and make a contribution to people who aren't just here in Los Angeles.

Patrick Day: Absolutely. And on that note, I did a *Criminal Minds* a few years ago. I never saw the director when I was on set. I was in a hotel and she was in another room. It was like being on Skype directing me from the monitor. So it makes sense. Two weeks ago, I had a client who we sent on tape, and the director was somewhere else in the world and wanted to do a Skype interview for final casting. So, it's happening.

There's no way to just say it's not going to work because you've just got to figure out a way to make it work.

Bonnie Wallace: It's reality, and especially with some of these bigger projects where maybe the director is in New York doing some Broadway show, and the producers are here in L.A. and the actors are wherever on set somewhere else, you can still make it happen. You can have these meetings, (i.e. final callbacks), thanks to technology.

Patrick Day: And it's happening more and more. It's not going to go away.

Bonnie Wallace: It's important to get comfortable with it, I think.

Patrick Day: Now on that note, we had a contributor here who was a casting director, and she gave us a list of things—because she's in casting and does some Skype casting—and some of the mistakes people make are just so ridiculous that you can't believe you have to say this, "You need to treat Skype like it's a job interview. Don't do a Skype in your pajamas."

People are doing it. She said, "You wouldn't believe how often I'm doing a casting and they show up in their pajamas or they don't know how to work Skype or they're late." And I'm thinking, "You're at your own home. It's not as if you're putting on a suit and getting in 110-degree heat and sweating so you don't want to wear the suit." Show up, treat it like a job, be early, and be appreciative. We're not being roofers.

Nothing against roofers, but they've got a tougher job than we do as actors.

So you should be appreciative of the fact that you're having this opportunity and it's just amazing that people forget that.

Bonnie Wallace: So treat it like the job interview that it is.

Patrick Day: That it is. 110%.

Bonnie Wallace: What is your advice for someone who's just trying to break into the business? What are some critical first steps that an actor needs to take to succeed?

Patrick Day: Read. There are so many great techniques and books out there. There's one right here I'm looking at, *The Hollywood Parents Guide*. There are so many opportunities for you to read and read out loud. When you're eating your cereal, read the cereal box out loud. When you're driving around, read the billboards out loud. Get used to reading out loud.

If you're in a smaller community, there's always theater going around somewhere. If you can't get into your local community theater, find a buddy down the street and read out loud with them. Put on your own scene work. Just explore and keep your eyes open. People watch, look at television features, films, theater, go see shows so you can see what's out there and see if it's really for you, because again, at the end of the day, if this is not fun, there is no reason to do it. It's too difficult. There's too much rejection out there, so it's got to be fun.

Bonnie Wallace: It had better be fun. I love all these things that you said that have nothing to do with say, moving to L.A. or New York or getting an agent or getting your head shots.

Patrick Day: Play.

Bonnie Wallace: Play. Get good at it, have fun with it. There's so much you can do literally from where you are, wherever that may be.

Patrick Day: And as you're aware, nowadays, if I have an idea, I can pick up my phone, record it and somebody in Australia could be watching it that night if it's good.

Bonnie Wallace: Are we talking about YouTube?

Patrick Day: YouTube, yes. YouTube and Instagram, and the blah, blah, blah, it keeps going on, but in reality, you can make content and have it seen. Years ago running around L.A., you would make content, you'd shoot on film, which was ridiculously expensive, you'd get three takes that you hoped were right, you'd have to wait to get it developed, then you'd have to transfer it to VHS or even Beta, and then you'd put it in the mail and snail mail it to ads you got out of Variety and hope the producers still had an office there, and then wait six weeks and hope to hear and send letters. Nowadays you can do all this stuff on your phone and have it out that night. So if you have an idea and it's good, get it out there.

Bonnie Wallace: We talked a little bit about this before, what somebody can do, who's trying to break into the business, but if you're a young person, and you don't live in L.A. or New York, what are some things that you can do right now wherever you are, if you're in Tennessee or Washington or whatever, to help prepare and move toward that dream you've got?

Patrick Day:	Find a kindred spirit and start creating content. That can happen wherever you are. Find somebody that you get along with that respects your work, that isn't going to tear you down, and start creating content, because we're in a world where you can create content and upload it every day, and as we discussed, getting into your local community theater or going to watch plays and people watch, all of that stuff is great.
Bonnie Wallace:	And totally available. One of the things that Dove did, that I know she's not alone in doing, is she deliberately went about watching classic top-notch performances and classic top-notch film from decades back. Not just whatever's out this week. You can learn so much by studying fine acting that may have been done before you were born.
Patrick Day:	Absolutely. There's a lot of content out there to look at.
Bonnie Wallace:	Any final thoughts for young actors who are hoping to make a career in film and TV?
Patrick Day:	Just have fun. That's the final thought. Oftentimes your entire career is based on the next person that says yes. You're going to hear, "No, no, no, no, no, no, no, no, no," and if you give up, we don't know if that next person was the one that says "Yes," and I have seen it many, many times. That first person that said "Yes," or that next person that says, "Yes" can change a whole career.
Bonnie Wallace:	Can change your life.

Patrick Day: Can change your life. 100%. As long as it's fun.

Bonnie Wallace: As long as it's fun. And if it's not fun, go find some other environment.

Patrick Day: Go find something that's fun.

JUDY KAIN

Founder, Keep It Real Acting Studios

"I feel that commercials are a little mini movie.
Almost 90% are directed by film directors."

Los Angeles acting teacher Judy Kain is founder of the award-winning *Keep It Real* Acting Studios. She is also the author of *I Booked It*, host of the podcast, *Hollywood Game Changers*, and an actress with over 400 commercial credits and over 110 film and TV credits.

Alumni include Storm Reid, Ethan Herisse, Ray Nicholson, Kecia Lewis, Wesam Keesh, Lawrence Chau, Bambadjan Bamba, Kai Wener, Deric McCabe, Chalet Brannan, Verona Blue, and Hala Finley.

Bonnie Wallace: You were a successful working actress before you opened your own acting studio. What made you decide to become an acting teacher?

Judy Kain: I started teaching for Caroline Barry. She was my commercial teacher and she had me subbing. My business partner at the time said, "Why are you working for somebody else?" And I said, "Well, I don't really want to enroll people," which I didn't at the time. I didn't want to enroll people to take my class. It sounded like selling cars, you know what I mean?

She said, "I'll do it," and so she did. She was the enrollment person, and I was the teacher, and I asked my friend and colleague, Francine Selkirk, if she would rent her studio and come in on the final class, and she was happy to do it. We ended up teaching together for 10 years.

My reputation as a commercial teacher was fostered by her, by working with her, and all the agents got to know us. I mean, they knew her obviously, but they got to know me. I owe her everything.

She's such a give-back gal, and she had a great studio, and she was already renting the studio on Sundays to somebody, so it was a good fit. I'd come in at night and started one class, then it grew to two classes, then I had three or four classes, and then I needed my own studio.

I made the move when I ended the casting business, *Talent to Go*, when I gave that to my business partner and opened this and just became a teacher. But I also saw the need for taping. This was about eight years ago. It was just beginning, and I could see the future.

Bonnie Wallace: We moved here about 10 years ago, just at the cusp of when people were starting to talk about self-tapes, and it's really important.

Judy Kain: It is critical. Of course, people have makeshift things in their homes. I know actors are putting little studios in their homes and doing the same thing that I'm doing, but there is a huge demand, so there are a lot of people that are offering that as a service, because it's very hard to do it yourself. Have you tried?

Bonnie Wallace: Of course. It's difficult to do well.

Judy Kain: I mean, first of all, just to get the whole setup together, unless it's already done, which is why I love this. But then to have a reader in a timely way, a good reader, somebody who can give you something, and then the editing and the compressing.

Bonnie Wallace: The uploading, the downloading. When we landed here, smartphones weren't really ready for what the requirements were, so I used a little camera on a tripod, and there wasn't a single blank wall in the little apartment that Dove and I were in, so we had to hang a blanket over a bookcase to make a background. Very guerilla.

Judy Kain: There's a lot of guerilla, and you see now in the instructions from casting that they are not liking it. They don't want guerilla anymore. They want well done.

Bonnie Wallace: I was just in a conversation with somebody else about this, and there's this kind of rising expectation around production values, if you will, around just auditions. I'm thinking to myself, "My gosh, production values around auditions-!" But at the same time, if casting is blowing through a thousand self-tapes, a thousand submissions over the course of a day to try and narrow it down to someone they want to bring in...

Judy Kain: They're going to pay attention to something that looks good.

Bonnie Wallace: And if something looks bad, it's going to turn them off. It's not fair, but it's the way of the world.

Judy Kain:	Well, it's not fair in a way because it's the actor's expense, but they always say, "But you can do it yourself," but you really can't, so it's a real catch-22. There's always going to be something for actors, a hurdle to jump over. I mean, back in the day we had to have 300 head shots stapled with the resume to your agent at all times.
Bonnie Wallace:	Luckily that part's changed too.
Judy Kain:	That's fine, but now you have the self-tapes, so there's always something.
Bonnie Wallace:	Do you have an overarching philosophy that guides your studio, would you say?
Judy Kain:	Well, obviously "keep it real" is the overwhelming philosophy. I think that all the teachers come from that perspective, but for me, I always hire people who are passionate about acting, not bitter, and they have to still be working, because I find that if you're still a working actor and you're still actively engaged in pursuing the jobs, then that keeps you passionate, and it offers the students a current perspective on the climate of the industry, which I think is important rather than what it used to be like. Because there are some people out there who are teaching who haven't really seen the inside of an audition room in a long time.
	And that I think is harmful to an actor, because you don't get a lot of chances to meet and greet a casting director to make an impression. I always say you have one chance to make a first impression. That's it, so if they're coming in green or dated or too presentational...

Bonnie Wallace:	Which may have worked 20-30 years ago, but it doesn't work anymore. Now, you offer a selection of commercial classes as well as improv and theatrical in your studio here in L.A. Can you tell me about these classes?
Judy Kain:	Well, the commercial class, A to Z, was the first one. That was the embryo, and I structured it, and it's literally the same structure that I've been teaching for almost 20 years. It's six weeks. It covers every type of commercial audition you'll go on. There are five types. So we go over a technique that I use to sort of master or get a hold of that type of audition. It's the personality style audition, MOS, no dialogue, it's the spokesperson, it's a scene, and the improv audition. Then the final week we have an agent come in.
Bonnie Wallace:	That's exciting. That's hard to come by. That's a big carrot.
Judy Kain:	They love coming, because they know they're going to see actors who at least have been trained and trained well. So we get great agents in here, and they often pick up people, so that's nice. Then I have a casting prep intensive, which is kind of the intermediate class where we just tackle more difficult things, and I try to work with them on honing their technique.
Bonnie Wallace:	Is this commercial or theatrical?
Judy Kain:	Commercial. Then I have an advanced commercial class, which I love, because I have a mock audition or a mock call back every week, so I have a casting office in,

or sometimes a director in, or a producer in the room. They come in one at a time or two at a time for a scene. They do their audition, they leave, and then we do a Q and A. That's all in the course of the first hour.

We give real feedback, and it's awesome, because then I can see what they're actually doing in the call back room, because once the first class is over, they're going to be comfortable, so I'm not going to see what happens when they get nervous, and then I address it for the rest of the class. We always go over the same five types of commercial auditions. It just gets increasingly more difficult with the advanced call back class.

Bonnie Wallace: So you've got a true curriculum for commercial?

Judy Kain: Absolutely. Then we have two theatrical classes. One is more of an audition technique. We call it either Pilot Season Prep or Booking the Theatrical Audition, which is basically auditioning, and everything is done with the camera, because that's how it's done.

But then we also have an ongoing scene study class, which is Meisner-based, and that is literally just to hone the craft, to keep the skills up, work on scene work. The nice thing is that you do work every single week. You get up at least two times, which I think is remarkable, so there's that. That's our theatrical department, and then we have Paul Hungerford who is, I call him the improv guru. He doesn't like to be called that. He's such an improv junkie, and he teaches an amazing class. It's eight weeks, and we have a performance at the end.

Industry people come to see it and have picked people up from it, so that's a great training ground. In that class, there's no shaming, there's no, "You're doing it wrong."

Bonnie Wallace: Improv is so scary. It's funny though, at the same time, every casting director, director, whoever I've ever spoken to who's a decision maker in this industry, they all say that improv skills are critical for a successful acting career, so you've just got to get comfortable with it. Even if you're never going to stand up on stage and "do improv," you have to feel loose, I think.

Judy Kain: Yes, I did take it when I was younger. Probably more brave. I did quite a bit. I studied with Paul Sills, who was Viola Spolin's son. I studied in Milwaukee. I studied at The Groundlings. And with Cynthia Seghetti. So I had some really, really good teachers early on, and I have absolutely no desire to perform in an improv troupe ever.

Bonnie Wallace: But you make it available for your students.

Judy Kain: Oh, absolutely. He's really the perfect teacher for that. And then we have kids and teens classes, same thing, acting classes, commercial and theatrical. We also have more for the whole actor. We have a branding class, we have a headshot class, and we have a class in what you're wearing. It's called, "*Really? You're Wearing That?*"

That's how the title came out. It's hard to get actors to understand how important the clothing is, but once they do, it blows their mind. It handles a whole area that you could be insecure about, or not even know that you're really creating a terrible impression.

Bonnie Wallace:	Yes. Just getting it wrong, firstly, and creating unnecessary impediments to being cast. Or taken seriously.
Judy Kain:	We have a class for four to six-year-olds. It's five weeks. It's awesome. They are so adorable. Donna Rush is a teacher, and Hannah, and boy, they really come out of there and book. It's so adorable. They're cute. They get comfortable and confident. And at that age, think about it. In kindergarten, what are they doing? They're repeating, they're repeating, they're repeating, preparing them to sustain for first grade. The same thing is happening in class: they're repeating, repeating, repeating, preparing them for that audition. It really works, and the parents love it because they see the difference … It's hard bringing a kid around to auditions when they don't book.

When they start to get callbacks, it helps tremendously. I know because my son was a child commercial actor, and there was a period where it was, "Do you really want to do this?" Driving to Santa Monica for auditions.

Bonnie Wallace:	Well, but that's what it takes. It also takes faith and perseverance.
Judy Kain:	Perseverance for sure.
Bonnie Wallace:	You also offer private coaching and self-taping services. We talked a tiny bit about the taping earlier, but can you tell me about these two services?
Judy Kain:	Well, taping of course comes in usually last minute. We get calls the day of. We have people sometimes

literally just show up and go, "Do you have any time?" And they'll wait. But we have two studios where we tape and we download it, upload it, compress it, and send it wherever it needs to go. We can put it right on the actor's Eco Cast if they need it. I do coach along the way.

Some actors don't want coaching, but some of them really just need that eye. A little tweak or something here, or just make this more intense. Yesterday this gal came in, and she wanted to tape a monologue just to have something on her Actor's Access. So I coached her for about a half hour or so, but it definitely went from 0 to 50, really.

And then I just do coaching if people have an audition where they're actually going into a person's office. With a lot of kids, the agents want the kids to not be coached by the parents. I don't know why the parents need to coach the kids, and once they coach them, it's etched in. It's hard to break.

Bonnie Wallace: Yes. You can do a lot more harm than good if you're coaching your kids, unless again, you're an actual professional. It's okay to let the professionals do it, or if you don't have a professional who can coach a kid, it's okay to let your kid's instincts rule the day. Because if they've got the passion to do this, they're going to be better anyway.

Judy Kain: They are.

Bonnie Wallace: What's the youngest age you work with at your studio?

Judy Kain: Four.

Bonnie Wallace:	I think when kids are younger than four, it's just tough.
Judy Kain:	Yes, there's really hardly any point. They hardly go out, and there's a big gap between a baby/newborn/six months old baby, to four years old. Once they're four, then they can begin. Really before that, there's very little. They're not going to be doing any work. They're too young.
	There's not much work, and there's no real time on the set, legally. The labor laws do not allow them to be on the set long enough, so if it's triplets, great. They'll hire the triplets and sub in.
Bonnie Wallace:	Or maybe twins, but otherwise, it's okay to let your kid just wait until they're at least four.
Judy Kain:	Exactly, because they need some skills to be able to listen, pay attention, and sit for an hour and a half in the class.
Bonnie Wallace:	Let's talk about auditioning. Obviously, auditioning well is the gateway to booking, to getting jobs. What advice do you have for actors approaching an audition, and do you think actors should approach commercial auditions differently than theatrical ones?
Judy Kain:	No, it's my pet peeve. It's my pet peeve that you walk into a lobby of a commercial audition, and everybody's talking. They're on their phone. They're not putting any attention whatsoever into the task at hand.
	I think it's the same. There's no difference. You still have to make choices, and that's what I teach in my commercial classes. Just the choices that you make are

145

the same choices that you would make. In fact, you almost have to make more, because you're given nothing. You're given no backstory, you're given no history. You have to create the relationship and most of the backstory and make everything personal. So anyway, I feel that commercials are a little mini movie. Almost 90% are directed by film directors.

Bonnie Wallace: People don't know this. The money that goes into them is astonishing. And the production values are top notch. In a way, it's like poetry versus a short story.

Judy Kain: Yes, and the trap with an actor, I believe, is they think the more they do, the better it will be, and that's not the case.

Bonnie Wallace: Less is more.

Judy Kain: Less is more, and keep it real.

Bonnie Wallace: Any special advice for audition self-tapes? We've been talking about taping. Not everybody has the luxury of being within striking distance of coming into your studio and being able to work with you. For example, what if you're further out, maybe not in a major market. Even if you're in L.A., you've got to be able to master it somehow. Maybe you're on location. You can't always pop into the studio in time.

Judy Kain: Right. I remember I was on location in Atlanta and had made friends with a dad of one of the child actors on the show, and I asked him, "Would you mind reading?"

Because I had a last-minute audition. He said, "Oh, I'll not only read it. I brought my camera."

I went out and got one of those kits. I got a little mini tripod. Obviously, you can use the iPad. I got the iPad clamp. I got a little light to attach to it with a mic, and I bring that with me wherever I go now.

Bonnie Wallace: That's a really good side note for everybody listening. Actors who are working, and parents of young actors who are working, if you're on location, make it part of your pack-up lists to make a little kit, because it's like a law of the universe: if you're on location, you're going to get a really important self-tape you've got to do in your hotel room after filming all day. So be ready.

Judy Kain: I think the main thing that actors somehow don't realize is you have to be off-book. You have to be at least 90% off-book, and we can't see the script. Don't show the script. Hide the script. Filter it into the scene, but do not come in and read and tape someone reading. That's not going to work.

You have to prepare. That to me is how the industry has changed tremendously. Everything is shortened. They have less time to cast, and they've left less time to produce. They have less time, so everybody's got to be prepared.

You've got to show the performance with choices and levels, and if you can't be off-book, where's that? How are you going to possibly do a choice?

Bonnie Wallace: On top of that, you're competing with people who are off-book.

Judy Kain: Oh, absolutely. And if you go in the room, it's the same thing. Have the script, but they're taping you too, so you can't be reading the sides in this scene. It makes the director nervous.

Incorporate that camera into the scene. Incorporate it in somehow. Be aware of it so that your face is really being seen. Make it a part of the scene. Make it part of your fourth wall.

Somehow, it really helps. Otherwise, it's like the forbidden fruit, and then you can almost see that you're avoiding it, and you organically turn away from it, and that never helps.

Bonnie Wallace: Talk to me about your book, *I Booked It.*

Judy Kain: I go over what I feel is important for an actor. It's called *The Commercial Actor's Handbook,* so I go over everything that an actor really needs to know to be prepared. I tried to skew away from actors who are just beginning. I tried to really approach an actor who's already in the business or at least familiar with the business, but I go over everything.

All of the different types of auditions, the traps that you might fall in, agents, managers, how to get one. I go over clothes to wear, I go over branding. Also, what I love about the book is I interviewed an agent, Hugh Leon from Coast to Coast. I interviewed a commercial producer, Anton Maillie, and I interviewed a director, who had directed me in 20 different spots. And a casting director, Ross Lacy. So it also gives their perspective as well, not just my voice, but theirs as well. They're great interviews.

Bonnie Wallace: It is really great because there are so many books out there on acting technique, and on this and that for the actor, and by and large, they're aimed at theatrical, which is great and very important, but there's not a lot out there for the commercial piece. Let's be honest, you can pay the mortgage and then some on commercials. Commercials can be really lucrative.

Judy Kain: I had a house, the Clairol house. The house that Clairol built. That was amazing. I had no idea that it was going to be that kind. It played all over the world. I was even spoofed on Saturday Night Live.

Bonnie Wallace: Commercial acting is its own universe, and it's really important if you want to do it to know how to do it right and do it well.

Judy Kain: And for somebody just beginning, most beginning actors are not in the union. They could actually get a lot of work doing non-union commercials to get their feet wet and to build their confidence and make money.

Bonnie Wallace: And then eventually join the union.

Judy Kain: Absolutely, and then tackle the theatrical world.

Bonnie Wallace: A lot of younger actors are often taken on by agencies in their commercial division to sort of see how that all goes. Get their feet in the water before they will consider taking them on theatrically. So commercials are a gateway to a lot of things, or they're also just their own thing.

Judy Kain:	Yes, and you can do them until you're 99 years old.
Bonnie Wallace:	That's actually a wonderful point. It's sort of like voiceover that way. The work doesn't dry up when you're at a certain age.
Judy Kain:	It's true. I mean there aren't as many jobs, but certainly seniors work. Oh, and I teach a free senior's class too. The first Monday of every month, I have a free senior's class from 4:00 pm to 5:00 pm on Monday, and they are adorable. A lot of them are working.
Bonnie Wallace:	What would be your advice for a young person who wants to be a professional actor, but they live far away from L.A. or New York, at least right now? What do you think some of the best ways for them to move toward that dream might be, right where they are?
Judy Kain:	Well, that's another thing that's changed tremendously in the industry: there is work everywhere. There is work in Alabama. There's a lot of work in Louisiana. There's a lot of work in Georgia. There's a lot of work in the Carolinas. In Texas, there's a lot of work. See if you can get a local agent to start submitting you. Obviously have some training, because you don't want to waste your time or anybody else's time, but train and find out who the casting people are and get to know them. Work where you are. Usually most of those states are *right to work* states, so you don't have to be in the union. You can do union work, but you don't have to be in the union, so I've told people who

are starting to try to get credits, to try a smaller market for a year.

Bonnie Wallace: It's actually a silver lining if you're not already in a major market to build up your resume as much as you can before you consider making a move, because it's easier. There's less competition.

Judy Kain: Right, and easier to be considered with footage and credits, when people have hired you and worked with you. So that's changing. You either had to be in New York or L.A. or forget it, but now that's completely changed. Even the coast, Oregon, Washington, they're shooting up there. Certainly Canada. If you're in Canada, you can have a career.

But you *have to have* Canadian citizenship. That is the caveat there. You can't just go up to Canada and hope to work, because they won't let you.

Bonnie Wallace: Exactly. Unless you're cast in L.A. and hired to shoot in Canada.

Judy Kain: Yes, of course. There's that. But you could go to Atlanta easily.

A lot of L.A. actors have Atlanta agents and are working out of there as well, which is also another thing you can do. You can live in L.A. but have your Atlanta agent ... The goal is not to make a lot of money, because you're going to eat it up with your flights and your lodging or whatever, but you will get the credits. If you really make that your focus, you could do that for a year, year and a half, build up your resume, and then hit the ground running here.

Bonnie Wallace: It's nice when you finally do get to the major market to have something on your resume as well as some experience and footage ready.

Judy Kain: I do think it's important to find a place you can go where you feel at home, where you can study all the time until you're so busy working that you don't have time to study, because it's kind of the Catch-22 of being an actor is it's an art form, but you can't really practice that art form by yourself. You need other people in order to stay in shape, whereas you can go to the gym by yourself, but you can't act by yourself.

Bonnie Wallace: You can write a book by yourself. There are a lot of things you can do by yourself in the creative field, but acting's not really one of them.

Judy Kain: No, it's not. People say they watch movies and stuff. Yes, but do you really watch them as a student?

Or are you just watching them to check out and to enjoy? I think it's really important to be in class and up on your feet and getting over those inhibitions, fears, blocks that you have. We all have them. Get rid of the tricks, and you can only really do that in a class when someone's calling you out on it.

Bonnie Wallace: To me, in anything, the real learning can only occur when you're on the field, whatever that field is. You can think about it all day long. You can think you know how to do it, but your body and everything needs to be fully engaged for learning to take place.

Judy Kain:	Absolutely. Just that one thing that happens to you when you go to an audition. You have anticipation or nerves or excitement or something of that nature happens to you, so you've got to deal with that. I think the only way you can deal with it is practice.

And the only way you can do that is in front of a group of people.

It's all learning experience. Even if money's an issue, which I always tell actors, money cannot be an issue in this career. It can't be an issue. You have to have something that is supporting you to do your craft. It's like realtors spend a lot of time canvassing areas and spending promotional money, materials to get new clients. They have to do that before they sell a home.

Bonnie Wallace: Well, and then showing and showing and showing different places to somebody that they're representing who's looking, with no guaranteed outcome and no money whatsoever. This is not different from that.

Judy Kain: Exactly. It's not at all. You have to have something that's flexible or find a way to trade skills. I've had people come in and do typing or filing or things in exchange for classes. You have to get creative. If you're a Pilates teacher, work out an exchange with somebody so that you can take class.

Bonnie Wallace: Or make enough money as a Pilates teacher to take class, or have a flexible schedule.

Judy Kain: And to get your head shots and to do the things that you need to do, but it just cannot be an issue. I find that if you really, really want something, if you really want to make it as an actor, you will find a way.

Bonnie Wallace: I will never forget talking to Garrett Clayton, who moved here at 19, and for three years, worked from 5:00 PM to 5:00 AM in a restaurant so that he would be able to pay the rent and be available during the day for auditions. I just thought to myself, "You know what? Basically, you need to be willing to do something like this." It obviously paid off for him, but that was three *years*. That wasn't three months.

Judy Kain: I know. I find this generation—or whatever, maybe it's just this time of life—people really want to learn this craft in four to six weeks, and it's not going to happen. It takes longer to become a manicurist. To go to cosmetology school takes at least eight months, and then you have to get good at it, too. No, it's crazy to think that four weeks would be enough training in anything.

Bonnie Wallace: It's a career, and the stakes are high with anything that you get hired for, millions of dollars are on the line. People don't just hand these opportunities out randomly and casually. You need to be genuinely ready to carry that.

Judy Kain: It's way harder than it looks. I mean, people think, "Well, people say I'd be great." Okay, good. Now let's see if you can do it. People say, because they are not experts. You have to have that experience under your belt. There's something that happens, and I see it when it does in an actor, where all of a sudden, oh, they got the confidence switch. It went on.

Bonnie Wallace: It is like a switch turns. I saw it in my daughter. When that switch turned, all of a sudden everything changed.

Judy Kain: Boom. But to get it to turn on means you have to keep practicing, practicing, practicing, and doing it. Whatever you have to do before it turns on. Do your own content. I saw my friend completely changed when he started doing his own content. All of a sudden he was in charge, and it changed his whole posture.

Bonnie Wallace: Can we talk about that for a second? I think a lot about mindset and the importance of mindset to success in anything, but especially for acting.

Judy Kain: Yes. To me, it has to start with, "I love what I do." So if I love what I do, I'm willing to do a lot. I'm willing to drive to Santa Monica on a Friday at 5:00 pm and be happy to have the audition most days.

    Because you love what you do, you're happy to be there, and you know what a gift it is to have the audition, the opportunity. Nothing's worse than a bad attitude, and it stinks up the whole room. Even if you don't say anything, we can tell.

Bonnie Wallace: Everybody in the business is a creative, and creatives are sensitive.

Judy Kain: They sense it. I do that in my classes too. I'll tell certain people, "You have an intensity about your face that could be read as F-you, and you need to be aware that you have to come in smiling. Even though you're going to play the tough guy, you've got to come in smiling, because it's off-putting."

Bonnie Wallace: You may be playing the tough guy, but the people who are hiring you want to enjoy working with you.

Judy Kain: Right. So yes, it is definitely a mindset to stay positive. I mean, listen, if you're auditioning for two years and nothing happens, maybe then reassess. Maybe think, "Well, maybe I'll go work behind the scenes or something," but you should be getting some kind of goodies, some rewards, some payback for the work that you're doing. If you're doing it right, you should be able to get a couple things to keep you going to the next thing, and then a couple things to keep you going to the next thing, right?

Bonnie Wallace: Some signs. Little breadcrumbs that you're on the right path.

Judy Kain: That you're on the right path, absolutely. Yes.

ANTHONY MEINDL

Founder, Anthony Meindl's Actor Workshop

"What I teach is so simple, it's just not easy."

Anthony Meindl is a master acting coach and founder of *Anthony Meindl's Actor Workshop*, which has locations in Los Angeles, New York, Atlanta, Chicago, Santa Fe, Vancouver, Toronto, London, Sydney, and Cape Town. His philosophy is radically different from the status quo. He doesn't use scene objective, sense memory or any of the standard 20th century approaches that most acting schools take as their foundation. Instead, he emphasizes living truthfully in imaginary circumstances. He's the author of *At Left Brain Turn Right, BOOK THE F*CKING JOB!* and *Alphabet Soup for Grownups.*

Alumni include Shailene Woodley, Ruby Rose, Pom Klementieff, Emma Kenney, Camilla Cabello, Trevante Rhodes, Brianne Howey, Sierra Capri, and Jenna Dewan.

Bonnie Wallace: Your approach to acting is really different from the standard ones. Can you explain your philosophy a little bit?

Anthony Meindl: Yeah. It's so weird because I'm reading John Cassavetes' *Lifeworks* book right now. For people, who don't know, John Cassavetes was really the forefather of independent cinema. He and his wife Gena Rowlands, maybe young audiences would know her from *The Notebook*. She played the mom. It was directed by their son, Nick Cassavetes.

Anyway, he was really the trailblazer of exploring just living on camera for American directors in the '50s, '60s, '70s. The opening quote of his book is, "Life class is the best acting class." That's what I teach. Even Stanislavski who came up with many different ways to try to get actors to be real, said, "I just do whatever I have to do to make people stop acting," basically. Right?

I think the truth about acting is that we come up with all these words, and definitions, and theories, and concepts, and names for something that is as simple as you and I right now, just listening and talking. The heart of it is all listening. I think people get stuck on the mechanics of something, but we're not fixing the inner workings of a car. We're not mechanics. You don't have to be a mechanic. Mechanics are for mechanics. We just have to try to tell the truth, which is very, very difficult. I find that if we do away with a lot of the things that put people in their heads, they're already more predisposed to do it naturally.

I'm just not invested in calling it something because I find that whether they're painters, or writers, or actors, or singers, it's literally about the person igniting their art through themselves, so that's what I teach. Be you, really, which is really very difficult to be.

Bonnie Wallace: I love that. We were talking earlier, and I shared with you my own philosophy about acting, which is that the actor's soul, their spirit, is like the light that shines through the stage light gel, and the gel is the character.

Anthony Meindl:

That's a beautiful way of articulating it. Gary Oldman says something similar: "The characters that you're playing are just basically prisms of yourself. That's all it is." He says, "When it says that a character is crying in the script, or you go and see the movie and you see a character crying, it's not the character crying. It's me, Gary Oldman, crying." That's the big leap that I think more and more actors are starting to have.

That's Gary Oldman and he's been around forever. You start to see that distillation of it, the talking about it in a way that moves beyond the concepts, and you can see very clearly that you can't become someone else. The physics make that impossible.

Bonnie Wallace:

Well, there's a kind of psychosis to that, too. You really are still you.

Anthony Meindl:

That's a good point.

Bonnie Wallace:

The crying is where *you* are. I watched my daughter do a very emotional scene a couple of weeks ago. You could tell her whole body was involved and engaged in those feelings and those emotions. It was real. Her body was experiencing it in a very real way. The tears were real and that was her, crying. That wasn't really her character.

Anthony Meindl:

Well, I guess another way of thinking about it is when we're watching them, the final edited program, movie, TV show, theater, whatever, the piece, the play, we're involved in the story so we're seeing the character ... the storytelling is occurring through the person playing the character. When we surrender to the circumstances in the story, then it's a subjective experience. Right?

We're imprinting on whatever it is that we're watching, filling in the blanks of who we think these people are or aren't. That, to me, is where a lot of the character development really occurs. When you're watching your daughter and you know that she's crying, if I don't know your daughter and I go watch the movie and I see her crying as "the character," yes, of course, I'm watching the story unfold, and she's doing it authentically, so I surrender to that narrative but it's still her. It's not Dove. It's Dove as Julie. It's Dove as Sabrina. It's Dove as whatever the character's name is.

I think those are huge light bulbs. You know what I mean? I had a guy last night in intro class where he's never taken an acting class before. Again, he's got concepts of it ... He gets up and he tries to show us the idea of a guy who's nervous or a guy who is ... right? He's acting.

Bonnie Wallace: The idea of it, that's so well put.

Anthony Meindl: That's totally it, but that's what people do. They play the *idea* of what they think the characters look like. I get it because we have to come from making a choice and we have to go for something. We have to understand the scene and figure out a way of how we're going to live in it.

I have found that if the actor is trying to listen, listening naturally evokes a response, a natural, authentic response in the moment. To me, 95% of the heavy lifting is about listening ... John Cassavetes' book says that as well. He says, "The best actors are the best listeners." The listening will do it for you. If I tell you some tragic news, we just heard some tragic news ... see? Right now, you still have a response to it. Listening does it.

Bonnie Wallace: Yes. It's physical.

Anthony Meindl: Physical, physiological, emotional, historical. The things that actors think they need to play, if they would just listen, it's going to do it for them. I think we're not taught to listen. I also think we think listening is so easy. It's so hard to listen. Do you know what I mean? It's really hard to just be. It's being.

Bonnie Wallace: People get in their heads and they're not really present. That's really what you're talking about. To me, it's about being present, and listening is a subset of that. People don't know how to be present. That's an issue for human beings in general, not just for actors.

How did you end up being an acting teacher and having all these schools?

Anthony Meindl: Well, I was an actor myself, and I was trying every kind of methodology in the book. Then I was working and I was doing really well when I moved to L.A. I found that my own exploration of, "What is acting?

What is it? What is living? What is being human?" You know what I mean? What is this thing that we're doing, that we're trying to capture on film, or on TV, or wherever in a non-actor-y way? What are the mechanics of it? What is the process of it? How do we find a way in that doesn't feel like it becomes false, or academic, or presented, right? I don't know. I just began to discover that, for me, my own spiritual evolution ... I've been to India a number of times and am reading a lot of books on science. I found that they're all dovetailing.

The beautiful thing about technology is we have access to information scientifically that we didn't have

20 years ago. Brain scans can show what happens, parts of our brain that are lit up creatively when we meditate. That's the same stuff that is lit up when we are present and creating in the moment. You begin to start these correlations between presence, and joy, and listening, and intuition, and instinct. All that stuff is, to me, the foundation of what I teach. It's spiritual. It's acting. It's a philosophy of acting. It's a philosophy into a way of life. It's physics. You know what I mean?

Even though we talk about acting in terms of understanding some simple concepts that I think everybody has to understand, because they're given circumstances of a scene, I really think our program is about the humanitarian aspect of what it means to be an artist. You have to be curious about the world and the social ... the conversations we have are about Black Lives Matter, and about tragedies of terrorism, and about empathy, and compassion, and ethos. We're not talking about what is your objective in the scene. It's so derivative.

Bonnie Wallace: Well, if you're living your life, you're not stopping and asking yourself what your objective is as you walk into somebody.

Anthony Meindl: That's totally it. You see, you should guest teach at the school. This is why right now my objective is not ... I don't even think about my objective. We're working moment to moment.

Bonnie Wallace: For just presence.

Anthony Meindl: Right? That's totally it. All I teach is that. Those are the grounding scientific principles of how the entire world works. The only difference is we're saying someone else's words besides our own words. That's the only difference, but to do that is very difficult. I like to say that. What I teach is so simple, it's just not easy.

The understanding of acting, I cannot make it any more understandable than I've done, than I think we're doing. That's beautiful. I mean, listen. I love actors. My whole life is about the arts. However, I think we're so much more powerful ... art is a vehicle for expressing the power of our humanity. Who we really are is ... the power isn't our humanity. It is in being human. In the face of tragedy, how do we face that with vigilance, and compassion, and peace although creating activism? You see what I'm saying?

I think that is the power of being a part of a studio, or a movement, or a philosophy. It's actually a philosophy based on love. I'm going to totally start crying. It's really what it is. I'm crying right now.

Bonnie Wallace: It's beautiful.

Anthony Meindl: That's what I teach.

Bonnie Wallace: You're speaking to the sacred work of being a human being. To me, part of what excites me about the work that you're engaged in, and the people who work with you are engaged in, is the fact that it is a deep reflection of the sacredness of theater for culture.

Anthony Meindl: Coming together telling stories.

Bonnie Wallace: Storytelling. It's how we communicate what it is to be human, basically.

Anthony Meindl: That's totally it.

Bonnie Wallace: That's why being an actor, at its best, at its highest, is a
                     true calling because you are called upon to live trans-
                     parently. Live so that others may see what it is to be
                     human. I mean, what a high calling.

Anthony Meindl: Well, I think the challenge you remind me about is that,
                     especially young actors, myself included, when I was
                     in my 20s and what we try to help them understand,
                     is that I think a lot of us don't believe that our stories:
                     A, anybody is going to be interested in them; B, they're
                     worth telling; and C, that they actually bring value. The
                     only story that brings value is your story. Then what
                     happens is when you tell your story personally through
                     the work, talking about it, sharing your challenges, your
                     hopes, your dreams, your tribulations, your stuff even
                     though it's very personal to you, it also becomes uni-
                     versal. It's all the same.

Bonnie Wallace: It's like poetry. The universal is always found in the
                     particular.

Anthony Meindl: That's totally it. My story is more valuable than the
                     story I'm making up about my character. The character
                     story can only come alive by me being brave enough
                     to find the intersection where I meet with this person's
                     story.
                          Ten different actors, by bringing themselves to that
                     story, are going to do it differently. Then we just have
                     to decide, well, whose essence or whose energy most
                     matches it? That's really how simple it is, but you've
                     got to be brave enough to realize, this is how I'm going

to tell the story. This is how I would play that character. That means *through you*. That's a huge departure I think from a lot of acting traditional methodologies. Although, I will just say one last thing, I think all acting methodologies are really trying to say that. They just get lost in the nomenclature, a good word ... or the theoretical, the academic, so they make it be about something else. Then they lose the thread. You know what I mean?

My thing is it's always evolving so why would I be teaching the same thing? It doesn't make any sense. This is my own personal opinion. I can't teach something that was being taught in the 1900s. Now, we can go back to the source material and all things come from the beginning. All things come from the Greek, our Greek ancestors who were performing plays, but the instrument has changed. Actually, the needs for actors have changed.

Bonnie Wallace: The consciousness has changed.

Anthony Meindl: Yes, that's all changed. All scientists talk about ... the world we're living in is constantly evolving and expanding, and so why would teachings about anything not continue to expand? If we have the technology to show that it's evolving, I can't hold onto those ... the world is not flat, people. There you go. Mic drop.

You talk in your book, which I love, about faith and resilience. It's a beautiful chapter. It talks about what not only young performers and parents have to do with their children coming to Hollywood, to have faith and resilience because it takes forever, but all of us. You know what I mean? Through life. I understand it.

Bonnie Wallace: You come from a very strongly held, distinct philosophy. How do you translate that into your acting workshops and all of your schools? What do you do in those workshops? How does that work?

Anthony Meindl: Well, I mean, the work ... even though I talk about bigger things that are always very, very personal, I think it's really about changing paradigms about how we hold ourselves. That's the big work. If you're listening in the scene in the way that this technique makes happen for you, you're going to start changing. In other words, you're going to start feeling things that normally in your day-to-day life you do not allow yourself to feel. For some people, it might be getting angry. For somebody else, it might be getting in touch with repressed sexuality. For somebody else, it might be just having fun. For somebody else, it might be being physical.

The beautiful thing about listening, again, is that it's going to start triggering your stuff. What the teaching is about is ... science talks about this. Without awareness, there can't be change. It's all awareness-based at first. You discover in the moment, in your work, "My gosh, I start to feel X, and I don't want to feel X so why?" Then you start to see in life when something happens and you start to feel X, right?

Last time I was teaching this intro and this girl in her scene has no feeling, yet. She's 21, right? Now, obviously, she's a feeling being. I can see it but she completely compresses it and shuts it down. It's like putting a cork on a champagne bottle. I said to her, "Ashley, what do you do with feelings?" She's like, "It's all shut down until it explodes." The work then is to learn how to have a new relationship with our feelings. That starts to get exercised through the work and our life.

Classes are a just way in. It has less to do with talking about the window dressing and instead just cleaning up the window so you can see through it, the transparency we're talking about. You've just got to get honest with yourself.

Bonnie Wallace:　I really like that. I've been thinking a lot recently about how critical it is for actors to be completely in touch with all of their emotions because, as you said, if any of it is blocked, you can't experience it. Therefore, you can't portray it.

You need to be an incredibly evolved, emotional human being, I think, to be a fine actor.

Anthony Meindl:　That's totally it. In my first book, I have an Al Pacino quote where he's being interviewed by Katie Couric. She asked him, "How do you play all these ... you play such explosive characters and blah blah blah." He says, "Well, you just get in touch with the primalness of what it means to be alive, and every single human being walking on the planet at some point wants to explode or implode." I remember that. I watched the video of it. I remember Katie Couric's eyes got really big. That doesn't register in her being.

Bonnie Wallace:　She has no space for that possibility.

Anthony Meindl:　Exactly, exactly. Well, it's there because she's human.

Her logical mind turns that off. That's the other thing, is helping actors to stop judging. There's no place for judgment in acting, in any art, I think, because it's incompatible with creativity. Real quantum creativity, real, full-on optimal creativity comes from your channel for it. If I'm pinching off the channel, then I'm not working optimally. What I try to do, what we try to do is just create a space. It's very safe and very nurturing, and it's nonjudgmental. You begin to see why am I judging all these parts of myself? I'm human. It's okay for me to think terrible thoughts. It doesn't mean I'm a terrible person.

Bonnie Wallace: Or that I'm going to act on them.

Anthony Meindl: That, too. I think we live in a very shame-based culture. I think because our religious history is very puritanical. The difference I think sometimes between Americans and Europeans is, I think Europeans are a lot more fluid in certain ways, sexually and with self-expression. You know what I mean?

Different cultures allow different things. The difference between guilt and shame is we may do something and be able to see, "That was just a silly act, or I didn't really use my head with that or that was kind of dumb." That's just like making amends for it and realizing you didn't think it out. That's guilt. It's processed and released. With shaming, you become the jerk. You start to shame yourself believing you *are* the act. It's really getting people in touch with their feelings.

Bonnie Wallace: That's powerful.

Anthony Meindl: It's intense, yeah.

Bonnie Wallace: It sounds like something a lot of people who don't even want to be actors might benefit from.

Anthony Meindl: Gosh. Yeah. I was just at my dentist yesterday and my dental hygienist asked, "Can I just come and take one or two classes? I just want to sit in and listen to you lecture." She doesn't know it's hard to act. It means a lot to me. I think good teachings are universal so it shouldn't just be about acting. It's not just about acting.

Bonnie Wallace: In addition to your work that you make available through different levels of classes, you also do regular workshops with casting directors and agents. They come in and do workshops under your auspices. What value do you think lies in having them come in? What does that do for your students?

Anthony Meindl: Well, as you know, again, you talked about it in your book. I think you've got to get seen, and it's great to get different opinions about your work because it's going to be subjective. You can meet me and not like me.

Somebody else could meet me and love my work. You know what I mean?

I think it's important for actors to get in front of people who are making decisions for casting, or producing, or whatever. Maybe more valuable is they're just getting insight about the business. I work with this really great group called Industry Hollywood that comes from overseas. They basically bring 20 students over who are in the process of maybe getting their green card. It helps a lot with immigration.

They go and meet a lawyer. Then they take different workshops in town. They always work with me. My thing is I think it's still amazing to meet agents, and managers, and casting directors, just meet everybody, but also take everything with a grain of salt because everybody is working for their own agenda. You know what I mean? For every absolute, you discover there are no absolutes. Information is really important, I think, especially if you're starting out.

Bonnie Wallace: I couldn't agree more. There's so much mystique around it and it's so abstract and, therefore, scary.

Anthony Meindl: Yeah, it's overwhelming.

Bonnie Wallace: It's totally overwhelming. The more you get a chance to get in front of, and meet with these people, you see they're just really people. They're just doing their best to do their job, and it's safe, and it's okay. You can learn some things.

Anthony Meindl: As Margot Robbie just said in an article ... I have this in both books. My philosophy is *nobody knows*. She used a swear word which I won't use here. She discovered, getting to the top, that nobody knows. What she means by that is you come to set, or you're at where you are in your career and you realize everybody is just trying to figure it out.

I think that is a real healthy way to stop putting so much pressure on yourself of having to have all the answers before you make the move, or before you get your headshot, or before you take the class, or before you book the job. You're never going to have it all together. I think the best people come together, and realize, and admit they don't know, and they figure it out together just as we're doing right now. It's collaborative. Nobody f-ing knows. You know what I mean?

Bonnie Wallace: You have worked with some incredible, incredible actors.

Anthony Meindl: I've met some great people in my life, yeah.

Bonnie Wallace: Shailene Woodley.

Anthony Meindl: I love Shailene.

Bonnie Wallace: Cory Monteith.

Anthony Meindl: It was just the anniversary of his passing, about two days ago, July 13th, I think. It's so bizarre to think he's gone.

Bonnie Wallace: Some of that stuff never really ... you can't really ever get over it. These extraordinary artists, most of whom luckily are still with us, they are still working with you a lot. They worked with you before they got somewhere and they're still involved with you.

Anthony Meindl: Yeah. I just coached Ruby Rose the other day for something. She's up for a big movie. She's got three big movies coming out this year. Shailene is an amazing, to me, example of ... she was just in class a couple of months ago before she went stomping for Bernie Sanders. I just really respect her wanting to be engaged in social causes. I think that's her own constitution but also, again, what the school is about. I think it's so great to be at the top of your game. She was back in class in March and April. She's working in front of 80, 90 people who are observing and she's falling flat on her face. That's huge. You know what I mean?

Bonnie Wallace: It's brave.

Anthony Meindl: It's really brave. You have to be able to take those kinds of risks and leaps. You know what I mean? I think the important thing that I always talk about, is you have to approach everything as a beginner because if you think you know, you're screwed. Even in my teaching, if I were to teach you, you're different than Shailene so I'm not applying the way I work with Shailene with you. Your needs, and temperament, and energy are ... you're different. I'm just working on getting more of you, so I can't approach something from my previous knowing. Does that make sense?

It's beginner's mind, Buddhist mind.

Bonnie Wallace: Now, you've recently started working with kids.

Anthony Meindl: Yes. We're excited about that. We just started last week. Well, we've done it on and off, but now we have a regular program. I've got an ongoing teen class on Thursday nights which is great. A lot of working teens in that group. We just started a summer intensive. They just started last week so we have a preteen class up to the age of 11, I think, or 12. Then we have a 13 to 17 or 18-year-old group. It's full so it's exciting.

I'm known for working with so many teens and starting them off. I don't know why I never really put two and two together.

Again, it's about staying a child in the work. It's about becoming a child, staying a child, working from a child, curiosity, play, non-judgment. I was just with my seven-year-old niece this past week in my hometown just watching her. There's no filter, with that expression.

We teach from, that kids already know. They're already codified to do exactly perfectly what they need to do because they're only going to be playing themselves at that age anyway. The acting "class" that they need is really a class that's supporting them in being more of themselves. Some kids might be a little bit more shy, so maybe we have to get them to be a little less shy. Some kids may grandstand or be showoffs so maybe we have to find the balance of reining that in but still keeping the essential energy of what makes them spirited, and funny, and out there alive.

Our work has less to do with training kids how to act. That's the worst thing. It's just getting them to play and be, especially with kids. If it's a scene where you're talking to your mom about wanting to go to the concert, and you're an 11 or 12-year-old girl, how would you do it? How would you go and ask your mom?

Bonnie Wallace: In every way that it took until I got the answer I wanted-!

Anthony Meindl: It's that simple. Kids are just playing kids. I also think it's really dangerous if you start to try to mold kids in the name of an acting methodology. Let them be who they are.

Why is it that all these movies that are successful with young kids, most of them have never taken an acting class? I was interviewed by *The Hollywood Reporter* for ... What's her name? *Beasts of the Southern Wild* and that eight-year-old girl. Again, no acting experience. They interviewed me about, "Should a child be considered for..." I think she got nominated for an Academy Award, but is that the work? Just because you're playing yourself, is that the work? I said, "Heck, yes." That's all it is. Being yourself is the hardest thing to be. Why is that any less so because she's an eight-year-old girl?

173

Bonnie Wallace: Let's tease this apart because this is going to be confusing to a lot of people. It's easy to think, "Well, I'm myself every day, and so is everybody else out there." How come all these people aren't really actors, or can't act, or wouldn't be good actors? There's a distinction in there somewhere.

Anthony Meindl: Well, that's a good question. Sometimes I get this. We start with this foundation. It's you all the time. It has to be you, and we have to start with you listening in those circumstances. The technique is based on always listening as you in these circumstances. Then, as we advance, sometimes a student will fight me. They'll say, "Well, Tony. You're telling me to do it like I would, and this is exactly how I would do it." I tell them, "No, no, no, no, no, no."

What you start to see is that a lot of times, as we progress, we start to see how we respond to things in life and in our work from a place of protection, self-defense, defaulting out of it, negating, shutting down. None of those things work in a storytelling way.

Bonnie Wallace: Being ourselves isn't necessarily going to lead to good acting.

Anthony Meindl: Well, it is, because it's all you're ever going to have, but then technique is born out of removing the blocks, and the withholds, and the patterns that keep you from being fully expressed. Juliette Binoche talks about this. Marion Cotillard talks about this. They say that acting can't be taught. What you can learn is how to feel and use your emotions.

Bonnie Wallace: Fully.

Anthony Meindl: Fully. That's the truth. If I am in life, and somebody yells at me and I shut down completely and just say, "Okay," and then I'm doing a scene where there's a huge amount of conflict and I shut down, that's not going to be enough. We have to look at how do we open you up to not shutting down. That's the real work.

Bonnie Wallace: That's the training.

Anthony Meindl: That's all it is.

Bonnie Wallace: That's a lot.

Anthony Meindl: It is. This is why it's so simple.

Bonnie Wallace: Not easy.

Anthony Meindl: You got that but not easy because it takes ... sometimes I'm working with people where 20 years have put something in place, and they have to unravel that. After three months, they're like, "It should be happening faster." I say, "Honey child, I'm working against 20 years of habits." That's what's exciting about it. It's detective work in a way.

Bonnie Wallace: You've also written several books.

Anthony Meindl: I have. I have. Two are right here. Bestsellers.

Bonnie Wallace: I'm so excited to read these. I haven't read them yet but I will be reading them this week. *Book The F*cking Job*. We need a kid's version of this, Tony.

Anthony Meindl:	I know I need to have a preteen, kid's version. Just *Book the Job*. I don't use the word that much in the book. We thought it was a good...
Bonnie Wallace:	It gets your attention.
Anthony Meindl:	Well, also because one of the chapters is, to me, you have to be in an eff-it space. You know what I mean? You just have to be in, "I don't care anymore." Now, that doesn't mean you don't show up, and you're not professional, and you're not accountable. It just means I'm not going to worry so much about what everybody thinks.
Bonnie Wallace:	Well, I do think there's a lot of truth to that. I love to tell the story about how Dove got the job for *Liv and Maddie*. She told me point blank in the waiting room, "I know what they want me to do for this, and I'm not going to do it because I don't want to do it that way. If I did it the way I didn't want to do, and then I booked it, I'd be in trouble because then I'd be having to play something I didn't really feel resonant with for who knows how long. And then if I don't book it, I'll kick myself," ... so she says, "I'm going to do it my way."
Anthony Meindl:	That's why she got it.
Bonnie Wallace:	"They're going to like it, or they won't, and I don't care."
Anthony Meindl:	This is the key.
Bonnie Wallace:	She got it.

Anthony Meindl: That's the breakthrough. The thing is I'm always telling people, Bonnie, is they don't know what they want ... once they give you the breakdown, or the brief, or whatever you want to call it, those are concepts, and ideas, and adjectives, and descriptions on a page. Then the actor goes in and tries to play those things. I keep telling the actor, "Those things are one-dimensional, two-dimensional words. They become a living, breathing thing when you discover and know that you are those things. You are edgy, and funny, and weird, and angry, and sophisticated. Even if you don't think you are, you are all those things so don't show them. Be your way of being it."

Then their idea of what they think it is, meaning the casting director, again, they don't know until it's in front of them. Most actors go in, "Well, she's supposed to be like that." They ask, "Is this what you're looking for?" You're screwed.

Bonnie Wallace: Right. Then they try to fit themselves into some pretzel-shaped thing, which is unnatural.

Anthony Meindl: This is why your daughter got it. I love the story you share in your book ... it made me laugh about the mud girl. She's like, "Well, if I can't be the mud girl." Is it mud girl?

Bonnie Wallace: Mud-covered girl.

Anthony Meindl: If I can't be the mud-covered girl, then I might as well give up.

Bonnie Wallace: Then *Shameless* cast her the next day. It's true. You can't give up. If it's your calling, then it's your calling like anything else in life.

Tony, what would you say are some of the differences between acting for film versus acting for TV? What are some similarities? Do you even like to go there because your philosophy is, well, it's all about being present?

Anthony Meindl:
That's all it is. Acting is acting is acting. I think the only reason why there is a distinction between one medium or the other, meaning theater and anything that isn't theater, is because theater is taught incorrectly.

Theater is taught to project and be theatrical. You can't be that when a camera is a foot away from your face.

Bonnie Wallace:
Yes. People don't buy that.

Anthony Meindl:
Right? That's how theater is taught. My thing is beyond the projection part which sometimes we have to do ... although everybody is mic'd nowadays. The *New York Times* chief critic Ben Brantley was reviewing a revival of *A Lie of the Mind,* I think. It was Ethan Hawke and I think his theater company. He was saying how he was so amazed by watching it because it seemed as if they were saying their lines for the first time and it was so in the moment. I thought, "Well, good God." This is what's so sad about theater is that's the exception that he has to spend a paragraph talking about it because most things are phoned in. Most things are, "I've memorized my lines a certain way and now I'm just going to project them because I've said them this way."

These are Broadway shows. You think, wait a minute. If I ask you, "Would you like a cup of coffee?" In real life you wouldn't say, "Yes, I would like coffee."

You say, "Yeah, I'd love some coffee." The inflection, the tonality, the heart part that surrounds the text comes from listening, not memorizing the lines.

Bonnie Wallace: I love that you brought that up because that is something that I've seen personally. You see these actors show up and they will, in every take, do the same inflection, the same cadences.

Anthony Meindl: Yes, I can't take it.

Bonnie Wallace: The same tone. Wouldn't it be better to be present and do it a little bit differently each time?

Anthony Meindl: No, it's too scary for people and they're taught to control it. They think they're doing good work because they're controlling the way they say something, or they're never taught to listen. The thing is, Bonnie, about TV and film, is it's an editing medium, so they can get around it and build a performance in many different ways. It's beautiful that he commented, "Wow, they feel so real and alive in the moment." It's a sad commentary on how much it's not. That, to me, is theatrical training.

My thing is, just be taught correctly. Meryl Streep never took ten thousand different acting classes. That's the other thing that's happened. Maybe we're living in a time of ... what would you call that? Fragmentation or micro-niche specialization. Good acting training is going to cover all bases. "Now, you have to take an acting class for this. Then an acting class for this and an acting class for understanding how your eyes go, and an acting class for don't stay a pigeon toe, an acting class for elocution on text and ..." You know what I mean? It's crazy town. The actor will go from class to class to class to class to class to class. I don't understand it. Find a great class. It doesn't have to be our studio. Find a great class that kicks your butt consistently. That's it.

Bonnie Wallace: The challenge is to grow and be better.

Anthony Meindl: Why is that hard? I don't understand. Then you're going to grow as a person and an actor, a human being, and get more confident.

Bonnie Wallace: What about audition classes...

Anthony Meindl: I've two thoughts about that. First of all, every casting director I know tells me the same thing which is often times actors are schooled to the hilt where they come in and they execute perfectly so they execute audition technique perfectly, but nobody wants to see that. It's not in the lines. It's what's going on in between the lines, which again comes back to listening.

Everybody says it is a different animal but I don't think it's a different animal. It's, again, you being brave enough to go in and do it your own way. If you do that consistently, eventually you're going to book. You just will because something is happening in the room that they pick up on.

There's a woman ... Ellen Langer is her name, I believe. She is a sociologist at Harvard. Her research is so fascinating. I'm so inspired by a lot of these people at TED Talks.

Ellen Langer does work on, again, the power of presence. She's not an actress. She's a sociologist.

I think she calls it imprinting. What I think is ... you're leaving your footprint, your emotional presence footprint everywhere you go. One of her studies that I think is so amazing is the correlation to what I teach and the power of the moment. She has a control group and an experimental group. It's a classical symphony. They're playing, let's say, Stravinsky. I don't know what it is. They're playing a classical piece and they play it exactly as they've been taught and exactly note for note, meter for meter ... good schooling.

Bonnie Wallace: The "right way."

Anthony Meindl: The "right way." That's the control group. Then she has the experimental group that is allowed to, in the moment, based on feeling, intuition, who knows what we call it?

Imbue it with whatever they feel in the moment. The research that came out of that is so outstanding ... they record them. Then they play this back ... this isn't even a live audience, right? They're listening to it recorded. 100% of the response preferred the experimental group.

Bonnie Wallace: That's fascinating.

Anthony Meindl: There is something tangible, alive, visceral. Look, I'm getting goose bumps. It's always the moment. My thing about any kind of training whether it's for auditions or whatever it is, it's fine if you've schooled yourself in learning things perfectly, but you have to then know it and then throw it and play ball in the moment. When you do, when you leave, as she says, you have left an impression, a footprint, an essence of something intangible but tangible, energetic.

The way you do it. That can't be taught. I mean, it is. That's what I teach, but it can't be taught as a mathematical equation because it's just your way. If you're not being taught to do it your way, nobody will stand out if everybody goes in and does things the perfect audition technique way.

Bonnie Wallace: Trying to do it "right."

Anthony Meindl: Yeah, that's totally it. Dove had her breakthrough by deciding this isn't how I want to do it. I want to do it the way *I* would do it. Every other girl probably went in and did it the way they thought they had to do it or the way that the notes were firing in their mind based on what the casting director said. You have to be willing to say, "I'm doing it."

Bonnie Wallace: Yes. I'm doing it *my way*. And that's perfect, because the consequences of not doing it your way are terrible in any case. In a way, it's the only choice you should ever make.

Anthony Meindl: That's totally it. I would say, too, they're going to like you or not like you regardless. Isn't it better for you to have the experience if you're firing from all cylinders as yourself and they don't like you? Well, so be it. Isn't that better for you than really holding yourself back and trying to be somebody you're not and they don't like you?

Bonnie Wallace: Being liked for something incredibly inauthentic that you then have to keep …

Anthony Meindl: The mask alive.

Bonnie Wallace: The façade for the next four years possibly.

Speaking of auditions, any hot tips for self-tapes?

Anthony Meindl: I think the key is in the eyes and, again, it's in listening. I coached somebody yesterday for something and he had all the lines memorized perfectly but ... right now, I'm looking at your eyes and you're processing what I'm saying through feeling and listening. Now, you would go to your text. Because we learned our lines, we just say our lines back. Actors end up getting ... I call it the deer in the headlights look in their eyes, right? They almost have it memorized but not quite. They don't really feel comfortable. They're scared to work with the page so they're trying to recall the line. They're not really listening. They're waiting for you to shut up with your cue so that I can now say my kind of memorized line.

Bonnie Wallace: You can actually almost see them reading it in their mind.

Anthony Meindl: That's totally it. When I coach somebody, I almost ... let's do it again in your own words. Let's do it again and improv it. Let's do it again ... It's the lines, the lines really mess with people's heads because they get scared if they deviate. Listen, I'm not saying you should do a full-on improv as your self-tape, but it's okay if you put a couple of words as filler words in there to help you reduce the amount of times you try to say something perfectly.

You're not going to get, or not get the job because you say the words "I think you should leave my home," and the line is, "I want you to get out of my house." If it's coming from the moment, and you say, "I think you should leave my home," that's fine. Nobody is going to notice that.

Nobody is going to notice because you're so authentic, in the moment. What actors do is they stop. "My God. I'm so sorry. Let me repeat."

My thing about self-tapes is, again, you've just got to listen. You've got to listen.

I always talk to agents and managers and they see the self-tapes of their clients. They always tell me the same thing. "Why are they acting? Why don't they just say it?" That's what I teach. Why can't you just speak it the way you speak in real life?

Bonnie Wallace: Right. Without some sort of layer of pretense on top of that.

Anthony Meindl: Yes, acting it. Stop acting it. See, even agents and managers know. Just say it.

Bonnie Wallace I've got a lot of young people who reach out to me who live nowhere near a major market. They're far away from L.A. or New York, and their dream is to be an actor. What do you think are some of the best ways for people who don't have a shot at being out here right now to move toward their dream right where they are?

Anthony Meindl: Wow, that's a good question. You do talk a little bit about success in your book. I don't know if this really speaks to that. What does success mean anyway? I think, again, it's like soccer practice. Do you enjoy it?

Are you having fun? Are you meeting friends? Are you playing? Is it something you've always wanted to do? Maybe you get involved in the community theater program or you get involved in something at your school. Nowadays, there are social media platforms where, not only just being your own YouTube spokesperson, like a lifestyle person, you can do skits and film them. Steven Spielberg started making movies when he was 14, 15, 16 years old.

Bonnie Wallace: With his family's video camera.

Anthony Meindl: Yeah, with Super 8 cameras. You know what I mean? If you don't have the resources to move to L.A. or New York, I think those are ways to start. You may discover you're also a filmmaker. You're also a poet.

You're also a theologian or a philosopher. It's so much more renaissance-like than if you're just an actor. That goes for adults as well. I don't like actors to constantly be defined just by their acting.

It's not healthy. If you look at actors and the way they're "mediafied," at the end of the day, they're just people. I talked about this in the first book. We have no mythology in our culture. We just have no mythology, so we mythologize. They're just like you and me. They're doing a job.

Bonnie Wallace: Because we mythologize actors, I think it makes it feel even more "all or nothing." If I live in Iowa and I'm 15 years old, and I can't go to L.A. right now because my parents won't let me, then it feels as if it's all or nothing, and I'm not even going to try out for the school play.

No, do try out for the school play and see what that leads to, because it will lead to more school plays, which may lead to you starting to write screenplays.

Which may lead to a writing program in New York or a film program in L.A. when you're 18.

Anthony Meindl: Again, you talked about that and the success stuff. Not going to an end product, you can't, especially at that age. Also, I know some adults in the business, and they have kids, who say, "If she or he wants to act, they can do it but not until they're 18."

Listen, I'm not a parent but I think that's also maybe great because the beautiful thing about acting, as long as you're a human being and you're going to be a human being your entire life, you can act whenever you want. Maybe you're not supposed to start acting when you're 12.

There's lots of 12, 13, 14, 15, 16-year-olds who get leads on their own shows. Those shows run for three years. Then those shows get canceled. Those kids never work again.

Bonnie Wallace: Then where are they?

Anthony Meindl: My God. If you don't have a relationship with your parents that's more than just being a breadwinner for the household, what happens when that dries up? You think you're a failure. That's just too much.

Bonnie Wallace: That's what happens if you over-identify with being an actor as you were just saying. That's dangerous for anybody at any age, maybe especially for kids. Adults can fall prey to that issue, too.

Anthony Meindl: We know we can name lots of tragic, fallen, beautiful child actors who then don't work. Their whole self-esteem and self-worth is tied up in it.

Bonnie Wallace: You need something that is bigger than this work, something like family, or a spiritual practice. Something that can't get taken away from you. I think that's the secret for people involved in this industry. It can be very unbalancing.

Anthony Meindl: The trick is I think I wanted that when I was 18 or 19 and I started. Then I realized ... it's not sustainable. It's just not sustainable. It's not real.

Bonnie Wallace: If you want your life and what you do with it to be sustainable, it has to be coming from an authentic place, not from a gratification that comes from the outside. It has to come from the inside.

Anthony Meindl: Totally. That's the path we're all on. It's an interesting challenge, right? You look at someone like Meryl Streep. She's never in the gossip rags. She's not out there, so she also has a control over it. Now, I would think that a lot of your handlers probably make you believe, "You have to be out there. You have to be doing this. You have to be with this person. You have to get seen at this event. You have to go out to this. You have to brand this thing." I don't know if you do. I don't think Meryl Streep did that. You know what I mean? Nicole Kidman doesn't do that. Ryan Gosling doesn't. You can decide for yourself. You also mentioned that in your book, which I thought was really great.

Are you choosing it because ... I get the monetary aspect of things and people want to make a living. Are you making choices only for that, which then corrupts the reason why you're doing it in the first place?

Bonnie Wallace:

Exactly. Let's be honest. Most actors don't make much money, if any.

From a numbers standpoint, it's not a good bet. You'd better be doing it because you love it.

Anthony Meindl:

Love it. Love it. Love it. I always say I'm the number one advocate of creatives and artists. I wrote a blog not too long ago about how everybody in Congress should take an acting class. I really believe acting is healing our planet. I think if there's something else you love as much as acting, you should pursue it. Another way of thinking about it is just be open to everything. You can be an actor and a writer, and a singer, and an astronaut, and a teacher, and a tapestry weaver. You can be a painter, and a musician, and a poet, and a dancer. You can make wine, and sell cheese, and have your own bistro, and tell stories.

ERIC MORRIS

Founder, Eric Morris Actors Workshop

"I deal with liberating the actor's instrument:
how to free the actor, the person, to be able to be impressively expressive."

Renowned acting teacher Eric Morris has been teaching in Hollywood for over sixty years. His books—*No Acting Please, Being & Doing, Irreverent Acting, Acting from the Ultimate Consciousness,* and *Acting, Imaging, and the Unconscious*—are used in colleges, universities, and private schools all over the world. His latest book, *A Second Chance at Life*, explores how some of the techniques he developed for actors can free all people from obstacles and emotional blocks so they can experience and express their emotions.

Alumni include Johnny Depp, Arnold Schwarzenegger, Jack Nicholson, Scott Wilson, Michael Parks, Brandon Lee, Peggy Lipton, Billy Hayes, Kelly LeBrock, Aaron Eckhart, Rick Fox, and Hampton Fancher. International movie stars: Turkish actor Meltem Cubul, Brazilian actor Rodrigo Santoro, Columbian actress Angie Cepeda, and Indian actress Daminee Basu.

Bonnie Wallace:	Eric, your approach to acting is rooted in Stanislavski's Method, but it's got a distinct system that you've developed over time. Can you explain your approach and why you think it makes for better acting?

Eric Morris: Sure. First of all, the foundation of everything I do comes from Stanislavski, but I've been influenced by Lee Strasberg also. I watched him for seven years at The Actors Studio on the west coast. And it's a hundred-year-old system. What has evolved over my years of teaching, out of necessity, is that I've gone ... I say this humbly in a sense, but I've gone galaxies beyond the original precepts because everything that has evolved from there has gone on from the base.

Now, without Stanislavski and without Lee Strasberg, there would be no Eric Morris. I'm very aware of that. That's the foundation of what I do. However, there is a missing link in the Method. Here is what I think is the uniqueness of what I've created over a period of sixty years. The missing link is that none of the Master teachers, none of them, including Lee and Stella ... Stella would say that acting is all imagination. Don't use your own life experience.

The whole thing is I teach people how not to act, and to become experiential actors. What does that mean? It means that the actor has to experience what the character in a piece, a film, a play, a television show, whatever the character is experiencing, the actor has to actually a hundred percent experience that. The only difference is that it has to come from the actor's own living experience, and the author's description of what the character ... it might be alien to the actor in terms of background and experience, so it has to ... I don't want to use the word substitute. It has to find a parallel in the actor's own life to create that experience.

I deal with liberating the actor's instrument: how to free the actor, the person, to be able to be impressively expressive, and able to express how they are affected by external, and internal stimuli. This is not being done, and has never been done on the level that I've gone into in terms of instrumental therapy exercises.

Now don't confuse therapy with psychotherapy. Therapy could be physical therapy. It could be any kind of therapy that is helpful, but it's instrumental therapy that I use. At one time I had 300 or 400 exercises that liberated the actor to be able to eliminate their obstacles, their problems, their fear, their emotional blocks, their dependencies, and all of the things that get in the way of being impulsively expressive. That I believe is the largest part of my contribution and the system that I teach.

The actual working with the actor on a very deep emotional, instrumental level. Even Lee Strasberg, I used to sit and watch him ask an actor, "What did you do? Tell us what you did." He said, "Well, I was working for an experience I had where I argued with my mother about..." he'd say, "Stop. Stop, I don't want to hear it. Save it for your therapist. Just tell me the nature of what you're working for. I don't want to hear that." He was terrified. He was almost paranoid about getting personal with actors about their life. The first ten years of my teaching was a nightmare. People used to make up stories about me. They used to say, "Oh, are you going to Eric Morris's acting class? Are you going to lay on the couch and tell everybody how your mother abused you?"

Nobody ever did any of this, but people made up stories. You know how it stopped? Finally, after ten or twelve years, people would go on the late-night talk shows, famous people. And they would say, "Well you know I thought I was an actor until I started working with Eric, then I really learned, I really experienced what it was like to have the experience and express that rather than assume it."

People say to me, "You know why I want to be an actor? Because I want to be a lot of different people." That's ridiculous. You can only be you.

You have to find the source of what you are, to bring to the fulfillment of the author's intentions and description, and do that.

Now, the other part of the instrumental work I do, and the liberation and the missing link in the Method, is that I have gone much further in the actual craft work, the usage of craft to fulfill material, dramatic material. Now I think Lee was a genius, and I think a lot of teachers have contributed a lot craftually. When I was working with Lee, he dealt with obligation. What is the obligation? The actor's obligation to the material. But even that was limited to what is the character feeling and what is your obligation to feel that. My interpretation of obligation is much more broadly related to. The obligation is, what is the need of the character in terms of that piece of material.

What is the obligatory need? For example, you would describe what that need is, and that leads you to your choice. There are three sections to my process. *Obligation, choice, and choice approach.* Now what I've been able to do over a period of at least fifty years is I have thirty-one choice approaches.

What is a choice approach? A choice approach is the way you create the choice that you work for, that will stimulate the experience or life that you're after. My choice is, I'm working for this time and place that I really experience that in, by creating it sensorily. I go back to that time and place, and it stimulates the life of the character in that scene. So it's obligation. There are seven obligations. You want me to name them?

Time and place. Where does this piece of material take place? Time and place. Time of day, time of year, time of season, time of night, time of day, time and place.

Relationship. The relationship has two elements. Who is this person to me, and how do I feel about them?

Emotional obligation. What is the character experiencing emotionally, and the emotional spectrum, and all of the colors of the emotional spectrum.

What is the character, its obligation? What is the character obligation? There are four parts to that. What is the character like physically, emotionally, psychologically, and intellectually, and how am I like that? How am I unlike that, and how do I assume and create and really experience those elements?

Historic obligation. Where in terms of the history of the world did this take place, 12th century England or 1957? And you have to actually deal with accommodating that historic obligation.

And then there's obligation of a thematic obligation. What is the author's statement, and is your character the character who carries the author's statement? It's a thematic obligation.

And then the last one is the subtextual obligation. What is the essence or ambiance of the piece? For example, a lot of plays were during the depression era, *Winterset, Awake and Sing.* And in I think in *Winterset,* Mio, one of the two main characters, his father was executed because of conspiracy. It was a time when there was a great deal of resentment for immigrants in this country, and they were from Italy and they were convicted on conspiracy and he was executed.

So the subtextual obligation of the actor, and it's a director's responsibility also, is to create the essence of the play or the piece. So those are the eight obligations.

Choices. Choice can be anything. It could be a sound. It could be a person. It could be an animal. It could be a taste of a food, something you're wearing, a phone call, a letter, a weather condition, rain on the roof, a distant whistle from a train whistle. A choice can be anything that you work for that will stimulate the life that you're after.

Bonnie Wallace: All of which will serve to make it more real to both the actor and the audience.

Eric Morris: Absolutely. Time and place particularly. Now, the choice approach is the approach to the choice. It's the way you create the choice. I've created thirty-one of them. I'd say four or five of them I came into teaching with, I got from Marty Landau, who I studied with, and Lee Strasberg. But of the others, the thirty-one, there are five "megapproaches."

A megapproach is a choice approach so powerful it can create a whole system of acting by itself. Sense memory is a megapproach. Affective memory is a megapproach. Sub-personalities is a wonderfully humongous megapproach. Externals, getting a sense of a person, an animal, an insect or an inanimate object and translating it into human behavior.

Johnny Depp is using my work in terms of all of the pirate movies. And I know for a fact he's doing that. And the last one is imaging. I wrote a whole book about imaging, *Acting, Imaging, and The Unconscious.*

Those are the megapproaches of the thirty-one choice approaches. Now, as far as I know there are no ... I've never run into anything that specific in terms of craft. And so this is not an ego trip. I learned a long time ago, you can say anything about yourself. It may sound like an ego trip, it may sound narcissistic, but it isn't if it's true.

Bonnie Wallace: How can people find your books?

Eric Morris: Well, they're in a lot of the bookstores, and they're all on Amazon. They're on Kindle. There are eBooks. There are several that are on iTunes. You can get them on Amazon or you can get them at Borders. You used to be able to get them all at Samuel French and other Drama bookstores in New York, et cetera.

Bonnie Wallace: Let's back up a little bit. How did you begin as an acting teacher?

Eric Morris: That's an interesting story. I graduated from Northwestern University. I was with a bunch of teachers before that, after that, et cetera. And I would always ask this question, "How do you do that?" I'm saying *HOW*, that's the biggest three letter word in the world. No one could give me an answer.

I couldn't get an answer. "Oh Eric, come on. Think about it. Just recall it. Just reimagine. Imagine that happening." None of that is process. It doesn't work.

So I was in a play at the Players' Ring and Barbara Bain, the wife of Martin Landau, was in the play, and

Marty used to come and visit. During intermission, we got to talking, and I told him how frustrated I was, and I wanted to go to New York and study with Lee Strasberg. But I was broke. I was married to my first wife at the time and I couldn't go. He said, "Well, why don't you come and visit my class? I've started a class." So I went and watched his class and I thought they were all insane. But I was in the play. It was $25 a month. And that's 1950s, it was '58.

By the third time I was hooked, and for the first time in my life I had a *how*, the beginning of a *how*. And so I was with Marty for two and a half years, and I'm forever grateful to the man, he started me off on this journey that I'm still on and the *how* drove me to create everything I've created. *How*.

Actor gets up on stage to do a scene or a monologue, and when he's finished, I say, "Well, how did you approach that? How?" And if he can't tell me after learning anything, working somewhere else, then he doesn't know if he can say how. My people, after a period of time when I say, "Okay, what do you want to tell us? How did you approach this?" "Well, my obligation was to ... I had a couple of choices. I went from one to the other. My choice was this, my choice was that, and my choice approach is gaza, gaza, gaza. And that's how I did it."

After a period of time they learned that, and that's what's missing. A lot of people come to my class and the first time they get up there I ask them to introduce themselves and then do a monologue, or anything they have worked on. And when they're finished, I say, "Okay, how did you do that?" 97% of the people who get up there can't tell me how because they have no *how*. It's all abstract, vague, theoretical, conceptual ideas of assuming or embodying the feelings. It's all nonsense.

Bonnie Wallace: No foundation.

Eric Morris: No. No know-how. No craft. Not to mention the fact that most people in the world are really blocked.

Bonnie Wallace: That's a big one. I think about that because I think the finest actors have complete access to their emotions, and wherever you have a block, you cannot express something that your character might need to.

Eric Morris: Or experience.

That's what the whole purpose for instrumental work is all about, liberating the actor's instrument. Now my book, *Freeing the Actor* is all instrumental. I couldn't have written that book when I wrote *No Acting, Please* because I didn't have the depth of knowledge that I do now. So that book is all instrumental, *Freeing the Actor*, and it's a popular book. I'm very pleased with it. But in answer to what we're talking about, that *how*, the how is the impetus of my life.

Bonnie Wallace: So you began as an actor, but the quest for the *how* turned you into a student and a teacher.

Eric Morris: Right, right. Well, I was struggling ... I did some very good work as an actor, but I'll tell you, I didn't know how or why. Sometimes I was awful, and I didn't know why. I didn't know. Somebody would say, "Eric, that was fantastic work. I believe it was wonderful."

Bonnie Wallace: Which is scary because then you don't know if you can repeat it.

Eric Morris: No, I didn't know how. I did three seasons of summer stock, had a ball, did some great work, fun work, et cetera, but I didn't learn anything, you know?

Bonnie Wallace: We're actually sitting in your theater right now, which is really beautiful.
                   And you offer acting classes here in the studio.

Eric Morris: Yeah, Monday, Tuesday, and Wednesday.

Bonnie Wallace: What do you do in your classes?

Eric Morris: Well, I do instrumental work, and I do scene work. I do monologues, I do all kinds of instrumental work. I do scene parallels, which I invented.
                   Why did I create scene parallels about 30 years ago? I'm not saying I'm the only one ever, but it's my thing. A scene parallel is exactly like doing the written scene, only you don't do the author's words.
                   You identify. And there's a reason for that. You identify the responsibilities, the obligations, select the choices and the choice approaches, and then you do the scene parallel, paralleling the material. But you use your own words. And the reason for that is words have meaning and they breed concept. So actors get stuck in the concept and meaning of words and they start tailoring their behavior to match a concept. When you're doing a scene parallel, you can't do that. So by the time they get all their ducks in a row, and their choices are working, their obligations are clear, and they have a

good choice approach or choice approaches, they don't fall into the trap of concept. That's why scene parallels work so well.

Bonnie Wallace:
That's neat. I am unfamiliar with that, and I totally get it.

There is a list of incredible actors that sing your praises. It's a long list. It's extremely impressive. Johnny Depp, Jack Nicholson, Arnold Schwarzenegger, are just three.

When I think about Johnny Depp and Jack Nicholson in particular, I think part of the hallmark of what strikes me about them as actors is that they are extraordinarily free.

I don't know that I can think of almost anybody else besides those two who are just so profoundly free in their approach, and clearly, based on what I'm learning about how you teach, there's a direct connection there.

Eric Morris:
Well you know, to this day, I don't claim Jack as a student. I claim him as a contemporary. And he did take my class.

I was doing an interview in Atlanta once, and the interviewer wanted me to talk about Arnold Schwarzenegger, who I was working with at the time, and I said, "You know, in this interview you're interviewing me. I'd rather talk about me than talk about Arnold." You know?

I mean, maybe that was a little rude or whatever, but I felt like it's a little tacky, and hanging on to the coattails of somebody who's a superstar, I don't like that feeling.

I'm on my own mountain. I don't need to grab hold of that, the tail of a comet, because that's not my thing. You know?

Bonnie Wallace:

I think people talk about that because it's a kind of shorthand for understanding, "Oh, your work is associated with people who are profoundly successful."

For people who don't know you, it can lend a certain instant legitimacy that then perhaps allows them to want to go further.

Eric Morris:

So how I started teaching … Marty gets a leading role in *Cleopatra* with Elizabeth Taylor and Richard Burton, and he's got to go to Rome for a year. I'm on a white horse in the middle of a stream trying to cross the stream, and all of a sudden, I have no horse. I've got nobody teaching. Jack and I went and audited a class, I won't mention her name. She taught out of her apartment on the corner of La Cienega and Fountain. And we were sitting on wooden chairs, and she was doing such nonsensical work. I'm sitting next to Jack. We were both looking for a teacher at the time. I said, "Jack, I got to get out of here. I can't take this." He said, "Eric, it's rude. Let's wait for the break, okay?"

At the break, we both split. So I'm sitting at home, I'm with my wife, and we're living in a house in Burbank. One of those gingerbread houses. And I'm thinking, "I'm so depressed. I don't know what to do. I don't have a teacher. I'm not really … I don't feel like I have the hands on the handle as tightly as I want to." So I was selling at the time, newspaper ads for the Green Sheet, the Valley Green Sheet, the B'nai B'rith Messenger, et cetera, and so forth, telephone soliciting. And I get a telephone call. I'm as low as I can be. I have no money. I can't go to New York. I can't go anywhere. I'm working as an actor, but not enough to pay all the bills.

Bonnie Wallace: It's not steady work.

Eric Morris: Yeah. And so I get this call from a woman by the name of Ann O'Hara.

She was in Marty's class with me, and we did a couple of scenes together. She said, "Hi Eric, how are you?" I said, "Oh, don't ask me how I am. I'm suicidally depressed." She said, "Well, I know that Marty's gone. Have you found a teacher?" I said, "No, and I'm just ready to jump off a bridge." She said, "Well, why don't you start a class? I learned as much from you as I did from Marty." I said, No, no, no, no, no, no. I'm not a teacher. I'm an actor."

She said the magic thing, and God bless her. She said, "Well, you can promote your own work by teaching." Bing, a light bulb went off. And she said, "I'll be your first student and I'll bring somebody with me." So I rented a little place on ... I forget where it was. It was just a house, but nobody was living there. So in the living room I was teaching. I had one student, I had two, then I had three, then I had two, then I had four, then I had two, then I had five and I had one.

Kurt Conway, who was a famous teacher in New York and a Broadway actor came in, called Marty, and he said, "I don't like teaching beginners. Can you recommend anybody?" He said, "Eric Morris. He was the leader in my class." So he contacted me. At that time I had four or five, six people, and I was teaching on

De Longpre and Highland and he said, "Can I visit?" I said, "Yeah." So he came in, he said, "I have to leave in about an hour because I have an appointment, but let me just watch." So he watched for about two hours, actually, and he gave me a note. And I opened the note after he left, it said, "Eric, you're a born teacher. It would be an honor for me to have you work with me."

So I was his associate, worked for him. And that helped bring more people, and the rest is history. And that's how I started teaching quite by self-defense. If not for Ann O'Hara I don't think I would've ever started because the idea of being a teacher was kind of like a violation of my journey as an actor. "What do you mean teacher, I'm an actor!" But what it did for me is it made me a much better actor.

Bonnie Wallace: It's true. Anytime you have to teach something, it makes you inevitably better at that thing, regardless of what it is.

Eric Morris: For sure. In one of my books I say, "I've learned more from the people that I've taught over the years than they ever learned from me." I really believe it's a true thing. I'm blessed. I'm blessed because if I hadn't found this, my whole life would not have evolved on the level that it has in terms of consciousness and awareness and perception. I have laser light perception. It's not just the talent, it's a facility that anybody can develop over a period of decades. I ran into Bruce Dern at the restaurant down the street that closed about a year ago.

"Hey Bruce." He was with a bunch of people and he turned and he said, "This is Eric Morris. And he has influenced decades of actors that you see in films now. He's influenced those people for decades." I was so blown away by that. I was speechless, speechless, and he wasn't just saying that because I hadn't seen him in 20 years, you know?

So it was really a compliment. And mostly, I have to say that of all my feelings, the biggest feeling I feel is gratefulness. I feel grateful.

Bonnie Wallace: I share that sense of gratitude. Back to your work, in addition to your classes here at the studio, you also offer intensives and there's also coaching. Talk to me about those two.

Eric Morris: My wife does. I used to do private coaching. I don't anymore.

My wife has taken that over, and she has a wonderful following. And we do once-a-month intensives with people we invite when we feel they're ready for it. She teaches most of it. I come in on Saturday and teach the craft. She works with people for a whole year on a particular monologue, particular scene. It's a very in-depth exploration of this process and her contributions to the process, and that's the intensive and it's once a month. And I have people repeating it 10 and 11 years, and longer, and some 2 years, some 3. Then we have jamborees. I've been doing those for about 35 or 40 years.

We go up to Lake Arrowhead, to the UCLA Conference Center. We have many jamborees that are three and a half days long, and we have a major jamboree in June that's six days. And in those jamborees we get people from all over the world to come and we do the work. We do scenes, monologues, scene parallels, and we do teach all five megapproaches. We explore all five of the megapproaches in that week. And people who've taken it 20 years ago are still talking about it. People leave on the last day just off the ground. It's a wonderful experience.

It's five-star accommodations, three gourmet meals. It's in paradise, 5,500 feet. Beautiful Lake, hot tub, tennis courts, swimming pools. Not a lot of time to enjoy them because we teach for 15 hours a day, for six days between 12 and 15 hours.

I alternate with my wife. So they get an intense thing. And when can they have time off? Lunch. We take two hours for lunch. You have your lunch, you go swimming, you want to go to the lake, you want to take a hike up the cardio hill, you can do that. And after we're finished, if it's not too late, which it usually is, they can take a hot tub, but it closes at 10 o'clock so they rarely do that. But they can jump into the pool and take beautiful walks there. It's paradise. And we've been doing that for 20 years there, and before that for 30 years, I have a house up in Lake Arrowhead, and I worked in the house.

I don't take anybody under 18. And the reason I don't take anybody under 18, the work is very, very intense.

A lot of language, a lot of foul language. It's just too intensive and too intense for anybody under 18 to assimilate. And even then, if somebody under 18 comes, I have to interview them. I've got to make sure that they're stable because I let people audit my class. I don't charge for the first audit. I don't think you should have to pay for something you're checking out. So what I do is I give them a chance to look me and the class over, and I get a chance to look them over because I've had some people come over the years who are very close to not being able to distinguish reality from fantasy. And I don't work with people like that.

I don't drop them like a rock. I just say, "You know, I don't think this work is really for you. From what I get from you, I think you'd probably be more comfortable in a scene study class."

It's not a good fit, because it makes me feel like it would be dangerous for them and for us.

Bonnie Wallace: Well, intensive psychological work can be risky if people are not stable.

It's really wise to make sure you are screening for that.

I want to talk about auditions. Auditions are critical if an actor is to actually succeed in the business. What advice do you have for actors approaching an audition?

Eric Morris: Well, I can talk about it on two levels. One, if you are equipped and knowledgeable and have a craft, I know what to do, I know how to do it, and I know I know what to do and I know I know how. That's 98% of doing anything, auditioning or working, whatever.

So training, being a craftsperson and being instrumentally liberated and free, that's the biggest part. Now, I do believe there are some people out there who teach audition techniques on a very technical level ... a couple of my students have taken those classes, and have profited; mainly in auditioning and booking because knowing the technical aspects of what to do in an audition technically is also very important.

So I don't look down on that at all. However, the most important thing is to know what to do, how to do it, and to know you know what to do and you know how to do it. And you have a craft and you're instrumentally free to function. That's the most important part. And if you have that, it shines through. You know the one thing I've learned in all the years? These casting directors and often the directors, they don't know how to get it, but they recognize it when they see it.

You see? They don't know how they can make that happen, but they can say, "Yes."

Now, it's a wonderful thing to know how to get it.

Bonnie Wallace: What about any special advice for audition self-tapes?

Eric Morris: Well, first of all it should be technically good. You should have somebody who shoots you who really knows what they're doing. The lighting has to be good. There's nothing worse than turning in a tape that is substandard because it colors the person's response immediately, number one. Number two, don't self-tape until you're ready to do it. Don't rush to judgment. Don't get so anxious you just want to get it out tonight, Friday, so they get it by Monday. Take your time. It's better to take the time and to be a little late, maybe, hopefully not, and to do a good self-tape because you're prepared to do it.

Rehearse it, use your process, repeat it, and don't do it until you're happy with it. Don't put it on tape until you're happy with it because it's not going to do you any good, and these people have long memories.

Bonnie Wallace: I talk about that a lot with casting directors, and all the ones I've ever met and spoken with, they do have incredibly long memories; generally there's a positive spin on that. For example, they may have loved you but maybe you weren't right for the role, but they'll never forget you. But it does go the other way too. So if you really do a terrible job, they will probably also remember that as well. And maybe not call you in next time or give you an invitation for a self-tape.

Eric Morris: Absolutely.

Bonnie Wallace: So, not to freak people out and scare you, but you do need to take a little care.

Eric Morris: This was non-existent when I was an actor, nobody ever asked me to self-tape. Come in and read for us.

Bonnie Wallace: It's like a do-it-yourself screen test.

Eric Morris: And so the computer and technology has changed the business dramatically. Dramatically. When I used to audition for something, I'd walk into a room and the same seven guys were there.

Seven or eight guys. It was like a joke. I'd walk in and I would see Warren Oats or some other actor that I knew. Sometimes I got the job, sometimes they got the job, but I would walk into a room and we started laughing, the same seven people.

Bonnie Wallace: That's not entirely changed. Just a few years ago when my daughter Dove was a teenager, it felt as if we would go into a room and it would be the same seven young actresses all across town in different projects. That's still pretty real.

What would be your advice for a young person who wants to be a professional actor but who lives far away from Los Angeles or New York? What do you think are some of the best ways for them to move toward that dream right where they are, right now?

Eric Morris: Well, I've got 50, 60 people out there all over the world teaching this system, specifically, that I know about. In Europe, in Asia, in America, and they can contact me on the website. My wife Skypes. There's a girl from Brazil who contacted us, and my wife works with her once a week on Skype. She's a fledgling actress who is pursuing a career, but she's at the beginning. And then my wife Skypes with people who are doing a film in Europe, whatever. So they can contact us. And my wife is open to Skyping with people. She's very busy, but I'm sure she can make room. She's working with a guy now from Utah who just got a lead in a film and he has no background and no training.

She's working with him every day. So all they have to do is either contact us here or look at the website, and hopefully those names will be on there ... or if they want, just call me. I'm very reachable, you don't have to go through any jumps or secretaries or anything. Just call and I'll talk to anybody that wants to talk.

LISA PICOTTE

Founder, Lisa Picotte's Young Actor Workspace

"What we believe is what we achieve."

Lisa Picotte and her husband David Kaufman run the Young Actor Workspace, which provides classes for young actors age 5 to 22, from beginning to advanced levels. The studio is in midtown Los Angeles.

Alumni include Millie Bobby Brown, Brenna D'Amico, Taylor Lautner, Haley Ramm, Rico Rodriguez, Raini Rodriguez, Nolan Gould, Joshua Rush, Parker Bates, Grace Kaufman, Henry Kaufman, Forrest Wheeler, Niko Guardado, Chloe Csgerney, Dash Williams, Danika Yarosh, Ty Simpkins, Tanner Buchanan, Soni Bringas, Jack Grazer, Christopher Paul Richards, Brandon Michael Hall, Holly Taylor, Ruby Jay, and Henry Greenspan.

Bonnie Wallace:	Lisa, there are a lot of different studios in Los Angeles. What is your studio's approach to acting? What's your philosophy in teaching young actors?
Lisa Picotte:	We believe that if you're confident and you believe that you can do it, you can, and our motto is, "What we believe is what we achieve." So we believe if a kid is confident, then the creativity is freed. It's a rough business and it's hard, so we build them up, because we know on the outside it doesn't always go that way.

Also, my husband and I have both trained our whole lives, but I personally was trained with Uta Hagen's *Respect for Acting* book, so that's how I approach the work. My husband also uses that book and my husband was at UCLA. I was at the Academy and I also studied at the Royal National Theater in London. So we take the work seriously. For us it's about the work and the approach to the work, and we're really not interested in making people famous. We're interested in artists and being creative.

Bonnie Wallace: I love that. I think it's really important for young actors especially to stay grounded in that truth, because it can't be about being famous.

Lisa Picotte: No, and it happens to so few people that if that's the goal, then this is not the right studio for you. Of course we do have high profile clients, but that's not ... none of us started that way with that idea. It was always about the work and work ethic. I'm very, very, very strong, even with the little ones about work ethic and about showing up and being prepared and being on time and being courteous. All the things that I think are super important for being successful as a child actor.

Bonnie Wallace: Well, it's obviously translating. I had Brenna D'Amico on my podcast last week and that is clearly a very central part of what she believes in and where she comes from is that strong work ethic. So congratulations.

Lisa Picotte: Thank you.

Bonnie Wallace: You and your husband, David Kaufman, both have incredibly impressive acting resumes. Between the two of you, you've starred and recurred in eight network TV series, and five animated series. You've starred and costarred in over 20 features and movies of the week. You've guest starred in over 40 prime time series and you've done over 100 commercials. You've also won the L.A. Weekly Back Stage West Garland and Drama-Logue Awards for your work in L.A. theater. That's amazing. How do you think all of this professional experience helps you to teach and coach your students?

Lisa Picotte: Well, I've been there. I've done it and I've probably done it five times, different ways. So I think I'm not just talking about it, I've lived it, I've experienced it. I think that really helps with the teaching. Also, we have insight that people that don't have our backgrounds don't have. We know what certain things are said in the room, what it means, and they might not understand, but we know.

We also know how a certain project's shaking down, by who's auditioning for it. You know sometimes it's one of those things where you think, "Oh my goodness, I wish I didn't know," because we do know a lot and sometimes, depending on the project ... for instance, if they're casting a pilot and you're seeing, say 9 to 12-year-old little Caucasian boys. Well, maybe one day you get a call and you start seeing 9 to 12-year-old Hispanic boys or 9 to 12-year-old African American boys. Well, we know they've changed their minds and we know they've made a decision to completely revamp the script, but the parents don't know that, and the parents think, "Oh my goodness, what did my child do or didn't do?"

Well, the kids didn't do anything wrong. They totally changed the concept of the script. So the parents ... we know things that they don't know. The years of experience ... just seeing year after year, pilot season after pilot season, it's garnered us a lot of knowledge.

Bonnie Wallace: I love that you point that out because this happens so commonly, in the middle of casting, producers will decide to go a completely different direction with something, and the people who then ... they know they were close, they have evidence that they were close. They think "What did I do wrong?"

Lisa Picotte: And they might not have done anything wrong. Actually, there's a project being cast right now, exactly that. They were looking for little 9 to 12-year-old Caucasian boys and now I'm seeing they completely re-conceptualized it and now they're looking for 9 to 12-year-old African American boys, and all those boys are looking at me asking, "What happened?" and I'm like, "Well, that's the business."

Bonnie Wallace: They went in a different direction.

Lisa Picotte: They went in a different direction and that is not personal, and that's what a lot of people need to take to heart. So much is out of our hands and it's not personal. All we can concentrate on is the work, and that's what my studio's about.

Bonnie Wallace: I love that. I feel like half of what comes out of my mouth is, "It's not personal." It's not about you. So, you're an actress obviously, how did you begin as an acting teacher?

Lisa Picotte: I was doing a play at West Coast Ensemble, and there was a little boy cast in the play and he was just really cute and his mom was really nice. Her name was Anne Henry and Anne had another child named Jill, and I became very fond of Jill, and Anne asked me one day to help her with an audition and that was that. I said to her, "I don't know whether to hug you or to choke you. I don't know which I should do with you, because what happened to me?" I somehow went from doing plays and it became not about me anymore, and that's totally fine and I'm so humbled and grateful for it, however it was very much surprising.

I feel like I have a very unique perspective, because I started as a kid actor. So I know what they go through, and now I'm a parent of two child actors. So I understand what the parents go through and I'm also the teacher and I know how I want people to treat my children. I try to treat other people's children the way I would want my children to be treated. So I do have a very unique perspective on this that I think most people don't have.

Bonnie Wallace: You do. It's very rare to have somebody who's so, literally, rounded in the industry as you are in your position. You offer a variety of acting classes in your studio here in L.A. What do you teach in your different classes?

Lisa Picotte: We do scene study. We also do improv, depending on what season it is, we do different things in the fall. We do drama in pilot season, which is January to March. We do pilot season preparation, character analysis, script breakdown, how to walk in the room in character, how to think fast, how to make the strongest choice. We do the moment before the scene starts, we work on the objective, we do all the things ... living the reality of the character, we do all of that stuff.

They don't know they're getting that stuff, but that's what they're getting—and we're talking about sometimes little kids, but that's what they're getting. And they just think it's fun and they think it's fabulous, but I am really ... I'm pounding them with really hard stuff.

And they don't know that. Little ones, they're like, "Oh, that's fun!" and I'm thinking, "Yeah, you have no idea what you just did, but that's great."

Bonnie Wallace: But you just internalized all the right stuff. I love that. Now on top of the classes, you also offer one-on-one private coaching. Basically coaching for everything: TV, film, theater, musical theater, voiceover.

Lisa Picotte: Yes. My husband is a big voiceover guy, he has done dozens and dozens of animated series and he's actually doing one right now called *Goldie and Bear*, for Disney. He's on that show right now and my daughter is also on a show, *Clarence* and *Bubble Guppies*, and then my son is on a show called, *If You Give a Mouse a Cookie*. So you try to keep all of that straight!

My scheduling is a nightmare, but that's okay. Anyway so, yes, my husband is an amazing actor. He has a ton of TV and film credits, but he's also an amazing voice teacher, and not voice as in singing, but we're talking animation. Animation and voiceover. He's super gifted. So that's a little niche that's his, but of course we do everything. We do comedy, we do TV drama; we have kids all over. On Nick, at Disney, on the network shows, on the cable shows, we have kids everywhere.

Bonnie Wallace:	Do you only coach in person or do you sometimes coach on Skype?
Lisa Picotte:	No, I have clients all over the country and Skype is not my first choice, but it is a very effective tool, because if a kid lives in say, Texas, and they're flying in for a call-back, sometimes there's no time to come to me before they have to go. So we'll Skype the night before or ... I've Skyped kids in cars; I've Skyped kids driving to auditions from 500 miles away; I've Skyped kids everywhere. You cannot believe where I've Skyped kids.

And also, when my children are working personally, kids meet me on their sets, because I can't stop my business just because my kids are working. I've always said it's so funny because I've coached kids at McDonald's; I've coached kids in parks; I've coached kids in cars;

I've coached kids behind trashcans; I've coached kids at picnic tables; I've coached kids in you name it. I said, "This is just the strangest, weirdest..."

Bonnie Wallace:	You could write a little *Green Eggs and Ham* soliloquy about this ... "and I will coach them in a box, and I will coach them with a fox."
Lisa Picotte:	"... and I will coach them in the air, and I will coach them with a bear, and I will coach them everywhere." Yeah. So anyway, I've just coached them everywhere. I mean if it has four walls, we're in. We're good. A box, fine, got it.
Bonnie Wallace:	I've actually become a big believer in Skype, or Zoom, as a way of getting things done.

Lisa Picotte:	It's effective. FaceTime too. Sometimes we'll have clients that'll have multiple auditions in one day and that's when Skype is really effective, because they might go to one callback and Skype me, and then we'll change what we're working on and then they'll go to the next callback and they'll Skype me. There's no way they could come to my studio three times.
Bonnie Wallace:	There's a long list of young actors that sing your praises. It's very impressive. It includes Taylor Lautner, Rico and Raini Rodriguez, Forrest Wheeler, Brenna D'Amico. These are just some of your successful young students. What do you think explains the success rate of your students?
Lisa Picotte:	I think my studio offers a safe place. I won't let auditors watch, I don't let parents watch. When they come through that door, what's said in this room stays in this room and they'll tell me things and we share things. I share things with my personal life and we get into it deeply, and so I think they've found a safe place here where they can really make mistakes, take risks and then go out on the outside and slay the dragon. I think that's what this is for them.
	I had something like this growing up. I had a company that I was in, and they were my best friends, and I got to go once or twice a week and I would count the days till I got to go back and it was my safe place, and I didn't purposefully aim to create that again, but I do think that's what I did.
Bonnie Wallace:	That's huge and that's important.

Lisa Picotte: I think they have a safe place here. I think they know that I want the best for them, and they know that I care about them and there are a lot of struggles on the outside. So they have to have a place where they can go and just let it all hang out, and that's okay, and I think that's what this is and that's why I've had kids from being little, little, and now they're in their twenties and they don't leave. They just won't go. I'm like, "Can you guys just go. Please."

And they still call me Miss Lisa. They still call me Miss Lisa, they're in their twenties, "Miss Lisa, I need to talk to you."

It's super sweet and it's very gratifying and I really do want the best for them and I think because of my confidence in them, they go out and they have confidence in themselves, and I don't think that they get that a lot of places on the outside.

Bonnie Wallace: That's so important. I think part of what a parent can ideally do for kids, that a parent isn't always able to do, is create a container within which the kids can feel safe and then, as you say, go out and slay the dragon. To have a place where they can internalize the confidence that you have in them.

Lisa Picotte: Yes. So an interesting story. My son is recurring on *Major Crimes* and he plays the Detective Sanchez's little foster child, and he got this big scene where he was supposed to cry on cue and he read the script and he asked, "Mom, what if I can't do it?" and I said, "Well of course you can do it," and he says, "But what if I can't?" and I said, "No, why would you not be able to. I have never had a child or a student not be able to do it," and he says, "But what if I'm standing there and they put the cameras on and I just can't?" and I said, "Well, you have to believe in yourself. I believe in you. I've never had a child not be able to."

So come the day of the shoot, he stands in the corner and he does the technique that I taught him and he just loses it. Turns around, gives an incredible performance, slays it and then they said, "Cut," and he ran up to me and he's like, "I did it! I slayed the dragon! I did it, I did it!" and I said, "Of course you did," and I think in that moment I was the most proud of him I've ever been in his life and I told him this and not because he cried on cue, because I can teach any kid to do that, but I was so proud of him because he was so scared, and he stood up to the dragon. He looked the dragon in the eye and he just cut the head off.

I was so proud of his approach and his courage, because it takes a lot of courage to get in front of people and be an artist. It takes a lot of courage. So when you teach them young that they're fearless, they take that all the way with them to adulthood and that's why I think my program works, because we build them up and build them up and build them up, and then they go into the next class and the next class and the next class and then they go out and they feel like they can take the world on.

Bonnie Wallace: I'm so happy that you brought that up. It takes a huge amount of courage and that's one of the reasons that I feel like, no matter what happens with the kid who pursues acting, no matter whether they end up doing it for the rest of their lives or not, those skills ... they can take you anywhere. And they serve you, no matter what you do.

Lisa Picotte: You can give a great job interview, you can give a complete presentation without being scared, you can think quickly on your feet if someone asks you a question. You can come off as completely comfortable in your own skin, which are really the people that get hired. The people that you want are people that are comfortable with themselves. And I do have people that don't go on to be actors.

There was one girl, Megan Broussard, she was 13 and her mom called me and she said, "Megan was just voted Student Body President and I want to tell you it's because of you and your classes." Megan was the very first girl ever to be nominated at her school and win. The news media came, they did all these interviews and she said she wasn't scared, she had intelligent questions, she laughed, she was totally relaxed, and the mom said, "That is completely from your training in your classes, because nothing threw her. Bring it, bring it on. I'm good."

It didn't translate into an acting job, but I know it translated for her. That was a huge win. People were sticking microphones and cameras in her face and she's 13 or 14 years old, she's a kid. So I know that changed her and that's good, that's fine, that's enough.

Bonnie Wallace: It's more than enough. It's great. I see from your website that you work with young actors age 5 to 22. Can they just sign up, or do they need to audition, or how does that work?

Lisa Picotte: Email me. We have all levels. If you're a beginner you're not going to get into the advanced classes. You have to work up to that, but we have all levels. We do not turn anyone away; however there are wait lists. So you can always come to my studio. I will say this: my studio is not for kids that are hobbyists.

It definitely is for kids that are serious. It doesn't mean you have to know at 8 years old if you want to be an actor when you're 25, but these kids that are here really want it. They're really passionate and they would give anything to succeed and do it. So it's not for kids that are not sure. It's for kids who know, "This is what I want to do. I want to go for it," and they're off.

Bonnie Wallace: Highly motivated.

Lisa Picotte: Motivated. They just want it so badly. It's their art, it's their passion, it's their voice. So it's not for kids that are just, "Well, maybe I want to be an actor." The kids that are in my studio are super serious and I'm super serious. I'm not interested in working with people that are not serious. If you want to come to my studio, we will welcome you with open arms, but you have to really want it.

Bonnie Wallace: Well, it makes the quality of the classes that much better too of course. What do you think are some of the biggest differences between acting for live theater versus, say, film and TV and what are some similarities? How would you parse that?

Lisa Picotte: I've always described the different genres as driving and being in different gears. So, as an example, first gear is theater. Second gear is comedy. Third gear is one camera comedy. Fourth gear is drama. Fifth gear is voiceover. Sixth gear ... I don't even know if there is a sixth gear, but sixth gear is commercials. So it's learning what genre you're in and what is appropriate for that genre and we do teach that.

You're going to give a completely different performance for a multi-camera show than you are for a single camera, than you are for auditioning for the Disney Channel. It's different and you just have to know what gear you're in and as the kids get older, they just automatically go into gear like a car does, but you've got to learn that when you're little.

Bonnie Wallace: That was a complete surprise to us when we moved here and all Dove had ever done was stage work and we're thinking, "What is multi-cam, single cam? What is this?" And really ... they are different genres.

Lisa Picotte: They are and they all have different expectations of what's appropriate.

What's completely appropriate in multi-cam, is not appropriate for drama.

Bonnie Wallace: You'll never get cast in drama if that's what you bring to it. I like that metaphor.

Lisa Picotte: So it's like shifting gears. I always explain that, especially with the younger kids, "Okay we're in gear one now, now we're going to go into gear two. You're changing gears right now, but it's all the same car."

Bonnie Wallace: And it's all driving.

Lisa Picotte: And it's all driving and all going forward. I highly recommend that you watch the shows that you're auditioning for. If you're auditioning for a multi-camera show, you need to watch some multi-camera shows. If you're auditioning for *Grey's Anatomy*, watch *Grey's Anatomy*.

Bonnie Wallace: They have different rhythms to them, for one thing.

Lisa Picotte: Different rhythms, different ... just tones. Different tones, so yeah, you just have to know what gear you're in, but that's the easiest way to explain that.

Bonnie Wallace: I love it. Thank you. Some people are really good auditioners, but they don't necessarily have the goods to back that up once they hit a show. Some people are brilliant actors, but they're not such good auditioners. What advice do you have for actors approaching an audition?

Lisa Picotte: You have to know the material really well. If you need an extra day, ask for it. They can always say no. They can always say no, but they might say yes. Dress for the character, but that doesn't mean if you're auditioning for a nun that you wear a habit.

But if you're auditioning for a very wealthy, proper lady, I would wear a dress. If you're auditioning for a sports jock, I would wear sporty type clothes. You have to give the idea. You don't want to hit them over the head with how you dress because then I think it insults them. You want to give the idea of the character and you want to make really strong choices and you want to go for it.

We don't get most jobs. That's just the bottom line. Actors don't get most jobs, so you've got to go in there fearless, and you've got to go in there with the strongest choices, and just go for it and then let it go. So that's my advice. Really know your material well.

Bonnie Wallace: What about taped auditions? Any hot tips for those?

Lisa Picotte: They're more difficult and certainly I've had many students book things from tapes, but I see more kids getting stuff by going in the room. I think with tapes they know you could redo a scene a hundred times till you get that one that's just perfect and then that's what you send, but in the room, you're in their face and you can't hide it.

If it doesn't go well, it doesn't go well and if you kill it, you kill it, but the tapes, I think you just have a good person tape you and also a coach if you can. Or you just keep doing it till you feel like you did the best take, however long that takes. Don't have a non-actor work with you, if you can have someone that acts read the other role. I think that helps.

A lot of these tapes are flat when the parents read with them, because the parents aren't actors and it's not their fault, but what are you going to do? You have who you have to help you, but I would get an actor or an actor-type person if you could, to read with you. Really know the lines well. Put up a background, a blue background, like a blue sheet so that it's not distracting, and then just go for it. But it's always better to go in the room. Always.

Bonnie Wallace: What would your advice be for a young person who lives far away from L.A. or New York, what are some of the best ways for them to move toward their dream, right where they are, that they can do where they live?

Lisa Picotte: I was one of those kids. I was in a children's theater program. We did five shows a year. We won the best children's theater in the United States for three years while I was there. We're talking 8, 9, 10-year-olds. You had to be either in the show, do props, do costumes, run the lights, or take tickets. It was all child-produced, the entire show. So you had 10-year-olds running light booths.

You had 10-year-olds running spotlights. You had 6 and 7-year-olds setting props and we did it, and we did it well and we worked really hard and we formed this little company and those people are still my friends to this day, from way back then. And I say just go into any theater, college, community theater and do plays. You can do it and get roles and learn ... just because those actors are not in Los Angeles or New York doesn't mean they're not good.

You can learn from them and sometimes in these little regional cities, sometimes they do have agents. Go get a regional agent. Go get pictures. Do what you can do in your town or your place, because that's what I did and I did get work, and not of course like the big markets, but for me at the time it was perfect, and it was enough. And so I worked really hard on my plays and my scenes and I was never not in a show. I think I had done 45 shows by the time I was 16.

Bonnie Wallace: That's amazing training.

Lisa Picotte: Sometimes I had two lines and sometimes I was the lead, but I was always learning, always growing. Watching the older actors, watching, reading plays, saying, "Oh, there's this play coming up. Let's all read it together so we can figure out what roles we want to do", and you know, that was exciting, and it was wonderful. I know it wasn't the level of Los Angeles or New York, but it was wonderful.

Bonnie Wallace: Well, and it's about the love of it and the passion and the work. And that's at center, to me, what it's always about.

Any final thoughts for young actors or parents of young actors who are hoping to make a career in film and TV?

Lisa Picotte: You just have to support their dream, whatever that means, and it has to be their dream. Their dream. But you have to support it. If your kid wanted to be a soccer player, you'd take him to the soccer field. If a kid wants to be a dancer, you'd take them to dance classes. If a kid wants to be an actor, you just do whatever you can do to help them and support them, but, again, it has to be their dream.

MAE ROSS

Founder, 321 Acting Studios

"Hollywood is not going anywhere."

Mae Ross is the founder of 321 Acting Studios, an acting school in Los Angeles, and she's an industry veteran. She began her career at the age of 10, with a 64-city tour of *The Music Man*, and quickly added singing, dancing, and modeling to her acting career but she discovered that her passion was actually working with children, teens, and young adults. Mae has taught acting for over 25 years and launched 321 Acting Studios in 2007. 321 Acting Studios offers training in scene study, improv, cold reading, auditioning, modeling, and TV commercials. They also offer talent showcases and acting career seminars.

Alumni include Diego Tinoco, Forrest Wheeler, Christian Isaiah, Riley Beres, Sanai Victoria, Tait Blum, and Teddy Blum.

Bonnie Wallace: Mae, there are a lot of different techniques and approaches out there ... different schools of thought ... how do you approach teaching acting to your students?

Mae Ross: I like to hire teachers that have a little bit of all of it. It's very similar to being a dancer. You know, a dancer studies ballet, jazz, tap, hip-hop, lyrical, and then they become that fabulous dancer, and that's very true to acting, too, because there's the Method, Stanislavsky, Uta Hagen ... there's the Going to Zero, and just doing the moment to moment, there's the Sanford Meisner, which is, "acting is reacting." So I love that the teachers that I hire are not only very nurturing and positive and experts but they bring themselves, and they bring all of the wonderful techniques to our children and we have fun. We have a lot of fun.

Bonnie Wallace: If you are not having fun, you are not going to learn anything. Fun is the ground.

Mae Ross: Oh, we have so much fun, it's almost serious.

Bonnie Wallace: You offer acting classes in your Los Angeles location and you also offer online courses. Can you talk to me about that a little bit?

Mae Ross: Yes! That was another thing that I really felt passionate about is getting the information out there. People that are out in other parts of the United States or the world who want to bring their children here really need more information and we've had the experience.

Bonnie Wallace: Information is everything. I focus so much on education with all of my work too, and what you don't know can really hurt you. So the more armed with real information you are, the more successful your kid's going to be. Or you, if you are the actor!

Mae Ross: Yes, and speaking of armed, my technique class is taught by John Walcutt, you can IMDb him. He is a master actor with 200 guest star episodes. He has been in *Titanic*, and *Little Miss Sunshine*, and he is the director of OCSA, Orange County High School of Performing Arts. He is a master teacher and we have 10 online lessons. It's a technique class, and it's where you really learn how to be a greater actor, and the better actors do get hired. Let's face it. So if you want to be really good, search for "10 Lessons to Great Film Acting." We have some free series too. Go to our website, *321talentshowcase.com*, and you can check it out.

Bonnie Wallace: It's true that the better quality of an actor you are, the more often you are going to be cast. It's not random.

Mae Ross: No, no, they see the technique. They see the talent and the technique.
You need all of it.

Bonnie Wallace: So your students range in age from 4, which is so little, to 27, which is kind of the upper limit for a youth actor, for people who are still going out for roles of high school and college students. Why do you focus on teaching youth as opposed to adult actors?

Mae Ross: Well, I love children. They're so much fun. They're so eager. They want to be there, you know, when they come to acting class ... it's not like they're in a science class, I mean no offense, but you know, they are just so positive. I just get the best students. That is what I really love. I also get to share my experience with these children that are really looking to build self-esteem and build their confidence and that is really my passion ... to instill greater confidence in the children, which they need for the entertainment industry and it parlays into all walks of their life.

Bonnie Wallace:	You and I both talk a lot about the long-term benefits of acting classes, and the importance that these skills can have for everybody, regardless of where their life takes them.
	You don't know when you are young and you want to be an actor, how it's going to go. You can't know that, but what you can do is get these amazing skills that will serve you for all of your life.
Mae Ross:	They're life skills. Acting requires focus, concentration, listening, word retrieval, taking direction, being a team player, empathy, communication, public speaking ... there's so much that acting affords children as they're growing that I think every parent should put their kid in a drama or acting class because it has myriad of benefits, of life benefits, social skills.
Bonnie Wallace:	I agree completely. And two side notes to underline what you are talking about: people always talk about the benefits of sports, and the teamwork, the life lessons that you derive from sports, and I would never disagree with that, sports are brilliant that way. I just think that acting is all that on steroids. It's all those things but it also provides a lot more emotional and soft-skilled stuff that we don't get on a field. It's the same thing but more complex, which in the real world is an incredible, important skill set.
Mae Ross:	Yes, they learn to take the challenges of life and be able to roll with them so it's amazing. That's what I love about teaching children is seeing their growth.
Bonnie Wallace:	And just as a cool side note, Tenzing Trainor, who plays Parker on *Liv and Maddie*, was signed up for summer

229

acting camp by his dad some years ago ... I think he was 10 or something ... not because his dad wanted him to become an actor at all but because his dad's an attorney and wanted him to feel comfortable standing in front of a room; be able to talk to anybody, and have that confidence.

Mae Ross: Presentation skills...

Bonnie Wallace: That was literally the whole point, and then of course it led to pretty big things.

Mae Ross: ...a huge Hollywood career, which is wonderful.

Bonnie Wallace: You never know where it's going to lead, but at the very least it's going to lead to a more successful, confident person...

You've got extensive experience working with young actors on both Disney and Nickelodeon.

Are there any differences in how you would approach an audition for those networks versus just a comedy show on a regular network?

Mae Ross: You know it's really funny because I'm dying to hear what you have to say about this, because what I tell the children, first of all, is to wear really bright colors, I mean look at Nickelodeon and Disney, so we want those hot pinks and turquoise, and wear those colors that are going to pop to make you look young, fresh, and clean, happy, and then, one of my mantras is, "Okay, Johnny, loud and proud."

I love to hear my teachers say, "Okay, so loud and proud," or, "Share your voice," because it's better, I always tell them to go in big, broad, loud or whatever and let the director take you down, let the director take your child down because Disney wants to know that they have an actor to work with. They don't want to light any fires under actors. So it's actually a good idea to be on the "loud and proud" side and don't be afraid to be.

And also with Disney, Nickelodeon, and the sitcoms, everything's important. Every single thing. We forgot to order the pizza!!! Hold the phone!! Do you know what I mean? It's very different. So it's driven with that "everything's important" and that's another thing to think about so don't just take a line and throw it away in sitcom, Disney, or Nickelodeon.

What is your take on this? You've got a daughter in the business.

Bonnie Wallace: I do. The funny thing was she'd never done comedy before she was cast on the Disney Channel.

She'd done a bunch of drama and stage work and we thought, okay, we are going to come to L.A. and she is going to do film, serious film...

And then of course, to our great surprise, she ends up cast in this Disney show. I always thought she was funny but I'm her mom, right? She's a funny kid. So Dove sort of had to learn, and the way she approached it was a little more of a hybrid, a little less broad, and I think *Liv and Maddie* in particular is a little less broad and big. But Disney in general because it's aimed at children, that's the kind of humor that they respond to and Disney knows that, and so that is the direction most of the time, and that is the writing most of the time.

Mae Ross:	Yes it is. Everything is important.
Bonnie Wallace:	You have to go with that when you are on that network, whereas when you are on film or doing an audition for film, at least, you can let the focus be on your face and let small things read out of your eyes. It's quite different.
Mae Ross:	It's more nuance ... I am not saying that Disney does not have nuance in their sitcoms, they do, they have brilliant actors, those kid actors are amazing. But we are talking about going to the audition. Let's show them that you can be big and let them discover your nuance.
Bonnie Wallace:	And they can always ask you to dial it back ... and sometimes they might, but that way they can see how big you can make it ... it is important also to know that different auditions require different skills.

I know that you teach that. Let's talk about auditioning a little further. It's really its own thing. And I think that people don't appreciate that until they're out there doing several a week.

What advice do you have for actors, for auditions? |
| Mae Ross: | The first thing I tell my parents—because again we are talking about the youth market here and youth actors—is I tell the parents that we have an acting career program, showcase and acting program, where we bring the talent agents up to my studio, 321 Acting Studios in Los Angeles. The agents just love coming to our showcases. I've had relationships for twenty years and they actually get a little mad if they aren't invited. I have to rotate them. |

But what I tell the parents is to really keep it fun. Try not to express your worry and your stress, because our children are little sponges and they're going to pick up that, "Mommy seems really stressed and worried about this and I don't know why," so keep it fun, keep it light.

Keep it light and have fun. I tell the children to just go in and do their best, and I actually tell them to just have fun even in a dramatic audition, because if they're enjoying themselves—if the actor looks like they're enjoying themselves—then it makes everybody around them relaxed and they are more at ease. I also tell the children that after they audition, they should just think, here's the mantra, "What's next, what's next." And I tell the parents not to ask how it went. Then it is a lot of stress on them or pressure.

Bonnie Wallace: Let's talk about the acting career program you just mentioned. What does that look like?

Mae Ross: Yes, the Showcase Acting Career Program is a program that is designed to get children and teens and young adults entered into the entertainment industry, a successful way to break in. Or for those children that already have a career, to move their career forward. So it is a program based on success, just like you've navigated everything in the *Hollywood Parents Guide*, which is a great book. I highly recommend it.

We've navigated the steps to get into the business. So we've got the right agents, how to get the work permit, we do a photo shoot ... we do a whole package that is geared towards getting the children noticed by the talent agents. We don't guarantee anything because we are not that kind of school.

Bonnie Wallace:	Nobody can guarantee anything. Honestly, anybody who's guaranteeing a career, it's not possible.
Mae Ross:	No, it's a scam.
Bonnie Wallace:	It's one of the red flags. Even the very best, most connected, powerful, experienced, big acting schools and coaches in L.A., they can't guarantee anything because so much of it is just serendipity.
Mae Ross:	Yes, it is. A lot of it can be the luck of the draw. But we do really prepare them, and the agents tell us over and over again how well prepared they are. We only showcase about 25 kids at a time and we do 4 showcases a year. There was one year we had 3 showcases in a row where 100% got callbacks. That's just insane, but yes, we have tremendous success in getting them talent agents, and I don't give up until they give up, so if the parents say we did not get an agent this time, well, we have an agent meet and greet they can come to. I am also here to help with my connections, too.
Bonnie Wallace:	Do you have any special advice for audition self-tapes? Even here in Los Angeles, and obviously if you are outside of L.A., if you are auditioning for bigger projects it is probably going to start on self-tapes. But even if you are here, you are still doing self-tapes sometimes. Sometimes the project has been cast in New York, or sometimes the timing can't work out, for example with kids who are in school. Typically for kids' auditions they try to schedule after school, but sometimes that doesn't work with the director's schedule or the casting director's schedule, so you still end up doing self-tapes no matter what.

Any advice for making a good self-tape for an audition?

Mae Ross:

Well I think there is the basic advice: good lighting like we have here today, just a plain background. You know the thing about self-tapes is that you can get your performance really great. Another thing, follow the instructions to a "T". If they want to see your hands, put the hands up. Follow it to a "T", because they are just going to flip to the next one if you did not follow the directions.

Bonnie Wallace:

Thank you for saying that. It blows my mind, but truly there are so many people auditioning for any given role that the people who are looking through the first round, they're looking for reasons to discard, they need to narrow the field so if you do anything silly, like not follow the directions, that's it. They are not going to pay attention to how brilliant you might be.

Mae Ross:

That's right! Follow the directions, and that will help you right off the bat. Wear something bright, I am all about bright colors. Not stripes or polka-dots, the eye goes to that, you don't want to wear that. Just make sure you have somebody who is working with you off camera and that their voice is not so loud. A lot of this stuff I have in a great blog on how to get a good self-taped audition. I am a *Backstage Expert*, which is where I have a column and I have around 43 articles, so you can search Mae Ross and Google me online, and you can find all kinds of information.

235

Bonnie Wallace:	Yes, and the more you understand about how it works, the greater your odds are of being genuinely successful.
Mae Ross:	Knowledge is confidence.
Bonnie Wallace:	And it is power definitely, too. What is some advice that you have for somebody that is trying to break into the industry? What are some critical first steps that somebody should take?
Mae Ross:	Well, come to our Showcase Acting Career Program if you are in Los Angeles. We have taken those steps for you and we have navigated it. But really if you are from out-of-town, I have told the moms and dads to make sure that you get your children in a drama program. Of course, and I am pretty sure that your book talks about this too, you want to make sure your children really, really like acting. That is one of the reasons why I want people to take this online course, as well, is that you will be able to determine if your child really wants to act, because this online course is an acting technique and it really shows what is needed out there, and so you will be able to determine if your child is really ready for something like the world of acting.
Bonnie Wallace:	I really appreciate that you brought that up. One of the reasons that I wrote my first book is because there are a lot of young people out there—especially with social media today—who want to be famous, because they equate fame with love and power basically. I mean who doesn't, right?

| Mae Ross: | Yes they do. |

| Bonnie Wallace: | And so they want to be famous, but that doesn't necessarily mean that they want to actually be an actor. What it takes to be an actor, what is means to act, they frequently know nothing about that and have never even taken an acting class or been in a school play. |

But they want to be famous, so they think they want to be actors, and you do your child a great disservice if you start to push them in that direction without having a chance to let them really explore it.

| Mae Ross: | They need to know what the craft of acting requires and that is why this online course, *Ten Lessons to Great Film Acting*, is so great. Because if they are teenagers, they all say they want to be on Disney, they want to be on Nickelodeon. We have kids coming into 321 saying that, but they change their mind, and then they say, "I really like acting." |

I see it all the time when kids come in and they're not sure, and then they discover they want to be an actor. We have Forest Wheeler, who's on *Fresh Off the Boat* on ABC, and he plays Emery and he came in a shy 9-year-old. I don't think he knew what he wanted to do. I spotted the talent and now of course he is on *Fresh Off the Boat*, which is a hit sitcom. So get into an acting class.

| Bonnie Wallace: | Say you talked to a teen that lives in the middle of the country. They are nowhere near L.A., and they can't move their family out. What can a young person do that's passionate about acting? What can they do where they are? |

Mae Ross:	Take an acting class. Show your parents just how passionate you are about it. Get into your little community theater, Dove Cameron did that … community theaters are all over the place, even in small town America. Get online and take some online classes. Again, *TenLessonstoGreatFilmActing.com*.
	Listen to podcasts, whether it be Bonnie's or anybody else out there, but definitely do get educated with it so you know what it is all about. Some parents say, "No, you have to wait until you are 18," so start saving money. And know that Hollywood is not going anywhere. You can get into it when you are 18, even if you are 12 now, and just let your parents know, you need to demonstrate how much you want to do this, so get into a class, get into a local theater and just show them.
Bonnie Wallace:	That literally gave me chills a second ago when you said Hollywood is not going anywhere. It's not. Hollywood is here. It's not going to be gone by the time you are able to get here, whenever that is.
Mae Ross:	Yes and remember, you are in it for the experience of acting. Just like a dancer loves to dance, you love to act. And when an agent says, "Why do you like to act?" you say, "Because it's fun. Because it is my passion." You do not want to say because of the money and the fame. But Hollywood is not going anywhere.

SCOTT SEDITA

Founder, Scott Sedita Acting Studios

"Keep it real, keep it honest. And if it's comedy, find the funny."

Renowned Los Angeles acting teacher Scott Sedita is the founder of the Scott Sedita Acting Studios, which offers a broad selection of on-camera drama and sitcom acting classes to enhance, expand and solidify an actor's craft. A former talent agent and casting director, Scott is the author of two books, *Scott Sedita's Guide To Making It In Hollywood: Three Steps To Success, Three Steps To Failure* and *The Eight Characters Of Comedy*. He's also the creator of *Scott Sedita's Actors Audition app*.

Alumni include Cameron Monaghan, Holly Taylor, Ross Butler, Haley Bennett, Chace Crawford, Brandon Routh, Josh Duhamel, Charles Melton, Lana Condor, Haley Lu Richardson, Kevin Alejandro, Chris Coy, and Joseph-David Jones.

Scott Sedita: Happy Pilot Season! I began my studio 22 years ago this month, and right at the beginning of pilot season. So, I was thrown into everything, which was kind of how I like it, you know what I mean? You learn as you go.

Bonnie Wallace: You told me as we were just sitting down that this is your eighth day working in a row.

239

Scott Sedita: Yeah, it's been busy. I do a lot of different intensives each weekend, so it keeps me busy, but I'm used to that. I was an agent in New York City when I was 22. After I got out of college … well, I had a job in Hollywood before I left college. I went to Boston University and studied film and acting and before I left, I had a job in the film industry in Los Angeles and then there was a writers' and directors' strike. I ended up having to go home to New York City and live with my mother in a one-bedroom apartment. So I took the first job I could get, which was that assistant agent job.

I kind of believe that everyone has different talents, and I have a talent to spot talent. That became very true and real when I was an assistant agent, because in no time I ended up leaving that smaller agency and going to another agency and becoming an agent. I was the youngest agent in New York City at 22. I didn't know very much, but I had a lot of things going on. I loved it and I believed in people and the people I believed in worked right away. I discovered Courtney Cox, Matt LeBlanc, Christopher Maloney, Michael Weatherly, Teri Polo. There were a lot of people there.

I was really good at what I did and I just burnt out of it, and I kind of wanted to go back to working with actors in a creative way. I also wanted to write as I did in college, so I gave it all up, I guess around 29 years old. And I moved to Los Angeles and I got some jobs writing, but in order to survive, my survival job was a casting director.

I worked for a great man named Danny Goldman, who was a huge casting director in that time. He mostly did commercials and infomercials and industrials and that type of stuff. And I went right into doing that.

And it was really interesting for me because as an agent you send people out, but you never get to see what they do in the casting room.

But as a casting director, I got to see what people actually did in the casting room. I got to see actors and how they could sabotage themselves in a casting room because, either they were unprepared or because fear set in or because they had certain expectations. So it was just interesting to me to see both sides of that. And during that time, Danny was so great, I ended up coaching actors during my lunch period. He'd let me do that and he lent me his studio at night so I could coach, and I ended up teaching classes there.

Then 22 years ago this month, in January 1998 I opened the studio. I had 10 students. Now we have hundreds. But at that time I had 10 students. There was that saying from *Field Of Dreams*, what was it?

Bonnie Wallace: If you build it they will come.

Scott Sedita: I know that's corny, but I think I said it to myself every day. And when you invest in yourself then you work really hard. I used to say, "I have a horrible boss, me." So I just taught and taught and I ended up building the space, getting more space. The interesting thing though, 22 years ago when I began, my classes were theatrical acting classes, and I concentrated on audition technique because that's kind of what I knew. I was an agent, and I was a casting director so it made sense that audition technique would be something that I would be good at.

I wasn't a scene study teacher but when I left Danny Goldman during that time, even just 10 years ago, the only casting directors that had cameras in the studio were commercial casting directors or industrial casting directors. Theatrical casting directors did not have a camera with the lights and the mic set up. That just hadn't started until maybe 10 years ago. So when I came over to do a theatrical acting class, I brought my camera and my lights and my mic and my blue backdrop that I had.

So I became the first theatrical acting coach who had a camera in the studio, and the interesting part about that is that I was ridiculed because a lot of people felt that an actor on camera in the process of learning how to act wasn't a good idea, and I understood that. But as I said, I didn't teach scene study, I taught audition tech.

People would say, "I mean the camera's great, but there are no cameras in auditions, so why do you have a camera in your theatrical?" I just felt it was really important for actors to see what they were doing on an audition. Also, to see how their essences were reading. And honestly, I was just comfortable teaching in front of a camera.

I think now every acting studio has a camera in the studio and just recently we completely upgraded our whole system here. We've been doing it throughout the years. But when I first started, I did mainly scenes that were dramatic, and the actors had to come and pick up the sides, like in real life back in the day. And then they had to come to class.

They weren't emailed out because there was nothing there. I got a fax machine and I started to fax them out, but that became a big pain. So I said just come and pick up your sides or it was a cold read, but the main things were always dramatic. I always did current TV and film type of stuff because I was a big TV watcher and I loved film. That's what I do on the weekend. I also was able, through my writing friends, to pick up pilots and scripts that were not yet produced, and I used to bring them into class.

I remember reading *American Beauty, American Pie, Sex In The City.* These weren't even out yet. I would bring them into class. It was fun. But this still stands when you come to study at the studio, you do a main scene and then you do what I call a "quick bit." That's the last thing you do at the end. It's like a dessert, and it's like a one-page scene. You might get a partner and you go out and you have seven minutes to put it all together.

I used to do comedy, and I realized by doing comedy that a lot of the students didn't really get a chance to do much comedy, because nobody was teaching text comedy. Not improvisational comedy or sketch comedy, but text comedy. So I gave them scenes from pilots, sometimes from *Friends*, but mostly from pilots they didn't know because I didn't want them to have some preconceived idea.

That is where my whole comedy side has come out in the studio. That's where *The Eight Characters Of Comedy* started, because it was actors who actually helped me. I saw the things that they were doing when they would do a comedy scene and they paraphrased, the rhythm was off, and it didn't work. And everybody looked around and asked, "Why wasn't that funny?" When they changed words or dropped words, they'd say, "Yeah, it's not working."

It's because comedy has a rhythm and I knew that from my writing comedy days. And I knew that there was a certain technique to do it. So I started to form a comedic technique 22 years ago in my class. As that progressed, I started making comedy the main scenes as well as drama, and that's where *The Eight Characters Of Comedy* started to bloom, because I saw different actors perform in different characters.

Bonnie Wallace: Can you talk a little more about *The Eight Characters Of Comedy*?

Scott Sedita: *The Eight Characters Of Comedy*, as I said, was begun 22 years ago as actors helped me kind of write it in a sense, because I could see what they were doing right and what they were doing, whether it was wrong … their mistakes really are what helps actors figure out what works and what doesn't work. And it began back then, but it was the eight characters of comedy that I started to see. If you had a particular actor who had an essence, let's say that was a little more sarcastic and cynical, they had a harder time comedically taking on a character that was hopeful and optimistic and perhaps naive. But if you gave that same cynical, sarcastic actor a role that had that essence in it, they were able to fit it like a glove and the humor would come alive.

That's when I started to discover. So I started to write *The Eight Characters Of Comedy* and that came out in 2004. It came out when there was no comedy on the air. So that's really an odd thing to happen. But it was the writers who really picked up the book first and they were writing their spec scripts for comedies that weren't on the air.

It was interesting because during that time, as the years went on, 2004, 2005, 2006, 2007, 2008, those writers would write me and say, "I'm writing my first spec script, I'm using your book, thanks." Or, "Now I'm a story editor" or "I got a job as a writer and I'm a story editor now," and all of a sudden, three or four years later, they were co-executive producers and the start of comedy was coming back. Not that my book had anything to do with it, but I feel like it obviously aided some of those people and kind of helped them.

I think it's the eight specific characters of comedy that writers use and work with, but the book has been out since 2004. It's sold over 250,000 copies. It's translated into Russian; it's going to be in Mandarin and Portuguese. It's helped me travel the world though I'm not a great traveler. I've gone to Australia, Sweden. I've gone all over Canada. I went to Norway. I always go to Canada now. That's fun. I've been to all of the United States really mostly doing the *Eight Characters of Comedy*... This is my second edition of the book, and it's ready to have a third edition soon. The second edition came out in 2014, and it's helped a lot of people and I'm really proud of that.

The class is still very popular. I do a one-day comedy intensive every month. This month I've done two of them. I'm going to do another one in a couple of weeks just because there's a lot of comedy right now.

This year is going to have a lot of comedy, especially multi-camera comedy. Thanks to Chuck Lorre. One of my students just booked a new series regular in the Chuck Lorre pilot.

Bonnie Wallace: Oh, that's fantastic! Congratulations. Would you say you have an overarching philosophy that guides your studio?

Scott Sedita: An overarching philosophy? Yeah, keep it real, keep it honest. And if it's comedy, find the funny because I've dealt with camera, I'm not theatrical. I'm not theater trained in that way to make something big and that's not my thing. I've always had cameras, so I've always made things ready for TV and film. Back 22 years ago as I started the studio, there's another thing I noticed.

The other thing I noticed was that actors didn't have a quick way to take their scripts and break them down for an audition. Now if it was a play, they understood what to do with that. But they didn't have necessarily an idea of how to take three-page sides and break them down. And that's where I came up with "WOFRAIM," which is my script analysis technique. That's what I put in my app. I was the first acting coach to have an app; that was about 10 years ago. It was funny because iTunes goes, "What's this?" They had no idea what it was.

And they didn't want to accept it. I had to go through a couple of variations of it for them to accept that this was interactive ... because they just didn't know what that was. But now it's done very well. It's still a very successful app and not only has my WO-FRAIM in it, but it has a bunch of other stuff, voice and speech exercises, practice scripts. I'm already starting to do a new version of it as well.

Bonnie Wallace: That is so cool. So you've got drama classes, and sitcom classes in the studio. Why do you break it down with these two approaches?

Scott Sedita: Because I have a method of how to do comedy. So in the method it's hard for an actor to delve deep into the trenches of drama and then the next week do a multi-camera comedy.

Bonnie Wallace: It's a big gear to change.

Scott Sedita: It's a big gear change, especially when classes should be a progression of things. I believe one week you're tackling this and then the next week you're tackling something that's close to the last thing, but it takes it to a new level so actors can grow in that way.

As I say, my classes are all audition technique classes. My Master Comedy class that I teach is for people who have gone through the one-day comedy intensive and who have already taken the ongoing sitcom classes here. Then they get to do my Master Comedy class, which is a combination of scene work and audition technique. The Wednesday is my Intermediate Audition Technique class. That's my signature class.

That's the one I've been doing for 22 years.

That particular class is an intermediate class. We do have classes for people who are new to that whole audition experience. I teach mostly advanced classes. We have other teachers here who teach, but Wednesday is open to people who have foundational acting and have studied and who have managers and agents who are about to get them. But my Thursday night class is called the Professional class and those are people who are series regulars.

Also, people who have worked their way up throughout, from this studio, from the nuts and bolts classes, to the scene study class, all the way up to my Wednesday Audition Technique class. And then they get to be invited to the Professional class, because I really feel like it's important for actors to know that they can grow at a studio and get to the higher tier class. That Professional class is a favorite class of mine. That takes all the different TV genres and every week you get to do something different, though we do not do multi-camera comedy.

Bonnie Wallace: What's the youngest age of a student that you'll accept?

Scott Sedita: Well, in the one-day comedy intensive, we do go younger than all our other classes. Our other classes really average the youngest at 15, 16. But we do take kids who we feel have foundational acting, who have agents, managers, who are not new to the business. So we had a 12-year-old yesterday in our class and you know what? He was great. It was great having him. But he's still 12. He's still 12 and he's in an adult class. I think it's a kid who can be in an adult class.

Once in a while I do the one-day comedy intensive for kids, which I really should do again. But otherwise it's mostly the one-day comedy intensive that we allow younger kids in.

Bonnie Wallace: So it sounds like your studio is mainly aimed at mid-teens into adults with the occasional exception, but you don't really have it striated, like this is the kid's class, this is the teen class…

Scott Sedita: Right. Absolutely. We do have people who are interested in the one-day comedy intensive who are kids and we meet with them. We meet with everybody. We're old school that way and we just see if we feel comfortable and they would feel comfortable in the one-day comedy intensive.

Can I tell you about my oddly favorite class? This is a new class and it's where I do ... I mean we have 53 people as series regulars. Yes. 53 alumni.

I'm very proud of that because people work at my studio ... if you know about my studio, you know that the people who come to my studio, especially in my classes, are people who work. Or people who are going to work, which is really more exciting to me. So I have this class, but it is once again for 15 and up, called the One Day On Camera Audition Intensive. But it covers—and this is the weird part about it—it covers how I have a method. I have found a method on how to book co-star roles.

Bonnie Wallace: Co-star. Not guest star. Not series regulars.

Scott Sedita: I went out to lunch with a manager who's a good friend of mine and I love her and she said, "What the hell are you doing? Why are you doing a co-star class? You're Scott Sedita. You have all these series regulars."

Because it's so much fun to watch somebody who's taken this One Day Co-star Intensive, so to speak, and then go out on a co-star audition, and book it. And it's their first job. It's like when I was an agent, it's so exciting for somebody to write me back and go, "I booked my first job." I am equally excited when someone says they booked a series regular, but I've also seen them book from a co-star to a series regular. So it's a new beginning for somebody, and for me, I'm happy that I could help them with a certain method I have for doing it that works.

Bonnie Wallace: That is so neat. You're the only person I've ever heard of who has a co-star class.

Scott Sedita:	I know. I started it about two or three years ago secretly and quietly. I love it. It's really fun. I get to work with these small roles that are so pivotal for a script. It teaches the actor the circumstances of a television show and understanding what your purpose is as that co-star role in that TV show. And it's important, and the acting has to be real. It has to be authentic. It has to be camera-ready. And you know what else it has to be? Because there are so many sight lines, you have to know sight lines. They have to see things that aren't there. I enjoy it. It's fun.
Bonnie Wallace:	I love it. It's interesting because everybody's always focused on being the big star. But how do you get there? Nobody goes from 0 to 60 in one jump. Co-stars are the gateway.
Scott Sedita:	They are. Commercials used to be, but you don't get as many commercials anymore. Back in the day, you'd book a lot of commercials, and the next thing you'd book is a co-star and then from the co-star the guest star. The reason the commercials and the co-star work well is because the commercials make you understand what look you have, and then what essence are you bringing forth.

In the old commercial you'd have the boy-next-door, the girl-next-door, the young mom, the young dad. So that gives you an idea of what kind of essence that you have. Now the co-star takes the same thing. It takes the look and the essence, but then it starts to filter more acting in, and the acting has to be real. It has to be honest. It can't pull focus from the series regulars, and that's an important thing.

Bonnie Wallace:	That is a huge thing.
Scott Sedita:	The week after, we get these emails going, "I booked my first co-star on *Criminal Minds* or *Modern Family.*" I feel good. I feel I can help somebody.
Bonnie Wallace:	Well, once you've booked a co-star it's like you're on the board now, right?
Scott Sedita:	Yes. It is a beginning. It's fresh. It's the beginning stages.
Bonnie Wallace:	Now you're on IMDb. Now you've got something, the little peg to hang your hat on. Now your agent and manager have something to send out.
Scott Sedita:	A lot of the upper agents and managers don't want to deal with them because they take a lot of time.
Bonnie Wallace:	Yes, but they can give you a little bit of a *real* reel, instead of a pretend reel, and suddenly they've got something to help shop you with, and get you in the door. That's so exciting. I love that you're doing that.
	You teach a lot of different classes that focus on auditions but for the people who may not be in L.A. and able to take your classes right now, any hot tips for auditioning?
Scott Sedita:	To be really honest, I would tell them to download my Actor Audition app. I know that sounds like a plug and it is. But at least you see a script analysis, an easy way. How to take a script and ask the questions that need to be asked, which is, what do I want from the other character? In this case, what do I want from the reader?

What do I want from that other person? Understanding that is the spine of any audition.

Because it's the spine of understanding the story that's being played. The other thing, I'm in the throes of writing my second edition to my book, *Scott Sedita's Guide To Making It In Hollywood*. So that's a very interesting book.

Bonnie Wallace: Let's talk about that because the subtitle is *Three Steps To Success, Three Steps To Failure* and I nosed around in that a little bit and it looked very interesting. I would love to have you talk about those steps.

Scott Sedita: It's not because of the three steps to success so much, because everybody has their thing. You know, mine is talent, competence and perseverance. But it's really about the three steps to failure, because the three steps to success is your want, but with every want there's an obstacle. And the obstacle for an actor is fear. So the book talks about fear and how it manifests into the three steps of failure. What actors do when it starts to happen.

See, actors don't have a blueprint. They don't go to school in the sense of a lawyer who has to go to four years of college and three years of law school and then doing an internship, or a doctor, or any of those, they don't have that. As an artist, you're more sensitive. You're more vulnerable. You should be because you're an artist. You're supposed to be there in the world picking up and absorbing what the world is putting out, so you as an actor can interpret that and be that.

But with actors, what happens is things go wrong, as every business does. As the start of rejection or disappointment sets in, fear sets in. Once fear sets in, then you're on the path of success taking a detour, and you're on the road to self-sabotage, and it starts very slowly, very slowly.

It starts very slowly and then all of a sudden it starts to hit. And it's important for actors to realize that, and to realize that how important fear is. The reason I wrote that book is from the perspective of me being an agent, a casting director and an acting coach. So that's the perspective of the whole book.

A few years ago, one of my actors who I really saw as someone who was going to be successful, started to show up to class late, and started not to do the work when he did show up. And so I went outside, where they were rehearsing. I went up to him and I said, "So what's going on?"

When you take my class, you're forced to read that book. And this is the whole reason because he looked at me and says, "I'm just self-sabotaging myself." Now, I can't help him necessarily stop self-sabotaging, but at least I pointed out that he understood that's what he was doing, because people don't recognize their fear, don't want to admit their fear, don't want to know that they're in their fear.

But the only way to deal with fear is first to acknowledge and then walk through it, work through it. Do whatever you need to do to work through it, because it's always going to be there, the more you work through your fear.

For example, I have no interest whatsoever in jumping out of a plane. You know, skydiving. Okay, that's not me. But I would imagine if someone was going to do that, first they prepared, took a class or were told how to do it, but as they're on the edge looking down, I'm sure there must be something that overcomes them, which is a sense of fear. Like, "Oh God, what could happen? What could go wrong here?"

But then because they want the joy of being able to do it because they practiced, they take the leap and of course they land on their feet.

That's exactly what actors have to do each time they walk into an audition, each time that they walk into their agent's or manager's office, each time they get up and do anything that has to do with their career, they have to walk through their fear and do the work.

Bonnie Wallace: To me, it takes profound courage to be an actor.

Scott Sedita: I agree.

Bonnie Wallace: And no less for really young people. I mean, regardless of age, to wake up in the morning, and do a bunch of work preparing for an audition that in your bones, you know your odds are not great at getting … and then to go out there, give it your very best shot, and get up and do it again the next day and again and again and again … talk about an act of faith and courage. It's incredible.

Scott Sedita: I agree with you 100%. It's tough, that's why you've got to love it. I think that when people come and study with me, I think that they think I'm very fair, and I guess funny, because we laugh a lot. It's important whether it's comedy or drama that we laugh a lot, but I think they would consider me very firm. And I think it's important to have that. I think sometimes they like to blow it up a little more that I'm edgier than I really am.

I think it's important for them to know that the business is a business, and that they can still be creative and still get support and love and still have a laugh and make sure that they have proper structure to be in this business. And with me, and the teachers here at the studio that they have someone who says, "This is the business, this is what happens in this business."

Bonnie Wallace: That creates a sense of safety, because it is a business. It's not just, "Oh I love to perform, therefore I should be an actress." Yes, that's a piece of it. It's an important piece, but there's so much more, which is what you're up to here in the studio.

What would be your advice on self-tapes? Self-tapes are a little bit different than auditions in the room, and they're here to stay.

Scott Sedita: Well, let me tell you my history of self-tapes, because you're talking to somebody who always had a camera in the studio.

The fact is that self-tapes always were a thing for me. What do I mean by that? I mean, we're talking about 20 years ago an agent would say, "Would you put somebody on tape and send it to me? A client of mine. I want to see how they're doing." Also, because I had a taping facility here, I became the person who would put people on tape for New York. A lot of the soap operas in New York and things like that.

Then we would send them home with a VHS tape, or a DVD later, and we were always able to do that so they could see their work and show their work to their agents and managers. Self-taping, the whole idea of what's happening in the business now, it's really only in the last few years that it's happened and it's an oddity that's happened. But it's not odd to me. Or for the actors that have been in my studio to self-tape, because that's a usual thing that they're doing over here. Of course, the audition class has helped them in that process, because they're constantly seeing what it should look like on screen through my lens, through my TV monitors as they're watching.

But also because last pilot season I added self-tapes to my courses, and to be perfectly honest, I really didn't know what I was doing. "Here's your audition, I'm giving you three or four days ahead of time, work on it, self-tape it and then bring it in." I have the capability in the studio to put it on the computer and to flash it up on the television. I'm giving you all my secrets away; I don't know if I should.

What I learned... first of all, I said to myself, "This is going to be interesting to watch 20 people in my class bring these back. But I'm sure the look will be great. I'll still have to work on the acting portion." Well I was surprised with what was coming down. People weren't necessarily on top of what the piece needs to look like, and also the sound of it. So I was able to help people and correct them and lead them into ways that was helping them. You can buy a light kit for 100 bucks, they're on Amazon.

Bonnie Wallace: Yes, you don't need a fancy studio.

Scott Sedita: Exactly. You don't. There are just certain angles that the camera needs to be that are important for self-tapes.

But this is ever the flow. It's going to change as we go along. Unfortunately, actors are going to need to be able to self-produce. We've got to self-produce which is really a good thing for actors in general to do, create their own material.

But self-taping is self-producing, which means you've got to get a reader who's good, who's not too loud, who is hopefully the right sex, even though that doesn't and shouldn't matter. It will start to matter. If you were doing a love scene in the old days, if you're a guy and the casting director's a male, you'd have to read it with him. That's the way it goes.

But because things have become so much more sophisticated, or you have more opportunities, I fear that the casting world or the world of who's accepting these self-tapes is going to want much better quality as it goes down.

So the best thing that you could do on a self-tape is make sure the sound isn't tinny, that you have a backdrop that brings the best out of you, and most importantly, that it's chest-up to give you a little head room, and the lighting's good. And then it's all about the acting. It's the first 15 seconds as I teach my actors. What happens in that first 15 seconds? Because now watching the self-tapes, there's a button just like when I was a casting director that you can fast forward.

Bonnie Wallace: Right. Or not even fast forward, just delete, and next.

And that's part of why they're becoming so popular because you can blow through a hundred auditions in an hour on tape.

Scott Sedita: I'm so happy you said, "Delete, next" because that's what I say, but I don't want to sound mean.

Bonnie Wallace: Unfortunately, it's a fact.

Scott Sedita: It's true. It's the first 15 seconds.

Bonnie Wallace: If you have a thousand people whose tapes you need to blow through in a day, I think it's human nature to want to eliminate as many as possible quickly, so you can focus down on the ones that seem promising. So anytime you see something that's like, "No, no, no …," you're buying yourself time to focus down on the ones who look interesting.

Scott Sedita: Right. You know what you're talking about. It's a phenomenon that's happening. I think I was starting to say that it wasn't until 10 years ago that theatrical casting directors had cameras, and it really was just little cameras with whatever lighting was available, fluorescent. Now they're starting to upgrade. So now all theatrical auditions are on tape. Very few are not on tape unless there's some sort of pre-read with the casting director that could be, but most of them are on tape.

So it's really important for an actor … it's so funny, I've been talking about this for 22 years … to make sure they understand their sight lines, and that they're not looking in the camera when they're trying to look at something, that it's not directly into the camera. And that they make contact with the reader and have a reader that brings out the best in them.

Unfortunately, now it's going to be up to them. My prediction, and it is not necessarily one I want to see, but if the scene is outside and I'm walking and talking at the same time, somebody is going to go outside and do a self-tape with someone filming them, walking and talking. And some casting director or some producer is going to say, "I like that.

That's good. Wow, this is what I want it to look like."

Bonnie Wallace: It's almost like you're talking about production values at this point-

Scott Sedita: Yes. Yes.

Bonnie Wallace: Which is interesting because at a certain level, it's not fair.

Scott Sedita: It's not.

Bonnie Wallace: It shouldn't be right that things other than the straight-up talent and look or the appropriateness of an actor for a role are being considered. But they are, because we're all human beings and we're affected by these things.

Scott Sedita: Yes, absolutely. And that's where I was when I looked at the self-tapes last year the first time I did it in class, and now we do them all the time. It was an education for me because I said, "This is annoying to listen to because it's so tinny. No one wants to listen to this sound. Even though your acting may be good, and it might possibly project from the terrible production of it, but your job is to do the best. And you don't need a lot technically to be the best."

In New York City, in the old days there were theater people who got together. We traveled, we helped each other. Somebody who has a really good setup for a tape should say, "Hey listen, you can use my

259

self-tape setup, if you will be my reader. Let's do it together. Let's form a group so we can help each other."

It would be much easier for people, and people just have to be willing to put themselves out to help others so they can receive help when they need it.

Bonnie Wallace: Community is important for all of us, but it is very important for actors because this life can be a little bit isolating.

Scott Sedita: Yes. It's Los Angeles. "Do I really want to go to Santa Monica? Chino Hills. I'm not sure." But that's what happens. I understand it.

It's part of fear. We let ourselves put things in our way that are not comfortable or pleasurable to stop ourselves from having a career. If you can, kind of get your work ethic over that and just do it.

See, parents know it. There are so many parents who will drive their kids for a freaking hour into an audition. You know what I mean? And on a continual basis, and do whatever they need, because they're adults and they understand what needs to be done.

But a lot of actors, especially young actors, don't realize. I've had so many actors who are older actors or started when they were older, and they've read the *Making It In Hollywood* book and they said, "Oh, if I just had this book when I was 20, 21 years old, because you're talking about all the stuff of fear that we encounter." Of course, you encounter it because you're artists. You're supposed to be vulnerable and sensitive. You're supposed to be that, and of course everything hurts more.

Bonnie Wallace: If you're going to be a fine artist, you're going to feel those feelings and then you have to develop the tools to deal with them. I really love your whole perspective in so many different ways, but I love the honesty of using taping as a really good tool to help an actor see themselves become better. I always thought that that's part of why my daughter Dove did so well so quickly. She would mercilessly, consistently watch herself on tape. She had me tape everything she did, and she would watch it like a football player watches playbacks of their own games to learn.

Scott Sedita: Well, she had a mother like you, as I was just saying. She had somebody standing in her corner for her and watching over what was going on. I give speeches at some things that have kids. I would say, "Mom, you need to read the book, if the kids are too young to read the book, because you need to see what's going to happen to them if they do get to success, or if they don't get it right away. So you have to make choices with that. And it's important for you to see that it is a career. It is a business and it takes time."

Bonnie Wallace: It takes time like any other career. You'd never in a million years think, "Oh you know, I want to be a lawyer tomorrow, or I want to be a professional football player tomorrow." And then step out on the field. You don't get to do that. You don't get to do that with acting either. You have to put in the time.

What would be your advice for a young person who's not in a major market right now? Not near New York or L.A.?

Scott Sedita:	Well, they get the best thing ever. This is the best time ever to be somebody who lives in mid-America. Number one, wherever you live, and as hard as this thing may be, you need to get into acting class. I realize a lot of schools are closing down their music and drama departments, which is just terrible. So whatever possibility you can, just explore in acting class, in improv class, anything you can possibly do.
	Then you have this great opportunity that so many actors before you didn't have. And once again it comes back to two words: self-tape. Find TV shows. If you have kids of the age of *The Goldbergs* or *Modern Family* at the beginning stages in 2008 when comedy started coming back, go watch them on Netflix or go watch them in syndication, and record them from your iPhone and then translate them for the young kids, and then put the kid on tape using that same dialogue and be the reader.
	You can look at *Modern Family* from the first two years and you have ages of all kids, because they started at 10, 12, 13. It's all around those ages. So that would be great. I think even Luke was maybe 8 if not 10. I'm not sure.
	The parent can transcribe it, have the kid work on it, and they can be the reader and they can put it on tape and they can find agents. Back in the day we only had a little book that had agents. Now you can go online, see if the agent or manager is legit. You can go with IMDb, you can see all the legitimacy. There shouldn't be any more, "I don't know if they're good or not." Go and check.
Bonnie Wallace:	IMDb Pro is your personal gold mine and it's worth every penny. The first month is free. My goodness, there's no excuse.

Scott Sedita:	Absolutely. Find if they take tape submissions. People realize that there are kids from all over the country. I also think that way back when, there were a lot more of those expos for kids.
	I think some of them were legit, and some of them weren't. I don't know. I don't think there are many of them anymore. Whether that's a good thing or a bad thing ... but what I mean by that is that you don't have that opportunity anymore, so self-tape is once again an opportunity.
	And you can do it all in your own time. You can do take after take after take after take until you find it's a good take.
Bonnie Wallace:	Which will help you get better and better, and also reminds you that there's no excuse for turning in something that's second rate, because everybody who looks at your tape knows you had time to put it together, so do your best.
Scott Sedita:	Right. This could be interesting now. This pilot season, I think a lot more self-tapes are going to be happening. We'll see. I've already coached four people in pilots, and three were going in and one was self-tape, but I'm doing one right after this.
Bonnie Wallace:	After we wrap here. Anything else you'd like to share, Scott?
Scott Sedita:	No. I think it's important for the actor to say to themselves, "What is it that I want?" And every day you have to get up and ignite that want.
	"I want to be a successful actor. How do I go about

263

doing that? How do I do that every day?" How do I invest in myself like I invested in myself 22 years ago with just 10 students to open up a studio in a beautiful location like Larchmont, which is way more expensive than I could do.

But I believed in myself and I believed that people would come, and I believe that if you believe in yourself and you work at it—I mean work at it—it will happen. The reason I know that is because I've seen a lot of actors who just booked their first co-star role and they went all the way to a series regular and are now all huge actors as well.

I hope I was helpful.

MARCIE SMOLIN

Co-Founder, The Actors Circle

"Try everything that we do. Figure out what works best
for you and put that into your bag of tricks."

Marcie Smolin is an acting teacher and co-founder of The Actors Circle, one
of the top acting studios for film and television studies. The Actors Circle
provides film and television workshops for actors of all ages and abilities in
their Los Angeles studio. They also provide weekly classes on film and TV
technique, private coaching, taping for auditions, and semi-private and corpo-
rate specialty workshops. Their actors have gone on to win Emmys, Oscars,
Tonys, and even a Grammy.

Alumni include Joseph Gordon-Levitt, Jason Reitman, Jessica Williams,
Sara Paxton, Miles Heizer, Ross Butler, Willa Holland, Wyatt Oleff, Jeremy
Sumpter, Thomas Ian Nicholas, Kelli Garner, Taylor Lautner, Nik Dodani,
Taylour Paige, Denzel Whitaker, Kristos Andrews, Cale Ferrin, Sara Ramos,
Marc Price, Drake Bell, Thomas Kuc, Erin Sanders, Matthew Underwood,
Guy Wilson, and David Lago.

Bonnie Wallace: Marcie, you started as a child actor yourself. And you
                    were a series regular on two different shows, as well
                    as a standup comedian for many years. Why did you
                    decide to focus on teaching?

Marcie Smolin:	I love teaching. It's my first love. Funny story though, how it happened. My former partner at The Actors Circle, who I started The Actors Circle with, Kevin McDermott, was my coach when I was a kid. At another acting school. And I loved his way. When he started his old studio, Center Stage L.A., I followed him there and he trained me to be a coach, and I would work with the young kids because I was only 18 or 19 at the time.

Then my career took off, and I went on my way, and then I got in a very bad accident and I couldn't work. I couldn't walk. I was in a wheelchair. I was sitting home feeling sorry for myself and I got a wrong number. I answered the phone, and I recognized the voice and I went, "Kevin McDermott?" And he said, "Yes." I said, "This is Marcy Smolin."

Marcie Smolin: And we talked for a minute and he says, "You know, you were my favorite coach." I told him about the accident and he said, "Have you ever thought about coaching?" And I said, "Well, I'm in a wheelchair. I can't walk." And he said, "You don't need to walk." And I went that night to his studio, I taught a class. It was like I was meant to be there. And the rest is history.

Bonnie Wallace: That is an amazing story. It really does make you feel like you have to pay attention to the clues…

Marcie Smolin: You really do. Sometimes the worst things can turn into the best forks in your road. Because I really, really love what I do. Kevin closed his old studio. We opened The Actors Circle together, and then he retired years ago. I've been on my own there for ten years. The Actors Circle's been in existence for 15 years.

I love it there. And I love the studio because we've been in the same location. We built it ourselves. I mean I built some of the walls. And my students have gone on and they've done other things, but you never know who's going to walk in the door. I'll be in a class and a former student will walk in, and they'll just sit down. "Do you mind if I sit in and do my thing?" And I love that they always have a home there.

Bonnie Wallace: That's a really special thing. There are a lot of studios in L.A., but probably not very many that fall into that category.

You've worked with some incredibly successful actors, including Joseph Gordon-Levitt, Jessica Renee Williams, Ross Butler, Willa Holland, and Wyatt Oleff. What do you think explains your students' high rate of success?

Marcie Smolin: Be good.

Bonnie Wallace: There you go. Okay, everybody, just be good.

Marcie Smolin: Be good. But work hard. Work hard. Work on your technique, be a good actor. Everybody on that list is extremely devoted to getting good, and getting better, and working on a project and then going back to class. Working on a project and learning and growing. We are in a time where social media is a deciding factor in who's being cast. Well those people, if they don't have any technique to back up with, they're not going to go any further.

Bonnie Wallace: There's a lot of anxiety around that right now. And what I've been seeing is that it's not typically so much that an actor or actress will get cast because of their social media following. It's more like if it's down to two people, and everybody in the room is saying, "I don't know, toss a coin. They're both fabulous. They'd both be great. I don't know." And then one of them has a significantly bigger social media following, that person will probably get the role. Is that kind of how you see it?

Marcie Smolin: That is what's happening. A friend of mine is the head of production at a big company. And when he came in and took over that job, he was told that he had to have a certain number of influencers in all of his shows. They do more kid-oriented programming and he's also a director and he was like, "Whoa." I had to go in to work with a lot of the people that they ended up casting because they didn't know the first thing about being on a set.

Bonnie Wallace: Just because you've got a bunch of Instagram followers doesn't mean you know what you're doing on a set.

Marcie Smolin: Listen, it is important. No matter what my feelings are about it, I do it myself. I treat it as a game. I have one for The Actors Circle. I have a personal one. My personal one, I created a whole character and I just decided to have fun with it, because I still do work in front of the camera. And I have to do this. I know for a fact that whenever any of my students go in and meet with new representation, they look at their social media before the actor ever walks in the door. And even if they decide they're going to sign them, they say, "You have to be this, you have to do this, and you have to get this many followers." There's a whole thing they have to follow.

Bonnie Wallace:	There isn't a contract that I've ever seen, that Dove's had to sign, that didn't have some stipulations around social media, in terms of what had to be posted, when it had to be posted, and what the requirements were around that. And then just as much, what couldn't be posted. It's just part of an actor's job these days.

Marcie Smolin:	That is something that I definitely talk about with my students. "Be careful what you put up there."

Bonnie Wallace:	You can take a photo that you feel is just a photo of you in your trailer, but you're unaware that in the background you're catching something that's a reveal, that production has spent maybe millions of dollars trying to keep the wraps on until the right day. And you've just revealed it. So mindfulness is really important. Again, these projects, these movies and these TV shows, nobody's going to throw away their years of work and investment by casting someone who doesn't have the chops. It's just that if it's down to a couple of people who've got the chops, it's the social media that may make the deciding factor.

Marcie Smolin:	And also, it's a factor in building your career. I said the most important thing is to be good. It's not the only thing. It's not. If that were the only thing, everybody that we know and love that's brilliant would be doing well, but some people don't do the other things. And there are other factors that go into it.

Bonnie Wallace: Well, let's move into some of those factors. Your school teaches five areas of concentration in your ongoing curriculum. You teach scene study, cold reading, interview technique, improv and character development. Could you break down the basics of those, and explain why they're important?

Marcie Smolin: Sure. Scene study, it goes back to what I said, being good. You need to know what to do with the script when you get it. How to break it down, backstory, character development, your relationships. You need to do all of that, and you need to know to spend time with the script, and spend time with the character, and spend time with the relationships. And take it to the next level.

But on the flip side of that is cold reading, where I will give my students a script and they have 10 minutes with it. You also have to know how to do that, because you're not going to get to the point where you're filming unless you can walk in the door and do a cold reading. And do it well.

Bonnie Wallace: And there are techniques.

Marcie Smolin: Yes. And, different techniques for different people. I don't have one cold reading technique. Because we are all different. Everybody's different. Some people are naturally great cold readers. Some people need help with certain ways of handling the script and all of that. Everybody's different.

Interview technique. Well, you're not going to get to the point where they're going to pay attention to your cold reading unless they've decided they like you.

You need to know what to do from the second you walk in the door. You need to know how to make connection, and eye contact, and be interesting.

Bonnie Wallace: An audition is an interview. And people don't really put that together all the time.

Marcie Smolin: No, it's true. There are actors who really feel that they just want to get to the script. They just want to get through that part. "Let me show you what I have." And that's all that should matter. But it's not all that matters.

Bonnie Wallace: Who you are as a person actually matters. Because it's a human endeavor. It's a true co-creation. And you've got to know that the people you're co-creating with are going to be pleasant characters.

Marcie Smolin: That you want to spend time with. Especially during pilot season.

When you're meeting an actor, and they're also looking at the actor thinking, "Do I want to work with them five years from now, day in and day out? Will they not disappoint me? Will they be pleasant? Will they be fun?"

Bonnie Wallace: "Will they be reliable? Will they be high maintenance?"

Marcie Smolin: "Will they show up?" Right, and you know what? Someone that walks in the door and says, "I just want to get to my script." That screams high maintenance right there. Right there, that's a red flag.

Bonnie Wallace: Everybody could probably use some interview technique. What about improv and character development?

271

Marcie Smolin:	Character development goes hand in hand with scene study, but we take it a step further. There are times people spend a lot of time with the same character. You, as an actor, you want to be different, and original, and make strong choices with characters, and bring characters that are rich and full of life, and that people fall in love with. And you have to spend time with them.
Bonnie Wallace:	I hear a lot of, "Make strong choices," in the industry. And I instinctively feel like I know what that means. But could you spell that out for the people who are thinking, "What the heck does she mean by that, make strong choices? How do I do that?"
Marcie Smolin:	That's a great question. I love that question.
	You get a breakdown for an audition. You've seen a million of them. Sometimes they just tell you very generic things: Girl, 15 to 18, blonde, sunny disposition. Well, okay. Why does she have a sunny disposition? Is she a cheerleader? Is she somebody who reads a lot and is very soulful?
	There are a lot of different choices that you can make. You don't want to go with just the obvious. And you don't want to just take everything at face value. But, on the other side of that, where people run into a problem … make a strong choice. But don't make a stupid choice.
	If a character is described as having a sunny disposition, don't come in dressed all goth with piercings. Because that's just not smart.
Bonnie Wallace:	You're just wasting everybody's time if you do that. Thank you for spelling that out a little bit better than most people do.

Marcie Smolin:	I'm very big on improv. Improv is really important. And having a strong improv background is a must. I love improv. We do bonus improv things at the studio all the time. We have improv jams once a month where everybody, past and present, comes down and for hours, we just improv.
	There are many casting directors, many directors out there, who work improvisationally in their auditions. There are times when you can walk in and they're just not going to use the script at all. There are many big films, I know, that students of mine have been at casting, where they didn't see a script until they showed up. There are big directors out there who don't like to release their material. And a lot of times, people want to see how directable you are.
Bonnie Wallace:	And sometimes they will deliberately set up scenes, and direct the actress to improv, and see how it goes. I've seen that myself. And you don't want to be the actor who freezes and says, "I need lines."
Marcie Smolin:	I have people come in sometimes and say, "Well, I don't really like improv. I just want to focus on scene study and cold reading." And I tell them, "Well, you're not in the right place. Because we're going to do all of that. You will improv here."
Bonnie Wallace:	It sounds like a place where you could really develop those skills. That's exciting. I mean, every casting director I think I have ever, ever talked to, that is one of the first things out of their mouths, is the importance of at least a comfort level with improv.

Marcie Smolin: Yeah. They look on actors' resumes to see what their Improv background is. It's important that people have an improv background. But don't lie and say you studied at the Groundlings, and then come in and not be able to improvise. That's bad.

Bonnie Wallace: Thank you for saying that. It doesn't get said enough, and it's really hard to understand if you're not in Los Angeles and really in this. But truly everybody is connected to everybody here at a certain level, and you just can't lie about anything. Because if you say you were in a particular show, chances are they know the person who cast it, or directed it, or wrote it, or something. It's likely they're going to ask you about it. And then, where are you?

Marcie Smolin: Well, there have been people who lie and put my name on their resume, that they've studied with me. And then they may go in, and they're reading for somebody ... I have a cousin who's a producer. "Oh, that's my cousin. Wait, let me call her." They'll call me and ... I remember everybody. And if I don't remember them, they're all on my computer. So I will double-check before I say, "I have no idea who that is," but basically, I remember everybody.

My basic philosophy at the studio is that everybody is different. Everybody, every actor comes from a different place. We don't all cold read the same. We don't all have the same skills. Some of us are stronger in some areas than others. There is no formula for being a good actor. That's why I teach a lot of different techniques, and then some of my own. Introduce people to everything. Because no one technique is the be-all and end-all for every actor. Everybody responds differently. And I always say to my students, "Try everything that we do. Figure out what works best for you, and put that into your bag of tricks."

Bonnie Wallace: And if it doesn't work for you, it's okay. Because it's not one-size-fits-all.

That makes so much sense to me. And I also love that you teach students of every age and ability. So how does The Actors Circle segment those students, age-wise? Obviously you don't have 5-year-olds working with 18-year-olds.

Marcie Smolin: No. The kids' classes are separated by age. So we have the younger class, we have tween class, and we have teen class. The adults, from 18 on, they're all together. We have a lot of adults at the studio. A lot of my students grew up and didn't want to go somewhere else, so that's how that started.

I have students at the studio who have been there from the beginning. Because they'll go, they'll work on a project, they'll come back ... and all abilities. Of course, I love working with amazing actors. But also, there is nothing like seeing the light go on in someone's eyes and watching them fall in love with acting. I'm going to cry. Watching them fall in love with acting, it's one of my favorite things. And also, it's okay to take acting class if you're not an actor, because it helps with so many other things.

Bonnie Wallace: I'm such a fan of that. I have felt all my life that acting classes are probably a good idea for anybody. They do so many good things for people, regardless of what you end up doing.

275

Marcie Smolin: I have a guy in my class on Monday night who's an E.R. nurse. He works 12-hour shifts and he needed an outlet. And he took my class, and after a couple months I said to him, "I hate to break this to you, but you're a really good actor." And now he's got an agent. I broke him. I broke this wonderful nurse. Nursing is actually a good actor job, because he works at night, and he goes to the auditions during the day. But I feel a little bad about that.

Bonnie Wallace: Well, and the truth is, mixing actors with different abilities is great because we can all learn something from anybody. If you see somebody in front of you doing really fine work, you can speed up your process.

Marcie Smolin: And on the flip side of it, it's really good for the actors who've been doing it a long time. Because you don't always work with someone on your level. You need to know how to make that work.

Bonnie Wallace: If you're on a set, it's not necessarily true that you're acting opposite somebody who's got the same level of ability you do.

Marcie Smolin: It's very often that doesn't happen. So you have to know how to make that work. You have to know how to bring that other person up, and work together, and not be an idiot about it.

Bonnie Wallace: Yes, you have to make your partner look good.

Marcie, in addition to your extensive experience as a professional actor, you have a bachelor's degree in theater arts and a master's in screenwriting. What are your thoughts about the pros and cons of going to university for acting training versus going straight to a more à la carte approach? In other words, skipping the university path. Because there are those two different choices: "I'm 18, do I just go straight to Los Angeles, or do I take four more years of school?" For many actors, it's a tough question.

Marcie Smolin: I did get my degree in theater arts because, back then, that's what everybody did. But for me, college theater does not definitely prepare you. It's fun. It's great. I loved college. My suggestion is... I never tell people, "Don't go to college." I think college is really important. Study something else and take acting classes.

I don't think a degree in theater is necessary. And a degree in theater will not really get you in the door anywhere. But if you have a degree in something else, you're a really interesting person.

Bonnie Wallace: I think it really varies from person to person, but getting a degree in theater, and spending all that money doesn't guarantee you anything.

Marcie Smolin: You will learn great things. I loved every minute of my college experience. I love college theater programs. When I talk about being good, there are things that you will do in college theater that you don't do in classes in Los Angeles or New York. Are they necessarily things that are going to help you on film and television? Probably not.

As a matter of fact, I have to spend time undoing things sometimes. Because ... I feel terrible saying this ... some people will get mad, but it's just true. If you want to be an actor in regional theater all of your life—and what a great life that is, by the way, I love theater—get your degree in theater. And that's all amazing. If you want to work in film and television, probably a college theater department would not be the route to go.

One of my former students, who was with me for years, is so talented. And one day he came to me and he said, "I don't like working in film." And he moved. He lives in Indiana, and he started a huge theater festival there, which has really taken off. And he and his wife make a living doing that. They have a life in the theater. And he is one of the happiest people I know. I'm jealous of him. So that's a great life. For film and television, for myself for example, I was lucky enough to have somebody in the audience of a play that I was in, in college. And the day after I graduated college, I was on a film set.

Again, I've had lucky moments in my life. After four years of college theater, my first line that I spoke on that set was so loud. And I was lucky enough to be working with Martin Landau in a scene. And he said, "Oh dear, come here." He pulled me aside.

He gave me several pieces of advice. And he gave me a great piece of advice that I share with my students all the time about finding your light. He said, "Whenever you're on a set, close your eyes, look up, and make sure your face is in the sun. Because if it is, you will have much less of a chance of ending up on the cutting room floor." And I swear to you to this day, I always close my eyes and ... it's a great tip.

Bonnie Wallace: So we've been talking about theater, and I want to talk a little more about it. A lot of young actors fall in love with theater first, before moving into TV and film. And they cut their teeth on theater because those opportunities are more readily available outside of L.A. They just are. What do you think are some of the biggest differences between theater versus film and TV? And what are some similarities?

Marcie Smolin: When someone comes to the studio from somewhere else, and they've done a lot theater, I can say to them immediately, "Ah, you've done a lot of theater." They will do their first scene in class, and they will project out to the audience. And I go, "You're on a film set now."

The studio is lit like a film set. And I block the scenes like film scenes. So if your back is to somebody, it's okay, because they're picking you up somewhere else. Theater actors will project too much. They will look out to the audience, they will cheat out.

Bonnie Wallace: It's true, that training gets into your bones. Your body feels that it's doing the right thing. It is doing the right thing, if you're on a stage.

Marcie Smolin: Sure. And on film, you have to remember that the camera picks up everything. It picks up nuance. So a lot of the things that you would do to play out to the back of the house, on camera, will look crazy. Too much. It will look like mugging.

And it's really hard for theater actors, a lot of times when they're training in film, because they don't think they're doing enough. And they think they're being dead and boring. And basically what you're doing on film is you're creating life.

And you have a job, you have one job. You want people to believe you. And you do that by being a believable human being. You don't have to be bigger than life. You don't have to cheat out. You don't have to do any of those things.

Bonnie Wallace: Some of my favorite actors are the ones who, when the camera runs across their face, you feel like you can read their thoughts just by looking at their eyes, by seeing something flicker across their eyes.

What advice do you have for young actors who are approaching an audition in general?

Marcie Smolin: Well, in the last five years, things have changed so much. So many auditions are taped now. Even if you're in L.A. or in New York.

I spend a lot of time during the day with people coming in and taping their auditions for them. And there are different things that are expected of you on a taped audition than an in-person audition. When you're going to audition in person, be prepared. Don't count on just getting the sides there and going outside and going, "I got this." Do whatever you can to have the sides. Get them at least 24 hours in advance. If you are doing a union project, they have to provide them.

If you are new and you're working off of Actors Access and L.A. Casting, and you're going for student films, and indie films, and web series, and things like that, you don't always get as much time with the material. So if they haven't provided the material, get there an hour early. Grab the material, don't sign in, go somewhere. Sit in your car.

Give yourself time with the material. Really know it. And, work on it out loud. Don't work on it in your head. Things sound different in your head than they do out loud. You don't want to ever walk into a room having the first time you've uttered those words be in there. Because you know how it is when you're reading something, and then you say it out loud, and you think, "Ooh, my voice sounds funny. What is that? That sounded so different in my head."

Bonnie Wallace: Your mouth handles the words differently than your brain does.

Marcie Smolin: Absolutely. There's reading words and speaking words.

Bonnie Wallace: Right. And there's always something you can do if there's a word you're not sure about. Look it up or ask the casting director.

Marcie Smolin: Yes. And the more you say something out loud, the more you're finding the nuances. Rehearsal's important. It's very important. Don't sign in until you're ready to go in the room. Sometimes people will come, and they'll sign in, and then get material, if there's a material provided. Or they'll go in and they'll look around, and think, "Ooh, okay, maybe I need a little more time with this...

I always tell people this: "You have enough friends. Do not make them in the waiting room."

There are very nice people in the industry, and there are some that are not nice. And there are people that are really good at psyching you out.

And they will say things like, "Oh, it's so good to see you. I have had 15 auditions this week. I love this casting director. I was at dinner at her house last night. She brings me in for everything." Most of it's not true, but it takes nothing, when you're nervous about an audition, to have your insides go, "Ugh."

If you can hear the people auditioning in the other room, don't let it change your choices. Don't make choices based upon things you might overhear. They might be laughing. It doesn't mean it's the right way. You don't know why people are laughing in the room. So stick with your choices. And going back to what we were talking about before, when you go in the room, make eye contact, be a nice person. Be interesting. When they ask you questions about yourself, don't answer with one word. Always find things to talk about, and have it not be about acting.

That's a big mistake a lot of people make. They'll come in and the casting director will say to them, "Tell me something about yourself." "Oh, I love acting. I act alone in my bedroom. I've wanted to be an actress since I was five." Well, how many times have they heard that story? Everybody in the waiting room is an actor because you're there auditioning. But if you talk about something really interesting, "I just climbed a mountain." "Oh really? Where?" "I just got back from this. I'm taking a tap dancing class, isn't that weird?" I mean whatever. Think about things that people might want to talk to you about. Be good and be interesting.

Bonnie Wallace: But authentic. Don't make something up.

Marcie Smolin: And don't lie, yes.

Bonnie Wallace: So any special advice for audition self-tapes? It is such an important skill at this point. And as we mentioned, even if you're in the major markets, they will do the first round of auditions more and more with self-tapes. So if you're not good at that, even though you might be blocks away from the casting office, you'll never get in there. Because you need to make the first cut. How can people do better self-tapes?

Marcie Smolin: There are things that people think are important that are not, and there are things that are really important that people will let go of. We do a lot of auditions taping at the studio just because I was so sick of seeing people's bad audition tapes. You don't have to spend a lot of money on an audition tape. As a matter of fact, sometimes that will be annoying. If directors and producers are looking through a bunch of tapes, they don't need to see fancy titles. "This is ...," with flashes of your headshot, and musical effects, and all of this.

Again, I'm going to go back to my theme, be good. It has to be well lit. It has to have good sound. You can do it in your bedroom if you have good lighting, but you have to have good lighting, good sound, and a plain background. And the person reading with you should speak in a whisper. That's all.

Bonnie Wallace: Just enough for you to hear, because they're not auditioning.

Marcie Smolin: I'm sorry to all the self-tape studios around here, which I think are great. And I would definitely call one in an emergency, if I had no one to tape me. But I always encourage actors to get a group of friends that you can get each other's backs. Because you're going to have to do so many of them, and you're going to go broke.

But there are also great self-tape places that, in case of emergency, you don't want to send in a tape that you've done in your car. With traffic and while you're driving on the freeway.

Parents will send tapes to me. "Can you look at this?" And I ask, "Why do I see you filming in the mirror behind them?" And sometimes people will build an elaborate set in their house, and it's too much. Or it's a sheet that's rippling. A plain wall is fine. If you're going to invest in anything, invest in some good lighting. Cheaply on Amazon, you can do it for under a hundred dollars. You really can. You can set up your self-taping studio. And a tripod, not a wobbly hand. Tripod, lighting, sound.

Bonnie Wallace: Tripods are so important because not only does that save you from being the next accidental *Blair Witch Project* and making everybody ill if they watch your video, but it frees up the hands of the person that you're reading with, so they can then turn the pages of the sides. It's just a good idea. And you can get little tiny adapters for cell phones, and that will allow them to fit onto a standard tripod. Or you can get a little baby desktop tripod.

Marcie Smolin: Or, I love the ones that bend. The gorilla tripods, they're great.

Bonnie Wallace: And they can wrap around things too. They're just fantastic.

Marcie Smolin: When I tape people, I have cameras. If they're in a hurry, I'll use their phone. So they can just upload it to Eco

Cast right there and then, we go over it, and I'll edit it for them. Have iMovie on your phone, if you have an iPhone. Have iMovie so you can put everything together nicely.

Another thing though, is if you can't find anyone to self-tape with you, there's a remote control that you can buy for your phone.

I make all my students buy them. It's about $10 on Amazon. It's a little remote control that works with an iPhone or an Android. You put your camera on a tripod, tape yourself, have a friend call you, and have them read with you over the phone or set up a computer. If you need to see their face, you can Skype in with them, put them under the camera. And I actually like it, personally ... it's like selfies. And they look fine.

Bonnie Wallace: That's brilliant.

Marcie Smolin: $10. Because you don't want to go broke auditioning. I coach people for auditions too, and sometimes they'll call me for coaching, and it's a three-line part. And I will say to them, "Let's just talk about it. Save your money for when it's something really chunky. You're driving Uber, you're waiting tables. Let's just talk about what you want to do. Let's talk about your choices." And I'll spend time, but I'm not going to charge them for that.

Bonnie Wallace: You don't need coaching for every single audition, you just don't. Some auditions carry more freight than others. Or carry less freight.

Marcie Smolin: Yeah, exactly. And some, you're crazy if you don't coach for.

Bonnie Wallace:	Let's talk about pilot season for a minute. There's a lot of anxiety about it in general for actors. Thousands and thousands of actors come out to L.A. every year between January and March or April. But, more and more shows are being cast year-round. Then never mind the fact that movies are cast year-round anyway. What are your thoughts about pilot season currently?
Marcie Smolin:	Well, pilot season has changed a lot. When I first started the studio, the Oakwood apartment was full of people coming from January to April. I always had to add classes during pilot season. I don't think people do that as much anymore. Because everything is being cast year-round. One of the things during pilot season that always sort of broke my heart a little bit was people thinking they were going to come out here from January to April, and that would be it. Sure, it happens for some people. But if you're going to commit to being an actor, and you want to be here in L.A., be here in L.A.
Bonnie Wallace:	You've got to give it more than a two or three-month shot.
Marcie Smolin:	It takes a while. And yes, it is possible. As you know. It is possible to be cast from other places. There are tapes, there are talent searches, there are casting directors who will ... Disney and Nick are great about that. They will cast a wide net. But bottom line, if you really want a career, you'll be in L.A. or be in New York. You just have to give it a shot. Start slow, and walk before you run. Sign up for Actors Access and L.A. Casting, Casting Frontier, Backstage.

Start with student films. Because no matter how much you take an audition class, every audition is different. Let them have some experience auditioning. This is for grownup actors too. I tell this to everybody. You don't want their first audition to be for Spielberg. Have it be for someone doing a thesis film. And then, the other thing about doing student films is you start to build up a reel.

Student films are great. I'm a big believer in them for many reasons. As I said, you don't want your first audition to be for Spielberg. You want to go in and get your audition skills sharp. A lot of times, students don't know how to audition people. So you really have to rally.

Student films are also a great way to build a body of work. Because, for your reel, you really want things that someone else has filmed with other actors. It's okay to have something they filmed in an acting class, or they've gone into a studio and they're doing a monologue. Really, a reel is showing a body of work.

Bonnie Wallace: Yes. A headshot will show one angle, and how you show up on film is different. But reel footage from class or a studio isn't the same, and it isn't a substitute for actual, authentic work.

Marcie Smolin: And then the more you work with people, different people, work begets work. Even with student films, work begets work. The more you're working, the more you're in that actor mindset.

Bonnie Wallace: That's a phrase that I repeat a lot myself. Work begets work. And it's true, I think, in all of life. But I think it's particularly true for actors because once you work with somebody, if it's a good experience for everybody, if it's an experience that people might want to repeat, then you've got a whole network of people who think about you when something comes up. Whether it's the casting director, or the director, or the producers, or the producer's husband who knows somebody who's producing something else. And that network can become exponential very quickly. If somebody has worked with you and you've delivered great work, and you were a joy to work with, who wouldn't want to work with you again? So a lot of stuff comes out of that.

Marcie Smolin: USC, for example, they have an amazing alumni association. And when they do their student film festivals, you do not know who's going to be in the audience there. I know students of mine did a student film, and they got the call, "Hey, I saw you in blah blah blah's student film. I'd like you to come in for this."

There are so many opportunities now. There are web series, there are indie films, there are all kinds of things that you could do now. All kinds of ways to build your body of work. You can be very busy as an actor.

Bonnie Wallace: To me, it's always two things, when we talk about a body of work.

There's the real work, which transforms you in the doing of it. It makes you a better actor, hopefully. It literally builds your experience and your capabilities, so that on the other side of it, you're better. But it's also another thing for your resume. And they're both important.

Marcie Smolin: Yes. I had a young guy start my adult class, he's 19. And he decided to go to acting class instead of going to college. And his parents were supportive, it was very sweet. And he said, "But here's the thing, I only want to do the work I want to do." And I went, "Mm-hmm ..."

Bonnie Wallace: Good luck with that.

Marcie Smolin: And he's never studied acting in his life. And, he was a beginner. And he said, "So I'm going on Actors Access, and I'm writing notes to the directors, like if I think that they haven't described the characters enough." I didn't know him yet when he told me this, and I don't think he'd do it now, because I pretty much set him straight.

I said to him, "Who are some of your favorite actors?" And he started telling me, and I would go on IMDb and say, "This was what they did as a teenager." You want to do some bad things. That's your life story.

Bonnie Wallace: You can learn a lot by doing projects that are not your dream projects. And I really do really recommend that anybody who thinks they might want a career in this industry, and any parents whose children think that they might, go to IMDb and go onto those pages of actors that you admire, who have careers that you would love to call your own. Go all the way down their body of work. It's chronological, so you can see what's literally at the bottom. And it's generally something like Spear Holder Number Four, in some forgettable, terrible B-movie. And it's okay, because everybody gets their start somewhere, and you can't hold out and say, "Well, I'm not going to start until I'm working for Spielberg."

Marcie Smolin: It's just not realistic. And also, you know what? Some of the things I worked on in the beginning, I wouldn't take back those memories for anything. Or the things I learned on the set from watching. Or that movie that I did where I got advice from Martin Landau, I didn't have a huge part in that movie by any means. I had maybe two scenes, but I loved every minute of it. You never know what's going to happen to you on a set.

Bonnie Wallace: You don't. And what relationships you are going to forge, and where those will lead. Possibly lifelong friendships, which are important from a quality of life standpoint, but can there can be important professional contacts as well. If you become a fan of someone, and they become a fan of you because of what you brought to that tiny role the two days that you filmed, years later, that can bear fruit. You just don't know.

Marcie Smolin: There are things, though, that I do think that people shouldn't do.

Things that will come back to haunt you.

One of my students recently got a script and it was a child. And she was about 12. And in her scene, there was not a lot of sexual activity, but the rest of the film there was so much, it was disgusting. The script was ... I'm not a prude, but it was disgusting. And I said to her parents, "Really?" And it was an indie, no money, and non-union.

That comes back to haunt you, those kinds of things. Nudity. I know there's protection in place for child actors. But once they turn 18, I think, you need to be so careful about that.

Bonnie Wallace:	I'm so happy you brought this up because it's truly the flip side of everything we were just saying a minute ago, "No, don't be afraid to do the weird little projects." The flip side is, for goodness sake, use your judgment, and trust your gut. And if something seems funky, don't do it. There is always another audition. There is always another project. You don't have to do everything that comes your way.
Marcie Smolin:	And also for safety purposes. It's great that we have all these resources on the Internet from which to get auditions. Use the reputable ones. Use Actors Access, L.A. Casting, Casting Frontier, Backstage, Cast It. Don't use Craigslist. Do not audition off Craigslist.
Bonnie Wallace:	Nobody legit is casting through Craigslist ever.
Marcie Smolin:	And then, to take it a step further, don't audition in people's houses. Or in a hotel room.
Bonnie Wallace:	It is not in any way, ever standard, to have an audition in a hotel room or in a house. If you end up showing up to one of those places because that's the address it turns out to be, and you already know it's non-union, just turn around, and don't go in.
Marcie Smolin:	And if you have representation, call your reps, and have them follow up on it. That's what they're there for.
Bonnie Wallace:	And when you see the sides, when you see a breakdown, something that gives you information about

the project … if it crosses lines for you in terms of your own personal comfort zones and integrity, don't do it.

If you have representation, let them know ahead of time what kind of material you're not comfortable with. So they don't send you over those projects, and you don't mess up your relationship with them. Because they'll think, "What do you mean? I worked so hard to get you this audition." And then you'll say, "Yeah, but I'm not comfortable with that kind of language. Or that kind of subject matter."

Well, they didn't know that if you didn't tell them. It's really important to stay inside the bounds of your own integrity. But again, if you've got reps, you need to let them know what those boundaries are, so you can work as a team.

Marcie Smolin: It's okay to have boundaries. I have boundaries.

Bonnie Wallace: It's healthy.

Marcie Smolin: Don't go to an audition that tests your boundaries, get the job, and then not take it though.

If you don't want to do the job, don't go to the audition. Don't waste people's time taking that audition, or thinking you're going to show up and they're going to say, "Oh, okay, you can wear clothes. Oh, you don't have to smoke. Oh, we'll change that word to 'oh fudge.'" It's not going to happen.

It's okay to have boundaries, it's okay to not want to do that, but then don't go to the audition.

Bonnie Wallace: That is a great point. Any other don'ts?

Marcie Smolin:	There are a lot of don'ts.

When you walk into the room, if you've been having a bad day, or having personal trauma, don't share it. I mean, I'm sure they're very nice people. But there are a lot of actors coming in. That's all they're going to see.

Don't go when you're sick. Don't go. If you go to an audition and you get someone sick, they're never calling you in again. You have burned that bridge. And it's not nice. If you have a cold, I'm sorry. We've all gotten a cold. But the nice thing to do, is to not go into a room full of actors, and then shake hands.

When you walk in the door, don't shake someone's hand unless they offer it first.

Bonnie Wallace: I have heard a number of casting directors say that. And if you think about it, it makes sense. Because they see so many people. It's just not nice, you know? And it seems nice, and it's counterintuitive, but … boundaries.

Marcie Smolin: Don't wear perfume.

Bonnie Wallace: People have chemical sensitivities.

Marcie Smolin: They do. And they want you out of the room. I have a girl in my Monday night class who wears too much perfume and I have told her, and she's gotten really angry with me. And she continues to do it, and I can't breathe around her. It's so bad.

Bonnie Wallace: And if you were in casting, you wouldn't cast her.

Marcie Smolin: No, they want you out of the room. So that's a big one.

Have good hygiene. Even if you're playing a bum, it's okay to look messy and rumpled and all that, but don't go so Method that you don't shower for five days. I know people who've done this, and you're going to stink up the trailer, and their office, and they'll have to all stand outside, and have somebody come in and spray it down.

Bonnie Wallace: All good advice. Some of it seems like it should be obvious, but we've all seen people, coming from a good place, feel they don't need to do that.

What would you tell a young person who lives far away from L.A. or New York, and this is their dream? What advice would you have on some of the best ways for them to move toward that dream where they are now?

Marcie Smolin: Wherever they are, be in acting class. You don't want to act just from audition to audition. Do any kind of theater you can. And also, any town pretty much has a college that's making student films. Call the college film department. They're always looking for kids. Register there. Pretty much every town has local agencies where they do regional commercials. It's not just L.A. and New York now. A lot of my students have Atlanta agents, and Chicago agents. They'll work as a local hire so they pay their own flight, but sometimes it's worth it. And find the sites that post open calls. Disney does it, Nick does it.

Bonnie Wallace: They do. As you said, they cast a wide net, especially when they're looking for an important role. They're going to beat the bushes until they see the right person.

There are also community theaters in just about every town and if you are fortunate, and you have some good directors, you can get some pretty good training that way. And do a lot of learning by doing. There's always something.

Marcie Smolin: There's always something. And for taped auditions, do it right. Get a coach. Probably get a coach from L.A. or New York.

Bonnie Wallace: And you can do that. That's what Skype and Zoom are for. And you teach and coach through Skype.

Marcie Smolin: I do. It is important because I see tapes done by acting teachers in small towns who've never left the small town and just ... they're good actors, they're wonderful people. But they don't necessarily know the ins-and-outs of an audition tape, and what it should look like to be seen for a project here.

Bonnie Wallace: Different sets of expectations. We've been talking most of the way through about The Actors Circle and what you do at the studio here in Los Angeles. And I think it's important to know, especially if people get excited about what you're up to, that they don't necessarily have to be in L.A. to have access to you.

Marcie Smolin: No, absolutely not.

Bonnie Wallace: Any final thoughts for young actors hoping to make a career in film and TV?

Marcie Smolin: Enjoy your life every step of the way. Everybody is on a different path. It happens for some people really quick, and then sometimes it happens for somebody a few years down the road. Doesn't mean you're any better or any worse. It's just the way it is.

You never know. Entering into this business is challenging. There are great rewards. And just live a good life while you're doing it.

Bonnie Wallace: Because it's your life.

Marcie Smolin: Exactly. And love your family, and love your friends, and continue to be interesting, and go to class, and get better, and don't let your emotional happiness be dependent on what auditions you had this week. You will be better when you walk in the room because you won't have an air of desperation. You'll just be cool.

Bonnie Wallace: That's wonderful advice. I hope everyone will just fold that into their hearts.

EPILOGUE: COVID-19 NOTE

As this book goes to print it is the unforgettable summer of 2020. Production in most film and TV is at a near standstill while the industry works together to figure out how to return to filming while keeping everyone safe on set.

It is a time of uncertainty, but also of opportunity.
When you look back on this time, what will you wish you had done? Will you use it to learn and grow and prepare for when the industry starts back up again?

Acting is a skill that grows with practice. Find ways to grow your skills now, so you can be ready to succeed when the cameras are rolling again. Read books, listen to podcasts, watch top quality fi lm and TV performances, learn everything you can about the industry, practice your self-tape skills… and get to class!

CONTACT

Zak Barnett Studios
Zak Barnett

332 South La Brea
Second Floor
Los Angeles, CA 90036
Phone: 323-746-5059

Website: www.zakbarnett.com
Email: studio@zakbarnett.com
Instagram: @zakbarnettstudios
Twitter: @zbsactingstudio
Facebook: @zakbarnettstudios

The Christiansen Acting Academy
Diane Christiansen

4934 Lankershim Blvd
North Hollywood, CA 91601
-and-
28328 Agoura Road, Suite 202 Agoura
Hills CA 91301 818.523.8283

Website: www.dianechristiansen.com
Email: actupdi@gmail.com
Instagram: @TheChristiansenActingAcademy
Twitter: @ActUpDi
Facebook: The Christiansen Acting Academy

Marnie Cooper School of Acting
Marnie Cooper

12801 Bloomfield Street
Studio City, CA 91604
Phone: 818-760-8009

Website: http://www.marniecooperschool.com
Email: marnie@marniecooperschool.com
Instagram: @marniecooperschoolofacting
Twitter: @MarnieCooper101
Facebook: Marnie Cooper School of Acting

John D'Aquino Young Actors Workshops
John D'Aquino

4150 Riverside Drive
Burbank, CA 91505
Phone: 818-588-3838

Website: www.johndaquino.net
Email: info@johndaquino.net
Instagram: @johndaquinosyaw
Twitter: @JohnDAquinosYAW
Facebook: John D'Aquino's Young Actors Workshops

Young Actors Space
Patrick Day

5918 Van Nuys Blvd.
Sherman Oaks, CA 91401
Phone: 818-785-7979

Website: www.youngactorsspace.com
Email: info@youngactorsspace.com
Instagram: @young_actors_space
Twitter: @YoungActorsSpc
Facebook: @Young Actors Space

Keep It Real Acting Studios
Judy Kain

4444 Lankershim Blvd, #203
North Hollywood, CA 91602
Phone: 818-901-8606

Website: www.keepitrealacting.com
Email: keepitrealacting@gmail.com
Instagram: @keepitrealacting
Twitter: @KeepItRealActin
Facebook: @KeepItRealActing

Anthony Meindl's Actor Workshop
Anthony Meindl

905 Cole Ave
Los Angeles, CA 90038
Phone: 323-450-9600

Website: www.anthonymeindl.com
Email: assistant@anthonymeindl.com
Instagram: @amawstudios
Twitter: @AMAWStudios
Facebook: @AnthonyMeindlsActorWorkshop

Eric Morris Actors Workshop
Eric Morris

5657 Wilshire Blvd. #110
Los Angeles, CA 90036
Phone: 323-466-9250

Website: www.ericmorris.com
Email: ericmorris19@sbcglobal.net
Facebook: @EricMorrisTeacher

Young Actor Workspace
Lisa Picotte

5571 West Pico Blvd
Los Angeles, CA 90019
Phone: 323-653-3318

Website: www.lisapicotte.com
Email: lisapicottestudio@gmail.com
Instagram: @lisapicotteworkspace
Twitter: @youngactorws
Facebook: @lisapicotteworkspace

3-2-1 Acting School
Mae Ross

3131 Foothill Blvd
La Cresenta, CA 91214
Phone: 818-248-5602
Call/Text/WhatsApp: 818-275-2740

Website: https://321ActingStudios.com
Email: contact@321actingstudios.com
Instagram: @321actingstudios
Twitter: @321acting
Facebook: @321ActingSchool

Scott Sedita Acting Studios
Scott Sedita

526 N Larchmont Blvd
Los Angeles, CA 90004
Phone: 323-465-6152

Website: www.scottseditaacting.com
Email: scottsedita@gmail.com
Instagram: @seditastudios
Twitter: @ScottSedita
Facebook: @scott.sedita

The Actors Circle
Marcie Smolin

4475 Sepulveda Blvd.
Culver City, CA 90230
(310) 837-4536

Website: www.theactorscircle.com/
Email: workshops@theactorscircle.com
Instagram: @theactorscircle
Twitter: @theactorscircle
Facebook: @TheActorsCircleCulverCity

A NOTE ON OFFERINGS AND PRICING

Until recently, you had to come to Los Angeles to learn from these top Hollywood acting teachers.

One silver lining in the COVID-19 epidemic is that these amazing teachers—and the top-notch classes they offer in the schools they founded—are now available to anyone, whether you live in Los Angeles or not. Most now offer online classes and coaching, and you can study with them from anywhere in the world.

The acting schools and acting teachers profiled in this book occupy a range of prices for their offerings, but most are surprisingly affordable. All of them cost much less than a college or university would.

Rather than list specific prices for different classes, workshops, and intensives that they teach—which would be our of date as soon as this book is published—I encourage you to go to their websites (which are listed on the Contact Info section of this book) and see what offerings speak to you, and then see what their current prices are. While you're there, sign up for their email lists so you can stay in touch as they offer new classes and workshops and opportunities.

Then take action, and sign up for something, so you can build your skills and get closer to your dream of a successful acting career.

GLOSSARY

10,000 hours	The idea that 10,000 hours of practice are necessary to obtain mastery of a skill. Popularized by Malcolm Gladwell in his book, *Outliers*.
Actor's Access	Online audition board owned by Breakdown Services. Services include posting casting calls & submitting talent online.
Actors Studio	Acting techniques based on a variety of methods were developed here by Lee Strasberg from the Stanislavsky System.
Agent	Someone who represents talent. Agents' chief function is to secure work for their clients. Theatrical agents represent talent primarily for film and TV projects; commercial agents represent talent primarily for print and ad work. An actor might have both kinds of agents. Agents must be licensed, and franchised by SAG or AFTRA.
American Masters	The five great American acting teachers to contribute to *The Method*, based on the work of Stanislavski: Stella Adler, Uta Hagen, Elia Kazan, Sanford Meisner, and Lee Strasberg.
As-ifs	A practice used to get actors to open up their imaginations in order to discover new and interesting things about the character they are playing.

Audition	A meeting between an actor and casting director through which the actor can demonstrate talent and ability for a certain role and the casting director can determine whether that actor is the person they want in the role. May be in person or on tape.
Backstage	An entertainment industry website and magazine aimed at people working in film and the performing arts, with a special focus on casting, job opportunities, and career advice.
Backstage Expert	Performing arts industry professionals who write advice columns for the *Backstage* website.
Backstory	A history or background created for a character.
Blocked	Being unable to feel certain emotions; suppressing feelings.
Blocking	The basic physical movements of actors on a stage or set. Blocking positions are often marked on the floor with tape and called "marks."
Booking	A commitment made to an actor for a job. Generally followed by a contract.
Branding	The conscious and intentional effort to create and influence public perception of an individual.
Breakdown	The detailed description of a project, including key players (director, producers, casting director) story line, and roles available for casting. Often includes estimated start date and location of production.

Breakdown Services	The primary distributor of Casting Breakdowns, used by CSA (Casting Society of America) casting directors throughout North America.
Callback	A request to return for another audition to an actor being considered for a role.
Casting	The process of finding actors, or entertainers, for a particular production. Part of the pre-production process.
Casting director	Also known (incorrectly) as a casting agent. Person responsible for choosing which actors will play the lead and supporting roles in a film or TV show, under the supervision of the director and producers.
Casting Frontier	An online audition board. Services include posting casting calls & submitting talent online.
Cast It	An online audition board. Services include posting casting calls & submitting talent online.
Character	The character is a being involved in the action of a story, as opposed to the actor, who is portraying the character.
Character development	The process of creating a believable character in fiction by giving the character depth and personality.
Choice	Emotional decisions that help define and shape the direction of a character. These are created by the actor and are not in a script.

Clip	A short excerpt from a video, film, or TV performance. Multiple clips can be linked to create a reel.
Close-up	A photograph, movie, or video taken at close range and showing the subject on a large scale.
Coaching	Helping an actor with a specific objective, such as booking a role in an audition, or having a breakthrough with a particular challenge.
Cold reading	An unrehearsed reading of a scene or sides. Used mainly in auditions.
Commercial	An advertisement; print, TV, radio, or web based.
Commercial class	A class teaching actors how to audition for, book, and perform in commercials.
Compressing	Reducing the size of digital files, such as self-tapes, for easier downloading, uploading, and sending.
Content	The ideas contained in a piece of creative work, such as writing, speech, or a movie.
Contract	A written or spoken agreement, enforceable by law.
Co-star	A small guest role on a TV show. Generally has under five lines, and one or two scenes.
Cue	In acting, the trigger for an action to be carried out at a specific time. Often the line of preceding dialogue.

Demo reel	A video compilation of an actor's best work that shows their range in two minutes or less, used to help agents, casting directors, and producers get a sense of the actor's abilities.
Dialect	A regional or social variety of a language distinguished by pronunciation, grammar, or vocabulary.
Director	Person responsible for the ultimate result of a film or TV episode. The major creative visionary behind the actors' performances and the aesthetic feel of the work.
Disney Channel	A United States basic cable and satellite television network, owned by Walt Disney Television.
Eco Cast	Eco Cast is a "virtual pre-read system" provided by Breakdown Services. With it, casting directors can send invitations to talent representatives or actors directly to record an audition themselves, expanding the range of people casting directors can see for each role.
Elia Kazan	Influential Greek-American director, producer, writer, and actor. One of the Five American Masters in Method Acting.
Episodic Season	Time of year when many TV series episodes are filmed and therefore guest star and co-star roles are cast, typically late summer to mid-December. This is a less clearly defined season as time goes by and more series are filmed throughout the year. Counterpart to Pilot Season.
Executives	Producers who make decisions on, and/or supervise

film or TV productions; on a TV show, may also be a writer or the creator of a series.

Executive session

One of the final stages of casting, where actors audition in front of the executives making decisions for the series regular roles in a new TV show. Precedes Network testing.

Eye line

Eye lines are where actors look while acting in a scene. Often, when an actor appears to be talking directly to another character, their eye line is directed at the camera, not at the other actor. Also referred to as sight lines.

Feature film

The Academy of Motion Picture Arts and Sciences asserts that a feature film runs for more than 40 minutes. Most feature films are between 75 and 210 minutes long.

Fourth wall

A theatrical term for the imaginary "wall" that exists between actors on stage and the audience.

Genre

Type or category of film or TV work, based on some set of stylistic criteria, including setting, characters, plot, mood, tone, and theme. For example, romantic comedy, action, adventure, science fiction, horror, procedural drama, historical drama, etc.

Going to zero

In an actor's imagination, the moment just before the scene starts. A method for grounding a performance in the truth of the character.

Green-light

Formal approval and commitment to production and it's financing, which allows a project to move forward from development to pre-production and then principal photography. The go-ahead for a film or TV project to be made.

Green room | The space in a theatre or similar venue that functions as a waiting room and lounge for performers before, during and after a performance or show when they are not engaged on stage.

Groundlings | A theater and school in Los Angeles. One of the leading improv training programs in the U.S.

Guest star | A larger role than co-star in TV, frequently one that drives that episode's plot. Guest stars may or may not be recurring.

Handler | A person who advises or manages someone in their work, especially someone important or famous.

Headshot | Photo of an actor, typically eight by ten inches and in color, used for securing auditions.

Hitting the mark | Doing an action, for example dialogue or movement, at a specific location on set.

IMDb | An acronym for Internet Movie Data Base. A free online database of information related to films, television programs, home videos, video games, and streaming content online – including cast, production crew and personal biographies, plot summaries, trivia, ratings, and reviews.

IMDb Pro | The paid version of IMDb, which allows users to see what productions are on the horizon, who is working on what, how to contact directors and agencies and a host of other resources.

iMovie — Video editing software application for Apple/Mac devices.

Improv — Short for improvisation; the art of spontaneously performing without preparation or script, often used in comedy.

Independent film — A feature film or short film that is produced outside the major film studio system.

Intensive — Short, concentrated series of acting training classes often focused on specific techniques, methods, or an aspect of the entertainment industry.

LA Casting — An online audition board, also known as Casting Networks. Services include posting casting calls & submitting talent online.

Les Mis — Common name for *Les Misérables,* an epic musical theatre production based on the novel by French poet and novelist Victor Hugo.

Line — The words spoken by an actor. Pieces or sentences of dialogue.

Major Market — Biggest centers for production in the U.S. for film and TV: Los Angeles and New York.

Manager — Someone who represents talent. A manager's chief function is to guide and advise actors on their careers. Not licensed.

Megapproach	Term coined by Eric Morris, referring to a set of tools that help the actor fulfill the character's obligation.
Meisner	The *Meisner* technique is an approach to acting developed by the American theatre practitioner Sanford *Meisner*. The focus of the *Meisner* approach is for the actor to "get out of their head," such that the actor is behaving instinctively to the surrounding environment.
Mentorship	A relationship between two people where the individual with more experience, knowledge, and connections is able to pass along what they have learned to a more junior person.
Method	A technique of acting in which an actor aspires to complete emotional identification with a part, based on the system evolved by Stanislavsky and brought into prominence in the US in the 1930s.
Mic	Common term for Microphone
Monologue	A solo performance used in theater auditions or agent auditions. Not used for film or TV auditions, which use sides, or scenes from the script.
MOS	A shot, a sequence, or a film that is shot without sound, which is added later. The origin of the term is cloudy, but one old Hollywood story says that *M.O.S.* stands for "Mit Out Sound."
Multi-cam	A method of production using a multiple camera setup. Several cameras simultaneously record a scene. Used primarily in sitcoms. Similar to live theater.

Morning Pages

Creative exercise made popular by Julia Cameron in her book *The Artist's Way*.

Network Testing

The final round of auditions before casting the series regular roles in a new TV show. Generally in front of dozens of network executives who have the final decision on casting.

Nick/Nickelodeon

An American cable channel specializing in children's programming.

NoHo

Common slang for North Hollywood, a neighborhood in Los Angeles. Home to many acting studios, dance studios, and people who work in the Industry.

Note

Direction given to an actor by a director, casting director, or acting coach.

Off-book

Performing from memory; not needing to look at printed lines.

On-set coach

Acting coach hired by the studio to work with actors while filming on set.

Pacing

The speed or tempo in which an actor picks up their cue and delivers their lines. Pace can also be the speed that creates a style for the piece.

Pauses

The space between lines delivered by an actor. Use of pauses is as important as the lines themselves.

Performance Art

An art form that combines visual art with dramatic performance.

Pilot	The initial, standalone episode of a potential television series. Used for testing and often not aired if the series is not picked up for production.
Pilot Season	The time of year when most pilots are typically cast, traditionally January through March. This period has become less clearly defined over time as more networks cast pilots year-round. Only applies to traditional network TV, not to film or web series.
Procedural drama	A genre of TV programming which focuses on how crimes are solved, or some other aspect of a law enforcement.
Producer	The person responsible for decisions on a production, from original concept to completion, and ultimately responsible for the success or failure of a TV show or film. Most projects have multiple producers who are responsible for different aspects of the production.
Producer session	One of the stages of casting, where actors audition in front of the producers for the series regular roles in a new TV show. Precedes an executive session, and network testing.
Projection	In stage acting, the strength of speaking or singing whereby the voice is used loudly and clearly. A technique used by an actor in a theatre in order to b e heard clearly.
Reader	A person reading/ acting opposite the person who is auditioning. For a self-tape, actors need to provide

their own reader. For an in-person audition, the casting director provides the reader.

Recurring	A recurring guest star in a TV series, who appears from time to time during the series' run. Contrasted with *series regular* characters, who typically appear in every episode of a series.
Rehearsal	A practice session or practice performance done prior to filming.
Rep (Representative)	Can refer to an agent, a manager, or a public relations representative.
Resumé	An actor's resumé, which shows their TV, film, theater, commercial work, relevant training and special skills, as well as their contact info, or agent and manager's contact info. Follows a special industry format.
Right-to-work state	A state where both union and nonunion workers have equal access to union jobs. Does not release union members from union rules and regulations. Specifically, the right-to-work means that employees are entitled to work in unionized workplaces without actually joining the union or paying regular union dues.
Role	The part, or character, an actor plays in a performance.
Room, the	Generally refers to the audition room, where an actor auditions for a casting director.
SAG	Acronym for Screen Actors Guild, a national labor union representing film actors and artists. Merged with AFTRA in March 2012.

SAG-AFTRA	A national labor union representing actors, announcers, broadcasters, journalists, dancers, recording artists, singers, voiceover artists, and other media professionals. Acronym for Screen Actors Guild—American Federation of Television and Radio Artists.
Scene-study	A technique used to teach acting. One or more actors perform a dramatic scene and are then offered feedback from teachers, classmates, or each other.
Scene objective	What a character wants more than anything throughout the scene. Drives the action of a scene.
Screen test	A final audition for studio and/or network executives. May be in a conference room or on a full soundstage.
Script	The written version of a play, movie, or TV episode.
Self-tape	A self-tape is an audition the actor films on their own and then sends in electronically. Casting provides the sides, instructions, and deadline, and the actor films, edits, and returns it to them.
Sense memory	A technique that involves recalling a sensual experience, such as sight, sound, smell, taste, or touch, to evoke an emotional reaction in an actor appropriate to their character in a scene.
Serial drama	A TV show which has a continuous plot that unfolds in sequential episode-by-episode fashion.

Series regulars	A part of the main cast contracted to work on a show for a period of time, often for multiple years.
Short Film	A motion picture that has less than 40 minutes running time.
Showcase	A chance for actors to show off their abilities, often in front of potential agents or managers. Not an audition for work.
Sides	Scenes or pages from a script used in auditions.
Sight line	Where actors look while acting in a scene. Often, when an actor appears to be talking directly to another character, their sight line is directed at the camera, not at the other actor. Also referred to as eye lines.
Single-cam	A method of production using a single camera set-up, used primarily in film, and TV shows filmed on location. As each shot is taken, the camera is moved and reset in order to get the next shot or angle.
Sitcom	Short for *Situation Comedy*. TV series that involves a continuing cast of characters in a succession of comedic circumstances.
Soap Opera/ Soaps	A TV drama series dealing typically with daily events in the lives of the same group of characters.
Spear-carrier	Euphemism for a character with a very small role and no lines.

Spec script	A movie or pilot written on "speculation"—without a deal or sale already in place, and without being commissioned.
Spolin	Viola Spolin; an actress, educator, director, author, and the creator of theater games. The modern improvisational theater movement is a direct outgrowth of Spolin's methods, discoveries, and writings.
Stella Adler	One of the five great American acting teachers to contribute to *The Method*, based on the work of Stanislavski. Adler later came to believe that actors should stimulate emotional experience by imagining the scene's "given circumstances," rather than recalling experiences from their own lives.
Stagecraft	The technical side of acting. It includes blocking, gestures and all the factors that are essential for an actor to be successful.
Stanislavski	A Russian actor, director, and producer born in 1863, who became renowned for his system of acting training. His books *An Actor Prepares*, *Building a Character*, and *Creating a Role* became the basis for what is widely known as "The Method."
Strasberg	One of the five great American acting teachers to contribute to *The Method*, based on the work of Stanislavski. Strasberg focused on the psychological aspects of the approach.

Strike the set	To tear down the set at the end of a production.
Studio	A place where actors train; a company that produces film or TV shows; a room or building where filming takes place.
Subbing	Substitute teaching.
Substitution	An acting technique involving the recasting of people, objects, and events in the script that the character must react act to, with real people, objects and events that the actor has known or experienced in their own life in order to create the appearance of emotional truth.
Take	A filmed version of a particular shot or scene setup.
Teaching	Teaching is focused on imparting knowledge and learning, where the teacher is in charge of the interaction. Distinct from coaching, which has more to do with the student as an individual.
Testing	Final stages of casting for a film or TV pilot.
Triple threat	A person who is proficient in three important skills within their particular field: in entertainment, this typically refers to acting, singing, and dancing.
Uta Hagen	American actress and theater practitioner, best known for her books *Respect for Acting*, and *A Challenge for the Actor*. One of the five great American acting teachers to contribute to *The Method*, based on the work of Stanislavski.

Variety	*Variety* is an American media company. *Variety.com* features breaking entertainment news, reviews, box office results, cover stories, videos, photo galleries and more.
Voiceover	Audio narration provided by a voice actor for a project or production. Voiceover plays a significant role in marketing, advertising, learning, broadcast, gaming and many other industries.
WOFRAIM	Scott Sedita's script analysis technique. *W.O.F.R.A.I.M.* stands for: (Wants, Obstacles, Feelings, Relationships, As-Ifs, Intentions, Moments Before).
Working actors	Actors who consistently work in commercial, television and film and yet are not household names to the average film and TV viewer.

ABOUT THE *HOMETOWN TO HOLLYWOOD* PODCAST

Since 2016, the *Hometown to Hollywood* podcast has been bringing intimate, authentic conversations with Hollywood's top talent to you in the form of twice-monthly interviews. With well over 100 episodes and counting, it's one of the best sources available for inside information, education, and inspiration for aspiring actors—or just people who are curious about how the Industry really works.

In the spring of 2020, Hometown to Hollywood moved to a subscription model, so it could become self-sustaining.

If you enjoyed this book—or have enjoyed the podcast—please consider supporting the work by becoming a Friend of the Podcast, for a small monthly fee. You can also give a subscription as a gift!

Just go to www.hometowntohollywood.supportngcast.fm and click on the level of support you can afford. For about the cost of a latte each month, you can have access to—or give access to—every new episode, as well as the entire collection of exclusive interviews.

Thanks so much for your support.

ABOUT THE AUTHOR

Bonnie J. Wallace is the founder of Hometown to Hollywood, dedicated to helping young actors build safe, successful careers.

She is the author of the bestselling *Young Hollywood Actors* and acclaimed *Hollywood Parents Guide*, producer of the *Hometown to Hollywood Podcast*, and writes a blog for parents of young actors, and young adult actors at *hometowntohollywood.com*, as well as articles for *Backstage.com* as a Backstage Expert. She teaches and speaks on the acting business at panels and events internationally.

Bonnie also offers one-on-one consultations with parents of young actors as well as young adult actors to help them build safe, successful careers.

Mother of Emmy Award winning actress and Columbia Records artist Dove Cameron, star of *Disney's Descendants, Liv and Maddie, Hairspray Live, Agents of Shield, Clueless the Musical, Light in the Piazza, Angry Birds 2, Vengeance, Isaac*, and more, Bonnie is dedicated to helping other young actors on this journey. She writes from her home in Los Angeles.

Find out more at *hometowntohollywood.com*.

Follow her on social media:

Instagram: @bonniejwallace
Twitter: @bonniejwallace
Facebook: @hometowntohollywood
Pinterest: @hometowntohollywood
Website: www.hometowntohollywood.com

To subscribe to the Hometown to Hollywood Podcast, visit:
https://hometowntohollywood.supportingcast.fm/

BONUS CONTENT:

Did you enjoy this book? Download the BONUS CHAPTER featuring an interview with actresses and acting coaches Audrey Whitby and Victoria Moroles at: www.hometowntohollywood.com/bonuschapter

PLEASE SHARE A RATING AND REVIEW!

Did this book help you in some way? I'd love to hear about it. Honest reviews help readers find the right books for their needs. Just go to Amazon and leave a sentence or two. Thanks!

Made in the USA
Coppell, TX
30 November 2020

42541693R00198